Losing Generations

ADOLESCENTS IN HIGH-RISK SETTINGS

Panel on High-Risk Youth

Commission on Behavioral and Social Sciences and Education

National Research Council

NATIONAL ACADEMY PRESS
Washington, D.C. 1993

NATIONAL ACADEMY PRESS • 2101 Constitution Avenue, NW • Washington, DC 20418

NOTICE: The project that is the subject of this report was approved by the Governing Board of the National Research Council, whose members are drawn from the councils of the National Academy of Sciences, the National Academy of Engineering, and the Institute of Medicine. The members of the committee responsible for the report were chosen for their special competences and with regard for appropriate balance.

This report has been reviewed by a group other than the authors according to procedures approved by a Report Review Committee consisting of members of the National Academy of Sciences, the National Academy of Engineering, and the Institute of Medicine.

Support for this project was provided by the Stewart F. Mott Foundation, The Medical Trusts of the Pew Charitible Trusts, the National Institute of Child Health and Human Development of the U.S. Department of Health and Human Services, and the National Research Council Fund.

Library of Congress Cataloging-in-Publication Data

Losing generations : adolescents in high-risk settings :panel on high
-risk youth / Commission on Behavioral and Social Sciences and
Education, National Research Council.
    p. cm.
  Includes bibliographical references and index.
  ISBN 0-309-04828-1
  1. Socially handicapped youth—United States. I. National
Research Council (U.S.). Commission on Behavioral and Social
Sciences and Education.
  HV1421.L67 1993
  362.7′4′0973—dc20   93-4358
                                                    CIP

Additional copies of this report are available from the National Academy Press, 2101 Constitution Avenue NW, Box 285, Washington, DC 20055. Call 800-624-6242 or 202-334-3313 (in the Washington Metropolitan Area).

Printed in the United States of America

Cover: Photograph by Eric Futran, copyright 1993.

PANEL ON HIGH-RISK YOUTH

JOEL F. HANDLER (*Chair*), School of Law, University of California, Los Angeles, California

GORDON L. BERLIN, Manpower Demonstration Research Corporation., New York, New York

THOMAS D. COOK, Center for Urban Affairs and Policy Research, Northwestern University

ALONZO A. CRIM, Georgia State University, Atlanta, Georgia

SANFORD M. DORNBUSCH, Center for the Study of Families, Children, and Youth, Stanford University

JOY G. DRYFOOS, Hastings-on-Hudson, New York

ROBERTO M. FERNANDEZ, Department of Sociology, Northwestern University

RICHARD B. FREEMAN, Center for Economic Performance, London School of Economics

JOHN HAGAN, School of Law, University of Toronto

CHARLES E. IRWIN, JR., School of Medicine, University of California, San Francisco

RICHARD JESSOR, University of Colorado, Boulder

GLORIA JOHNSON-POWELL, Camille Cosby Center, Judge Baker Children's Center, Boston, Massachusetts

AARON SHIRLEY, Jackson-Hinds Comprehensive Health Center, Jackson, Mississippi

BARBARA STARFIELD, School of Hygiene and Public Health, Johns Hopkins University

LLOYD STREET,* Department of Human Services Studies, Cornell University

R. Shepherd Zeldin, *Project Director* (through September 1992)

Susanne Stoiber, *Director*, Division on Social and Economic Studies

Barbara Briston, *Senior Project Assistant*

---

*Due to extended travel and fieldwork out of the country, Dr. Street did not see the final draft of the report.

The National Academy of Sciences is a private, nonprofit, self-perpetuating society of distinguished scholars engaged in scientific and engineering research, dedicated to the furtherance of science and technology and to their use for the general welfare. Upon the authority of the charter granted to it by the Congress in 1863, the Academy has a mandate that requires it to advise the federal government on scientific and technical matters. Dr. Frank Press is president of the National Academy of Sciences.

The National Academy of Engineering was established in 1964, under the charter of the National Academy of Sciences, as a parallel organization of outstanding engineers. It is autonomous in its administration and in the selection of its members, sharing with the National Academy of Sciences the responsibility for advising the federal government. The National Academy of Engineering also sponsors engineering programs aimed at meeting national needs, encourages education and research, and recognizes the superior achievements of engineers. Dr. Robert M. White is president of the National Academy of Engineering.

The Institute of Medicine was established in 1970 by the National Academy of Sciences to secure the services of eminent members of appropriate professions in the examination of policy matters pertaining to the health of the public. The Institute acts under the responsibility given to the National Academy of Sciences by its congressional charter to be an adviser to the federal government and, upon its own initiative, to identify issues of medical care, research, and education. Dr. Kenneth I. Shine is president of the Institute of Medicine.

The National Research Council was organized by the National Academy of Sciences in 1916 to associate the broad community of science and technology with the Academy's purposes of furthering knowledge and advising the federal government. Functioning in accordance with general policies determined by the Academy, the Council has become the principal operating agency of both the National Academy of Sciences and the National Academy of Engineering in providing services to the government, the public, and the scientific and engineering communities. The Council is administered jointly by both Academies and the Institute of Medicine. Dr. Frank Press and Dr. Robert M. White are chairman and vice chairman, respectively, of the National Research Council.

Contents

Preface

The title of this report is *Losing Generations*. In an important sense, it is another in a long list of studies, books, and reports that have said the same thing—many of our nation's children and youth are in trouble. The fact that this report is another in this long line should increase everyone's concern. We believe that the problems of America's young people are getting significantly worse, not better. This is a human tragedy, and it is a national tragedy that will have a serious impact on all of us.

This report is different, though, in that by focusing attention on the settings or environments in which young people and their families are living, it fixes responsibility where we think it belongs—on ourselves. The vast majority of those who write and read these reports were born in healthy, nurturing families who loved us and were able to guide us on our way. We grew up in safe, supporting neighborhoods, went to decent schools, were healed when we got sick, and, in time, secured rewarding employment. Some of us stumbled along the way, but we had second and third chances. Today, not only are such nurturing, supporting environments denied to large numbers of children and youth, but also, in many instances, the environments in which they live have actually increased the dangers to them. Many young people survive and lead productive, contributing lives, but large numbers of others do not; the odds against them are simply too great. This is not fair. High-risk settings do not just happen: they are the result of policies and choices that cumulatively determine whether families will have adequate incomes, whether neighborhoods will be safe or dangerous, whether schools will be capable of teaching, whether health care will be available—in short, whether young people will be helped or hindered while growing up. That many of the results described in this report may be unintended should not deter us from examining the policies that led to them and considering how they might be changed. It is our hope that the analysis contained in this report will assist the process of reappraisal.

Putting together the story of this report was a difficult, sometimes frustrating, but, in the end, exciting experience. The panel has incurred more than the usual number of debts, and on its behalf I would like to express our appreciation to those who helped us. Shep Zeldin directed the study from its beginning until September 1992. He had the difficult task of organizing the project, attending to the myriad details of budgets, meetings, and facilities, and, at the same time, listening to the multiple voices of an interdisciplinary collection of academics and practitioners. In addition to his intellectual contributions, Shep organized the work, helped put together an excellent group of consultants, arranged for a stimulating site visit and workshop at The Door, a New York City youth services center, and, on top of all of this, produced a first draft. Shep worked hard and well, and we thank him.

The difficult task of completing the project, putting the final pieces together, drafting and redrafting the report, and steering it through the review process was taken up by Susanne Stoiber. Susanne worked tirelessly, efficiently, and above all, brilliantly. She is a master at capturing ideas coherently and with passion, and, at the same time, forging a consensus. All of us are in her debt.

Many others contributed. Eugenia Grohman was our excellent editor and also provided valuable advice throughout the project. Elaine McGarraugh was the manager of the manuscript, with the thankless task of keeping track of hundreds of changes and verifying information and references. Barbara Briston provided valuable administrative support. Michele White, administrator of The Door, arranged a warm, informative meeting for the panel, and we appreciate her hospitality. Karen Pittman, vice president of the Academy for Education Development, Washington, D.C., and Howard Spivak, Harvard University, moderated our workshop with intelligence and skill. All of these people made our work more efficient and informed and helped us produce a better product. They have our heartfelt appreciation and thanks.

The study was sponsored by the Stewart F. Mott Foundation, The Pew Charitable Trusts, and the National Institute of Child Health and Human Development of the U.S. Department of Health and Human Services. We thank our sponsors for their patient support.

Finally, I would like to thank the panel members. This was a long, sometimes bumpy road, but the members stayed together to the end. We shared excellent discussions, worked through difficult ideas, and, I think, made good decisions. The members did this because they believed in the importance of the issues. It was a pleasure to work with such a fine group of people.

Joel F. Handler
Chair, Panel on High-Risk Youth

Losing Generations

ADOLESCENTS IN HIGH-RISK SETTINGS

Summary

Americans are concerned, even alarmed, by the apparent increase in the numbers of adolescents who engage in high-risk behaviors—behaviors that compromise their health, endanger their lives, and limit their chances to achieve successful adult lives. Adolescence is a natural period of experimentation and risk taking, but some young people—whether poor, middle class, or rich—appear far more likely than others to adopt "risky life-styles," life-styles characterized by drug use, unprotected sexual behavior, dropping out of school, delinquency, and violence.

The work of this panel began as an attempt to better understand why some adolescents are drawn to risky life-styles while others, similarly situated, engage in only normal adolescent experimentation. As our work progressed, however, we became convinced that a focus on individual characteristics of adolescents would contribute to the overemphasis of the last two decades on the personal attributes of adolescents and their families at the expense of attention to the effects of settings or context. We concluded that it was important to right the balance by focusing on the profound influence that settings have on the behavior and development of adolescents.

It is a truism that behavior and development are the outcome of an interaction between context and person, not of context alone. The focus on context in this report does not mean that the personal characteristics of individuals are unimportant, nor does it deny awareness of the individual differences that can be observed in every setting. Yet there are compelling reasons for our focus on context, on the role of settings: most simply, over the past two decades the major settings of adolescent life have come under siege in many different ways. For more and more children and adolescents—especially those who are poor and those who must deal with discrimination—the settings of their everyday lives fail to provide the resources, the supports, and the opportunities essential to healthy development and reasonable preparation for productive adulthood.

FINDINGS: DETERIORATED SETTINGS

Adolescents depend on families, neighborhoods, schools, health systems, and employment and training opportunities, and these institutions are under severe stress. As the fault lines widen, increasing numbers of youths are falling into the juvenile justice system, the child welfare system, and other even more problematic settings. This report attempts to improve understanding of the forces tearing apart the critical institutions in the lives of adolescents, as a first step in developing a viable plan to strengthen them.

Among the many factors that contribute to and shape the settings in which adolescents live, family income is perhaps the most powerful. Housing, neighborhoods, schools, and the social opportunities that are linked to them are largely controlled by income; a family's income and employment status also determine its access to health care services and strongly influence the quality of those services. Opportunities for advanced education and training and entry into the workforce are also closely linked to family income. On a more fundamental level, income is a powerful influence in shaping that most important of settings, the family itself. Thus, the decline in economic security of young families has had important and far-reaching consequences for children and adolescents.

Since the late 1970s, structural and demographic changes in the U.S. economy and society have caused a substantial and broad-based deterioration in the economic position of prime-age young adults, those aged 25-34. These young adults are the primary means of economic support for the majority of children in the United States (52.1%). A combination of declining real earnings and rising levels of unemployment has pushed a large percentage of these families into poverty. In 1991, 23.1 percent of families headed by an adult aged 25-34 had incomes below the poverty level: for whites, the percentage was 18.6; for blacks, 46.0; and for Hispanics, 38.0.

The decline in economic security has been severe—between 1973 and 1990, the median inflation-adjusted income of families with children headed by a parent under age 30 dropped by 32 percent. The economic security of young families has declined for many reasons, including the lack of growth in high-wage, high-benefit jobs, such as those in manufacturing; the decline in unionization; competition from recent immigrants for lower wage jobs; the isolation of inner-city residents from suburban jobs; and the inadequacy of worker skills for technically demanding positions. Demographic changes have also had a powerful effect: over the past two decades there has been an almost 40 percent increase in the number of female-headed households with children under age 18. The incidence of poverty among female-headed families with children is consistently 7 to 8 times higher than that among married-couple families with children. Although the increase in single-parent households has been an important factor in increasing the number of children living at or near poverty, two-parent households have also suffered. Most two-parent families have maintained their relative standard of living only by having two wage earners: in 1970 just under 39 percent of children had mothers in the workforce; by 1990 the proportion was 61 percent.

The increase in single-parent households and the reduced time that most parents are able to spend with their children materially reduces the effectiveness of families in providing the guidance and support that young people need. Although family income is the most powerful predictor of adolescent outcomes, other factors—such as family structure, home environment, childrearing practices, and child-parent relationships—are independently important to adolescent health and behavior. At all socioeconomic levels, single-parent families and stepfamilies are far more likely to have adolescent children who engage in health- and life-compromising behaviors (dropping out of school, early dating, truancy, running away from home, contacts with the police, smoking) than are two-parent families.

The combination of financial insecurity for an increasing proportion of families, increased work effort by parents seeking to maintain their living standard, and the demographic changes that have so dramatically increased the number of children and adolescents living in single-parent households result in increasing numbers of adolescents who do not receive the family nurturance necessary for positive development.

The child welfare system in general, and foster care in particular, is supposed to provide a "safety net" for children and adolescents from destructive or dysfunctional families. The total number of children in foster care has increased dramatically in the past decade, but the number of adolescents in the system has remained constant. Because their share of the total child welfare population has declined, there has been a reduction in the resources and attention committed to meeting the developmental needs of adolescents in foster care. As a result, the child welfare system is doing an inadequate job of preparing these adolescents to make the transition to productive, independent adulthood.

Adolescents who pass through the child welfare system are at high risk of educational failure, unemployment, emotional disturbance, and other negative outcomes. Studies show that adolescents released from foster care fare far worse then either low-income youths or a cross-section of the general adolescent population. Adolescents released from foster care are far less likely to complete high school or hold jobs. In one study more than 60 percent of the young women with a foster care background had given birth to at least one child. Granted that the adolescents were at risk before they entered the system—indeed, many entered the system precisely because they had already been abused or neglected, become truants or runaways, or experienced other serious problems. The findings nevertheless suggest that the child welfare system is unable to meet their needs. On the contrary, there is evidence that the system often excludes adolescents, does not protect them from known abuse, and then, in effect, abandons them.

Many children placed in foster care are likely to be emotionally disturbed, in large part because they have been raised in pathological families in which they were abused or neglected. In addition, the very act of separating a child from his or her family is traumatic and may itself cause disturbance. Yet the child welfare system has not been successful in providing mental health services for foster care children.

No one in the child welfare field holds any illusions that the system is currently able to provide adequate resources to promote adolescent development or that it has been able to do so for the past decade. Although foster care may sometimes be better for the adolescent than remaining at home or living independently, it is unable to provide the support that is required to help young people—most of whom have gone through very damaging experiences—to avoid health- and life-compromising behaviors that mortgage their future. Foster care is now itself a high-risk setting for most adolescents.

Outside their families, the most immediate setting of adolescent lives is the neighborhood. Most of the social interactions of families and adolescents are embedded in neighborhoods. They are a place for social interaction, a place for education and human service, and a place for preparing for and engaging in employment. In short, neighborhoods are a key setting for adolescent development.

During the 1970s the social composition of an increasing number of neighborhoods deteriorated: there was a 75 percent increase in the number of census tracts with concentrated poverty, and a 331 percent increase in the number of "underclass" neighborhoods. An underclass neighborhood is characterized not only by concentrated poverty, but also by a high degree of social disorganization. By 1980 more than half of all neighborhoods classified as poor in 1970 had become underclass. Underclass and concentrated poverty neighborhoods are a very high-risk setting for adolescents.

Most poor neighborhoods are racially stratified as well as being economically isolated. The average black family lives in a census tract in which 30 percent of families are poor; for Hispanic families, the figure is 23 percent; for non-Hispanic whites, 14 percent. The poorest neighborhoods remain the most highly stratified: an estimated 87 percent of all residents in such neighborhoods are members of racial or ethnic minority groups.

Adults in poor neighborhoods differ in important ways from those in more affluent areas: high-poverty neighborhoods have much higher proportions of unmarried mothers, single-parent families, and unemployed young men. There are fewer good role models for adolescents and a far higher percentage of adults who are involved in illegal markets. As their economic and social systems break down, the poorest of neighborhoods seem increasingly unable to restrain criminal or deviant behaviors. Not surprisingly, with little legal economic activity, few public and social services, limited recreational and youth development programs, and high levels of crime, adolescents lose hope and often cannot use the few opportunities that are available.

The growth in crack and cocaine markets since the early 1980s has placed additional stress on poor neighborhoods. The highly visible, lucrative, and violent drug markets have simultaneously accelerated the exodus of stable families and undermined the authority of long-term community leaders. Adolescents who are not involved as participants in drug markets are still influenced by their presence: some are victims of drug-related violence, and many more are unable to engage in normal neighborhood activities because of the dangers associated with drug markets.

The increasing numbers of adolescents who are victims of the drugs, poverty, and violent neighborhoods has in turn focused attention on the lack of adequate health and mental health care for many young people. Adolescent health has been identified as a problem by policy makers and researchers only in the past decade. There is emerging recognition that adolescent health issues are different from those of children or adults and that the health status of adolescents has failed to improve over the last two decades. Since the early 1980s, for example, adolescent deaths from suicide and HIV/AIDS, as well as from homicide, have sharply increased. Furthermore, the prevalences of teenage pregnancy, sexually transmitted diseases, and drug use have either increased or remained at high levels relative to those in other Western countries.

The American approach to financing and delivering health and mental health services serves most adolescents poorly. Many of the serious health problems faced by adolescents—substance abuse, sexually transmitted diseases, mental disorders, and physical or sexual abuse—are not covered by most health insurance plans, or the coverage is severely restricted and not adequate to provide effective treatment. And increasing numbers of adolescents are without any insurance coverage at all. Even when paying for services is not a problem, appropriate care is often hard to find. Few physicians specialize in adolescent health, and other practitioners are poorly trained in recognizing adolescent health problems, particularly when the symptoms are psychosocial rather than physical.

The overall U.S. health system is fragmented, and especially so for adolescents because of the diversity of their needs. Adolescents are unlikely to know where to go and are likely to be referred many times before finding an appropriate setting. The adolescent health and mental health care system lacks all of the essential elements of primary care: a consistent entry point into the system, a locus of ongoing responsibility, adequate backup for consultation and referral services by specialists on adolescence, and comprehensiveness. As a result, the health care system is poorly set up to help adolescents overcome problems resulting from poverty, dangerous neighborhoods, and an inadequate social environment including school and home.

The current trends for adolescent health services are not promising. Families, communities, and the society at large are generally reluctant to accept adolescent values that diverge sharply from community norms: to the extent that adolescent health problems stem from generally unaccepted behaviors, health services are not responsive to their needs. A movement of the U.S. health system into managed care, with tight controls on the number and extent of services that will be covered, may further place adolescents in jeopardy because of the dearth of knowledge about effective treatment for adolescent problems.

The formal institution that directly affects virtually all adolescents is school. Schools are critically important because education is the means by which individuals from economically or socially disadvantaged backgrounds can build the skills and credentials needed for successful adult roles in mainstream American life. Despite two decades of public debate and reform, however, schools do not now work this way for many students. Adolescents from low-income families and neighborhoods are at much higher risk of educational failure than their more affluent suburban counterparts.

Because of residential stratification, most of these adolescents attend schools with the fewest material resources. In 1991, for example, per pupil expenditures in the 47 largest urban school districts averaged $5,200; in suburban districts, the figure was $6,073. Although an $875 per pupil funding gap may not appear significant, in an average class of 25 students, the difference is almost $22,000—enough to hire an aide, provide special instructional materials or computers, pay significantly higher teacher salaries, or improve a dilapidated classroom. When the relatively greater need of urban children for special services is taken into account (for health needs, language instruction for non-English-proficient students, etc.), the resource differences are even more critical. Differences in funding of this magnitude can make a clear qualitative difference in the total educational experience.

Traditional education practices contribute to the high rates of failure for low-achieving students. Historically, schools have addressed the diversity of student achievement by tracking students into homogeneous ability groups and by retaining students who fail courses because of poor attendance, grades, or test scores. Contrary to expectations, these practices have consistently shown negative academic and social consequences for low-achieving adolescents. For example, research shows that ability grouping does not improve learning among low-achieving students. Rather, placement in a low-track program reinforces, compounds, and often exacerbates preexisting differences among students in competency and self-perception. Students placed in lower tracks rarely move into higher tracks: the inferior quality of instruction and learning environments in the lower tracks is one major reason that students seldom move from lower tracks into more advanced programs. In addition, instruction in the lower tracks emphasizes basic skills rather than higher order learning, effectively sorting students' future educational and career options. Adolescents in these classes are keenly aware of their reduced opportunities, and this contributes to their loss of academic interest and motivation. Grade retention has been shown to be similarly ineffective in improving the performance of low-achieving students.

Alternatives to tracking and retention are being tried and show promise of effectiveness. However, they require flexibility, a high quality of instruction, and the resources necessary to provide students with individual attention. These are very difficult for most poor school districts to provide, and even school districts with adequate resources have been slow to learn from the research on the needs of low-achieving students.

Thus, school systems very often compound the problems that students from low-income families and poor neighborhoods bring to their doors. As the numbers of students who need compensatory attention continues to increase, school systems that serve poor and low-income neighborhoods must struggle to provide not only education, but also health and social services. They will not succeed without adequate resources and without major innovations in their approaches to both education and involvement with the communities they serve.

After the structured settings of schools comes the completely unstructured transition to work, one of the keys to productive adulthood. About one-half of high school graduates in the United States do not go on to college, and of those who do, less than half obtain 4-year degrees. Despite the fact that 75 percent of high school graduates will not finish college, far less commitment is made to helping these students prepare for and find work than is made to helping students prepare for and enter college. The result is that most high school students—or college dropouts—have poor information about the occupational choices open to them or what is required to prepare for a field of work and how to obtain the requisite training. Left to themselves, they flounder in the labor market, either jobless or obtaining jobs with low wages and little opportunity for advancement.

Adolescents from low-income families face the greatest difficulties. Not only are they the least likely to attend college, but they also fare substantially worse on all measures of employment success compared with adolescents from more affluent families. For those under age 20, being raised in a low-income family is the strongest predictor of labor market inactivity.

The United States differs from most other industrialized countries in its reliance on market forces to effect the transition of young people from school to work. There are many federal, state, and locally supported programs, but it is difficult to consider them a system, and few have been targeted specifically to adolescents. There are also few structural links among the various programs: in fact, there are strong policy disincentives to such program collaborations. Further, the school-to-work transition system in the United States currently acts almost exclusively on the supply side of the labor market equation.

Vocational education and employment training have moved away from their immediate constituencies: vocational education is isolated from the academic curriculum; employment and training programs have moved away from serving youth who are out of the labor market. Vocational education programs do not offer a sequenced series of courses throughout high school, building an integrated academic and applied knowledge base related to the learning and skills required in specific occupational sectors. Although innovative programs have been developed to bridge high school and technical school experience, they are few in number and reach a very small proportion of students.

Because they lack support and direction, large numbers of high school graduates (and even higher proportions of high school dropouts) do not acquire the academic and technical skills that are needed to obtain well-paying jobs as adults. Although a certain amount of testing in the labor market is predictable among young adults, far too many churn through jobs without acquiring any training or experience that can lead to careers or good jobs. The failure of the school-to-work transition "system" to adequately respond to the needs of the majority of high school graduates contributes materially to the economic insecurity that characterizes a high proportion of young families.

For increasing numbers of adolescents, the second formal institution in their lives is the juvenile justice system or the criminal justice system. These systems assume major roles in the lives of many adolescents, especially the adolescent children of racial and ethnic minorities and the inner-city poor. Economic and residential stratification in the United States concentrates crime, particularly violent crime, in low-income, urban neighborhoods. Young black males, in particular, have a disproportionately high risk of encountering the juvenile and criminal justice systems, both as victims and as violators. Young black males who experience education and employment problems have a high probability of being arrested, imprisoned, or criminally victimized. (Involvement in both violent and property crimes peak in mid- to late adolescence.)

Because such a large proportion of low-income, minority adolescent males are involved in criminal activities, their treatment at the hands of the juvenile and criminal justice systems is enormously important in determining whether they can be brought back into mainstream society or whether their adult lives will be marked by unemployment, low-wage jobs, ill health, and participation in illegal activities.

Both the juvenile and adult criminal justice systems are generally failing in their efforts to rehabilitate adolescent offenders (an increasing number of whom are now consigned to the adult justice system because of participation in drug-related homicides and other particularly violent crimes). The decline of the rehabilitative ideal, a new emphasis on deterrence, and escalating rates of imprisonment affect adolescents as well as adults.

The high rates of arrest and imprisonment have many ramifications. Because community-level policing practices display discriminatory patterns, and because the justice system is nevertheless expected to embody high standards of fairness, the justice system has become a particularly difficult forum for black-white relations. The juvenile and criminal justice systems are perceived with suspicion, hostility, distrust, and despair by minority citizens, who too often are treated as suspects. Thus, it is not surprising that ghetto youth who come into conflict with the justice system have self-concepts, attitudes, and interests that aggravate those contacts and, in the longer term, are predictive of poor occupational and other life outcomes. Those contacts in turn do nothing to improve this situation; they are more likely to perpetuate and intensify the negative results.

The justice system is unquestionably overburdened. Its emphasis on punishment is expensive, has not resulted in reducing levels of official crime, and probably increases hostility toward the system in ghetto communities. For juveniles, the most effective treatment programs are implemented outside of public facilities, custodial institutions, and the juvenile justice system. They also tend to involve nonpunitive behavior and skill-orientation, multipart treatments that offer alternatives to the more socially and fiscally costly mechanisms of justice system involvement. Because involvement with the justice system has such devastating consequences for the future of adolescents—particularly minorities—it is increasingly urgent that alternatives be tried.

CONCLUSIONS: GOOD PRACTICE AND NEW RESEARCH DIRECTIONS

In response to the failures of many of the major settings in which adolescents are growing up to provide the guidance and support they need for positive development, many community-based service providers have developed new programs that attempt to compensate. The panel found examples of programs organized by local governments and nonprofit groups that appear to be effective in addressing the problems facing many adolescents and their families. Most of these programs are designed to support families and strengthen communities. The overall goal of such efforts is to enable and empower parents and community residents to increase their capabilities to nurture young people.

The specific programs are extremely varied in their methods and philosophies, but they have a number of common characteristics. First and foremost, their services for adolescents are comprehensive: the programs transcend categorical labels, organizations, and funding sources to bring together a coherent package of services to young people. Whether programs are offered in a single site or through interagency collaborations, their goal is to provide services that ensure that the emotional, recreational, academic, mental and physical health, and vocational needs of adolescents are explicitly addressed.

Although individual programs have shown impressive results and have provided a life raft for some adolescents, they are not a substitute for fundamental improvements in the major settings that are the framework of adolescent life. Those primary settings are crucial, and the first priority must be to strengthen them. It is neither feasible nor desirable to substitute comprehensive service programs for families, schools, neighborhoods, or ongoing health care. Moreover, knowledge about which programs work and why is painfully limited. If the role of community-based programs is to be expanded, major investment is required in rigorous evaluations with carefully defined outcome measures. The models that show success through such evaluations deserve to be more generously supported and replicated.

The focus on settings reflects the panel's appreciation of the profound influence that context has on adolescent behavior and our judgment that the power of settings on adolescent development has been underappreciated. The lack of attention to settings has resulted in an incomplete picture of adolescence and an excessive concentration on individual adolescent behaviors and programs, such as teenage pregnancy prevention, drug abuse prevention, smoking prevention, and dropout prevention. The categorical focus on individual behaviors has been largely ineffective because behavior is the result of individual and group interactions with the environment. Primary, sustained attention must be paid to reducing the exposure of children and adolescents to high-risk settings, because reducing the risks generated by these settings is virtually the precondition for achieving widespread reductions in health- and life-compromising behaviors.

Describing the destructive effects of high-risk settings is far easier than recommending specific policy and program changes to improve them. The demographic changes that are creating large numbers of poor, single-parent families are not well understood, and it is not at all clear what effect specific changes in public policies might have on those trends. Therefore, we have limited ourselves to describing the broad changes that we believe are essential if settings are to become less dangerous for a large proportion of American adolescents and to describing research priorities to improve understanding of the particular policies and programs that might be effective in changing these settings. We note, however, that the problems described are serious and urgent. Although current knowledge of how to improve settings is limited, we believe the nation should give a high priority to beginning the process of research and commitment to improve the security and well-being of its children.

1

Adolescents at Risk

Increasing numbers of America's youth are growing up in circumstances that limit the development of their potential, compromise their health, impair their sense of self, and generally restrict their chances for successful lives. For more and more children and adolescents—especially those who are poor and those who must deal with the discrimination that often faces racial and ethnic minorities—the contexts of their everyday lives fail to provide the resources, supports, and opportunities essential to healthy development and reasonable preparation for productive adulthood. Disorganization of the key settings in which poor and minority young people live their daily lives—schools, neighborhoods, families, and, sometimes, the health care and law enforcement settings—poses a daunting challenge for their successful development during childhood and adolescence. Those settings have deteriorated considerably in recent decades, reducing their contribution to healthy adolescent development.

Those settings—the major contexts in which young people are growing up in contemporary American society—are the focus of this report. To the extent that those contexts or settings, instead of being benign and supportive, have become more dangerous and destructive, the lives of America's youth have been placed at risk. In such settings, the likelihood of healthy or successful development—of doing well in school, of achieving a sense of competence, of involvement in prosocial activities, of being prepared to assume adult roles, of avoiding too early childbearing or encounters with law enforcement agencies—is acutely jeopardized. And when danger comes to characterize most of the settings in a young person's life—a decaying school, a dangerous neighborhood, and a broken family, for example—that youth is, quite evidently, at high risk of failing to become a healthy, competent adult. Indeed, under such circumstances, the risk of health- and life-compromising experiences, such as school failure or dropout, trouble with the law, or heavy commitment to substance abuse, becomes substantially greater.

Over the past two decades, the major settings of adolescent life have become increasingly beleaguered, especially where the number of families living in poverty has expanded and where their concentration in the inner cities of large urban areas has increased. Schools in such areas do not have the resources needed to sustain their mission, school buildings are in disrepair, and there is often the threat of violence in classrooms and corridors; neighborhoods are more disintegrated, buildings more dilapidated, and streets often physically dangerous; communities are also fraying as ever-rising mobility destroys personal ties and traditional institutions, such as churches, and local businesses suffer from disinvestment; families are more frequently headed by a single parent, often a working mother unable to obtain competent child care or by two working parents with less time for childrearing because they are striving to maintain their standard of living in the midst of a general decline in wages. Such settings have become the crucible in which the lives of increasing numbers of America's youth are being shaped.

SETTINGS AND INDIVIDUALS

The decision to focus this report on the major settings in which young lives are formed reflects the profound influence that context has on the behavior and development of children and adolescents. It reflects, too, awareness that the elements essential for healthy and positive development—resources and supports and opportunities—are differentially distributed and differentially available among sectors of American society, generally present in the more affluent settings and often absent or limited in poor and racially or ethnically separate communities. Settings are important not only the "first chances" they provide, but also for "second chances," those opportunities to redeem past failures or inappropriate choices. Such second chances are clearly less available when settings are in disarray, limited in resources, and subject to continuing pressure toward illegitimate activities.

It is, of course, a truism that behavior and development are the outcome of an interaction between context and person, and not of context alone. This report's focus on context does not mean that the personal characteristics of individuals are unimportant, nor does it deny awareness of individual differences within every setting. Whatever the context, individual differences are ubiquitous, and there will always be some people who overcome adversity and thrive, even as many others do not. Yet there are compelling reasons for the focus adopted in this report: to give primacy to context and to illuminate the role of deteriorating settings in putting the lives of many young people at risk.

First, in the history of inquiry about the development of youth, the focus has traditionally been on individuals rather than context, and the latter has generally been ignored. This is a good time to right the balance, to extend understanding, to acknowledge and elaborate the pervasive influence of contexts or settings. Second, the role a setting plays must actually be seen as twofold, and thus, doubly important: it influences the development of a person over time, through experience, socialization, and exposure in various contexts, and it also interacts with that person at any given time in influencing the specific behavior that occurs. Third, it is evident that there are large variations in rates or levels of health- and life-compromising experiences and behavior associated with different contexts, especially for differences that relate to the level of poverty (for example, rates of school failure and dropout, unprotected sexual intercourse, aggression and violence, and drug and alcohol use).

Fourth, as this report clearly details, the significant and noticeable changes over the past two decades have indeed been in the contexts or settings of adolescent life. Thus, it seems especially important to consider the reverberating effects that such changes might have on the behavior and development of youth. Finally, policy efforts to prevent or ameliorate bad outcomes (such as school failure) are clearly more feasible and more likely to be efficient when targeted toward changing contexts or settings—using what is known broadly as a public health approach—than when targeted at changing individuals on a one-by-one basis. For all of these reasons, this report articulates the ways in which the major settings of adolescent life, and especially their recent deterioration, have contributed to placing many of America's adolescents at risk.

In describing the impact of settings on adolescents, the panel is cognizant of the difficulty in disaggregating the influence of specific parts of environments: family, neighborhood, schools, the health care system, etc. (For a discussion of these methodological problems, see *Inner-City Poverty in the United States*; Lynn and McGeary, 1990.) We instead call attention to the fact that all of the major settings or contexts of adolescent life are under stress.

This report uses the term adolescents to describe young people in their teenage years (13 to 19). The concept of "risk" as used in the report is drawn from the tradition of epidemiology, reflecting a concern for adverse outcomes. The definition of adverse outcomes, however, extends beyond morbidity and mortality to encompass the failure to acquire the academic knowledge, social skills, and personal behaviors required to succeed in contemporary American society.

THE ROLE OF FAMILY INCOME

Family income is perhaps the single most important factor in determining the settings in which children and adolescents spend their lives. Housing, neighborhoods, schools, and the social opportunities that are linked to them are largely controlled by income; a family's income and employment status decide its access to health care services and strongly influence the quality of those services. Opportunities for advanced education and training and entry into the workforce are also closely linked to family income. On a more fundamental level, income is a powerful influence in shaping that most important of settings, the family.

Although the nature of the causal relationships remains unclear, a family's financial status is the single most important factor in predicting differences in socioeconomic attainment of children, whether from two-parent or other families. Children who experience poverty at any time during their lives are three times more likely to be poor as adults than children who have never been poor (Hill et al., 1985; Hill and Duncan, 1987). Furthermore, prolonged exposure to poverty is more damaging than short episodes of poverty, perhaps because in short episodes, the assets derived from prior financial security exert some protective influence. Persistent poverty has a strong racial bias. Although white children account for the largest proportion of all poor children (42 percent in 1990), persistent long-term poverty (more than 6 years) is relatively rare for white families. Fewer than 5 percent of children from poor white families experience sustained poverty. The experience of black families is different: almost 40 percent of black children experience persistent or long-term poverty (Sawhill, 1992).

   This report gives particular emphasis to the adverse effects of poverty-related settings on the lives of adolescents. We chose this emphasis because of the large and still increasing numbers of children and adolescents whose developmental years will be spent in settings of extreme deprivation. As this report is about adolescents, the consequences of impoverished settings on younger children are not discussed in detail. However, it is important to note that a large proportion of the adolescents growing up in impoverished environments were born poor and have lived in poverty for significant periods of their lives; this is particularly true for black adolescents. Many of these children enter adolescence with a set of vulnerabilities (physical, developmental, psychological, and emotional) that are not only additive in their effects, but also negatively interact with the deleterious effects of the settings discussed in this report.

   In 1990, 9.8 million children under age 6—more than 4 of every 10 in the country—lived in low-income (poor and near-poor) families, families with incomes of less than 185 percent of the federal poverty level ($13,924 for a family of 4 in 1991) (National Center for Children in Poverty, 1992). Although it is generally recognized that poverty can be harmful to children, the diverse mechanisms by which lasting damage to a child's health and development occurs are not widely appreciated. Poverty affects children directly by limiting a family's ability to purchase goods and services essential to health, including adequate housing and food (Klerman with Parker, 1991). Children in poor households are also more likely to be exposed to health risks and to experience events that damage their health, such as lead-based paint and home fires. Families living in poverty are subject to multiple stresses and constraints that lead to feelings of hopelessness and helplessness and often reduce parents' ability to provide children with the emotional support and stimulation critical to healthy development (Zill et al., 1991). Poverty may also limit parents' ability to engage in health-promoting activities, resulting in unhealthier life styles (National Center for Children in Poverty, 1990). Together these forces serve to place a highly significant proportion of American children at high risk for physical, mental, and developmental disabilities that will influence the remainder of their lives. It is important to note, however, that even among children exposed to long-term poverty, the risks to children's development vary greatly and may be mitigated by such factors as the availability of positive social support (Cochran and Brassard, 1979; Wilson, 1989), neighborhood cohesion (Garbarino and Sherman,

1980), extended family networks (Furstenberg et al., 1987; Kellam et al., 1977), and the resilience of the child (Werner and Smith, 1982).

The increased risk starts before birth. Poverty has been shown to be a consistently important predictor of inadequate or late prenatal care. Poor women are also less likely to eat a nutritious diet and to experience adequate weight gain (Brown, 1988). Whether poor women are more likely to abuse substances during pregnancy is unclear. Poor women are less likely to smoke or drink alcohol than are higher income women, but poor women who do smoke are more likely to continue smoking during pregnancy (Henshaw and Silverman, 1988) but less likely to drink alcohol (Pamuk and Mosher, 1988). The reported increased use of illegal drugs during pregnancy by poor women may depend more on which drugs are studied and the study site (U.S. General Accounting Office, 1990; Chasnoff et al., 1990; Frank et al., 1988). Pediatric AIDS is closely associated with drug abuse among pregnant women and their partners in impoverished neighborhoods (National Commission on AIDS, 1992).

These factors help to place infants born to poor women at higher risk of being premature and low birthweight (Berkowitz, 1981). Low-birthweight babies are nearly twice as likely to suffer severe developmental delay or congenital anomalies (Institute of Medicine, 1985). They are also at significantly greater risk of such long-term disabilities as cerebral palsy, autism, and mental retardation, and vision and hearing impairments and other developmental disabilities (Shapiro et al., 1983). These detrimental health and developmental effects of preterm delivery and low birthweight are all greater among poor children (Wise and Meyers, 1988; Parker et al., 1988). Both premature and low-birthweight infants are believed to be at increased risk of abuse because they exhibit "abuse provoking" characteristics, such as prolonged and irritating crying, and often demand a great deal of care (Frodi, 1981; Ammerman, 1990, 1991). However, this association was not found in a predominantly middle-class sample (Crnic et al., 1983). Thus, difficult babies may only precipitate abuse in parents who are already stressed because of such factors as economic deprivation (Ammerman, 1990).

Early childbearing is associated with many adverse developmental outcomes, even if a child is carried to term and is born at a normal weight. In 1989, slightly more than one-half million children were born to mothers under the age of 20 (Children's Defense Fund, 1992). Children of adolescent mothers score lower on standardized tests of language and intellectual functioning, beginning in preschool and continuing in elementary grades (Marecek, 1979). They are also more likely than children born to older mothers to exhibit behavior problems, ranging from hyperactivity to poor impulse control (Brooks-Gunn and Furstenberg, 1986; Hofferth, 1987).

Poverty is often linked to early childbearing. Among poor children under age 6, 47 percent had mothers who first gave birth before the age of 20; among nonpoor children, the proportion was only 17 percent (National Center for Children in Poverty, 1990). The child of a poor mother faces the double jeopardy of exposure to poverty and a mother who may lack the emotional maturity or knowledge to be a good parent. Being single, young, black, and poor is the combination most likely to be associated with a lack of success for the parent and poor caregiving (Egeland and Erickson, 1990).

All children who experience inadequate attention, maltreatment, abuse, or neglect are at high risk for developmental, learning, emotional, and academic difficulties, and the more such experiences a child has, the more negative the developmental outcomes will be (Sameroff et al., 1987). There are strong links between economic deprivation and child maltreatment, although the exact processes that mediate between poverty and developmental risk are controversial. Abuse and maltreatment are not confined to poor families, but successive studies have documented the highest incidence of child neglect in families living in extreme poverty and the most severe injuries from abuse or neglect occurring in the poorest families (Pelton, 1981; Wolock and Horowitz, 1984; Giovannoni and Billingsley, 1970). In fact, neighborhoods that are socially impoverished as well as economically stressed have higher rates of abuse (Garbarino and Sherman, 1980). Mothers of young children who are living below the poverty line are at the greatest risk of violent behavior toward children (Gelles, 1992), and living in poverty also appears to increase the likelihood of continuing abusive patterns across generations (Egeland, 1988).

Poverty exposes children to a number of other environmental risks of physical injury that strongly influence a child's socialization and success in school. For example, at least two major causes of brain dysfunction have a high correlation with poverty: head injuries (whether intentional or accidental) and exposure to lead (Reiss and Roth, 1993). Accidental injuries occur more frequently among poor children (Rivera and Mueller, 1987) and appear to be the result of living in dangerous housing and neighborhoods, as well as inadequate protection by parents and other caregivers (National Center for Children in Poverty, 1990). Both exposure to lead and blood-lead concentrations in children under 5 years have been shown to increase as family income decreases (Mahaffey et al., 1982). Even a low level of exposure to lead in childhood may result in higher rates of learning disability, low achievement, and failure to graduate from high school (Needlemen et al., 1990).

In summary, the evidence is clear and compelling that persistent poverty exacts a significant price on children's health, development, educational attainment, and socioeconomic potential, even though the causal relationships are not well understood in all cases. These effects become more pronounced by adolescence. The economic and demographic changes of the last two decades have led to a significant increase in the proportion of adolescents who have lived in poverty for prolonged periods. In 1991, the poverty rate for all children under 18 years was 21.8 percent (Bureau of the Census, 1992). Although the majority of such children will survive the experience and go on to a productive adult life, many will not. And the increasing proportion of all American children who will live in poverty at some point in their lives means that a steadily increasing percentage of adolescents are at risk of a compromised future.

Though this report focuses on adolescents, their life settings, and the changes that have occurred in them over the last two decades, we note again that the adolescents who enter these settings are a product of their early life experiences. Those whose early experience was marked by poverty suffer increased vulnerability to many of the settings discussed in this report.

REFERENCES

Ammerman, R.T.
  1990   Etiological models of child maltreatment: a behavioral perspective. *Behavioral Modification* 14(3):230-254.
  1991   The role of the child in physical abuse: a reappraisal. *Violence and Victims* 6(2):87-101.
Berkowitz, G.S.
  1981   An epidemiologic study of preterm delivery. *American Journal of Epidemiology* 113(1):81-92.
Brooks-Gunn, J., and F.F. Furstenberg, Jr.
  1986   Antecedents and consequences of parenting: the case of adolescent motherhood. In A. Fogel and L.G. Melson, eds., *The Origins of Nurturance: Developmental, Biological, and Cultural Perspectives on Caregiving.* Hillsdale, N.J.: Lawrence Erlbaum Associates.
Brown, S., ed.
  1988   *Prenatal Care: Reaching Mothers, Reaching Infants.* Committee to

Study Outreach for Prenatal Care, Institute of Medicine. Washington, D.C.: National Academy Press.

Bureau of the Census
1992   *Poverty in the United States: 1991.* Current Population Reports, Series P-60, No. 181. Washington, D.C.: U.S. Department of Commerce.

Chasnoff, I.J., H.J. Landress, and M.E. Barrett
1990   The prevalence of illicit drug or alcohol use during pregnancy and discrepancies in mandatory reporting in Pinellas County, Florida. *New England Journal of Medicine* 322(17):1202-1206.

Children's Defense Fund
1992   *The Health of America's Children, 1992.* Washington, D.C.: Children's Defense Fund.

Cochran, M., and J. Brassard
1979   Child development and personal social networks. *Child Development* 50:601-616.

Crnic, K.A., M.T. Greenberg, A.S. Ragozin, N.M. Robinson, and R.B. Basham
1983   Effects of stress and social support on mothers and premature and full-term infants. *Child Development* 54:209-217.

Egeland, B.
1988   Breaking the cycle of abuse: implications for prediction and intervention. Pp. 87-99 in K.D. Browne, C. Davies, and P. Strattor, eds., *Early Prediction and Prevention of Child Abuse.* New York: John Wiley and Sons, Inc.

Egeland, B., and M.F. Erickson
1990   Rising above the past: strategies for helping new mothers break the cycle of abuse and neglect. *Zero to Three* 11(2):29-35.

Frank, D.A., B.S. Zuckerman, H. Amaro, K. Aboagye, H.J. Bauchner, H. Cabral, L. Fried, R. Hingson, H. Kayne, S.M. Levenson, S. Parker, H. Reece, and R. Vinci
1988   Cocaine during pregnancy: prevalence and correlates. *Pediatrics* 82(6):888-895.

Frodi, A.M.
1981   Contribution of infant characteristics to child abuse. *American Journal of Mental Deficiency* 85:341-349.

Furstenberg, F., J. Brooks-Gunn, and S. Morgan
1987   *Adolescent Mothers in Later Life.* New York: Cambridge University Press.

Garbarino, J., and D. Sherman
1980   High-risk neighborhoods and high-risk families: the human ecology of child maltreatment. *Child Development* 51:188-198.

Gelles, R.J.
1992   Poverty and violence toward children. *American Behavioral Scientist* 35(3):258-274.

Giovannoni, J.M., and A. Billingsley
1970   Child neglect among the poor: a study of parental adequacy in families of three ethnic groups. *Child Welfare* 49:196-204.

Henshaw, S.K., and J. Silverman
1988   The characteristics and prior contraceptive use of U.S. abortion patients. *Family Planning Perspectives* 20(4):158-168.

Hill, M.S., and G.J. Duncan
1987   Parental family income and the socioeconomic attainment of children. *Social Science Research* 16:39-73.

Hill, M.S., S. Augustyniak, G. Duncan, P. Gurin, J. Liker, J. Morgan, and M. Ponza
  1985   *Motivation and Economic Mobility.* Research Report Series. Ann Arbor: Institute for Social Research, University of Michigan.
Hofferth, S.L.
  1987   The children of teen child bearers. Pp. 174-276 in S.L. Hofferth and C.D. Hayes, eds., *Risking the Future: Adolescent Sexuality, Pregnancy, and Childbearing,* Vol. II. Committee on Child Development Research and Public Policy, Commission on Behavioral and Social Sciences and Education, National Research Council. Washington, D.C.: National Academy Press.
Institute of Medicine
  1985   *Preventing Low Birthweight.* Committee to Study the Prevention of Low Birthweight. Washington, D.C.: National Academy Press.
Kellam, S., M.E. Ensminger, and R. Turner
  1977   Family structure and the mental health of children. *Archives of General Psychiatry* 34:1012-1022.
Klerman, L.V., with M.B. Parker
  1991   *Alive and Well? A Research and Policy Review of Health Programs for Poor Young Children.* New York: National Center for Children in Poverty, Columbia University.
Lynn, L.E., Jr., and M.G.H. McGeary, eds.
  1990   *Inner-City Poverty in the United States.* Committee on National Urban Policy, Commission on Behavioral and Social Sciences and Education, National Research Council. Washington, D.C.: National Academy Press.
Mahaffey, K.R., J.L. Annest, and J. Roberts
  1982   National estimates of blood lead levels: United States, 1976-1980: association with selected demographic and socio-economic factors. *New England Journal of Medicine* 307(10):573-579.
Marecek, J.
  1979   Economic, Social and Psychological Consequences of Adolescent Childbearing: An Analysis of Data from the Philadelphia Collaborative Perinatal Project. Institute for the Continuous Study of Man, Philadelphia.
National Center for Children in Poverty
  1990   *Five Million Children: A Statistical Profile of Our Poorest Young Citizens.* New York: Columbia University School of Public Health.
  1992   *Five Million Children: 1992 Update.* New York: Columbia University School of Public Health.
National Commission on AIDS
  1992   *The Challenges of HIV/AIDS in Communities of Color.* Washington, D.C.: National Commission on AIDS.
Needlemen, H.L., A. Schell, D. Bellinger, A. Leviton, and E.N. Allred
  1990   The long-term effects of exposure to low doses of lead in childhood. *New England Journal of Medicine* 322(2):83-88.
Pamuk, E.R., and W.D. Mosher
  1988   *Health Aspects of Pregnancy and Childbirth: United States, 1982.* Vital and Health Statistics, Series 23, No. 16. Hyattsville, Md.: National Center for Health Statistics.
Parker, S., S. Greer, and B. Zuckerman
  1988   Double jeopardy: the impact of poverty on early childhood development. *Pediatric Clinics of North America* 35(6):1227-1240.

Pelton, L.H.
1981   *The Social Context of Child Abuse and Neglect.* New York: Human Sciences Press.

Reiss, A.J., Jr., and J.A. Roth, eds.
1993   *Understanding and Preventing Violence.* Panel on the Understanding and Control of Violent Behavior, Committee on Law and Justice, National Research Council. Washington, D.C.: National Academy Press.

Rivera, F.P., and B.A. Mueller
1987   The epidemiology and causes of childhood injuries. *Journal of Social Issues* 43(2):13-32.

Sameroff, A.J., R. Seifr, R. Barocas, M. Zax, and S. Greenspan
1987   Intelligence quotient scores of 4-year-old children: social-environmental risk factors. *Pediatrics* 79(3):343-350.

Sawhill, I.
1992   Young children and families. In H.J. Aaron and C.L. Schultze, eds., *Setting Domestic Priorities: What Can Governments Do?* Washington, D.C.: Brookings Institution.

Shapiro, S., M.C. McCormick, B.M. Starfield, and B. Crawley
1983   Changes in infant morbidity associated with decreases in neonatal mortality. *Pediatrics* 72(3):408-415.

U.S. General Accounting Office
1990   *Drug-Exposed Infants: A Generation at Risk.* Washington, D.C.: U.S. General Accounting Office.

Werner, E.E., and R.S. Smith
1982   *Vulnerable but Invincible: A Longitudinal Study of Resilient Children and Youth.* New York: McGraw-Hill.

Wilson, M.N.
1989   Child development in the context of the black extended family. *American Psychologist* 44(2):380-385.

Wise, P.H., and A. Meyers
1988   Poverty and child health. *Pediatric Clinics of North America* 35(6):1176.

Wolock, I., and B. Horowitz
1984   Child maltreatment as a social problem: the neglect of neglect. *American Journal of Orthopsychiatry* 54(4):530-543.

Zill, N., K.A. Moore, E.W. Smith, T. Stief, and M.J. Coiro
1991   *The Life Circumstances and Development of Children in Welfare Families: A Profile Based on National Survey Data.* Washington, D.C.: Child Trends.

2

Earnings and Employment

$\mathbf{W}$e begin our analysis of the settings in which adolescents are growing up with a discussion of the economic position of prime-age young adults (aged 25-34) and a review of the changes affecting this group over the last two decades. Although many factors form the settings in which adolescents live, and these are discussed in subsequent chapters, family income is the key influence on all settings. Therefore, to understand why increasing numbers of children and adolescents are spending their formative years in high-risk settings, it is first necessary to understand the economic position of their parents. This chapter reviews the current economic position of prime-age young adults—the parents of 52.1 percent of children under the age of 18. The earnings of this population are the primary source of economic support for the majority of children in the United States (Centers for Disease Control, 1991).

TRENDS SINCE 1970

American family incomes increased almost continuously from 1949 through 1973 but have slowed dramatically in the last two decades. The 1973-1982 period marked the first sustained decline in real earnings for many workers since the Great Depression, and the recovery since then has not significantly improved the incomes of families with children. The income gains from the economic expansion of the 1980s produced increases in real per capita income. However, the gains were highly concentrated in the upper income brackets, and both earnings and per capita income became more unequal over the decade. The increases brought little real gain to the great majority of young adults with children (John et al., 1989; Danzinger and Weinberg, 1992).[1]

Since the late 1970s, structural changes in the U.S. economy, coupled with demographic changes that have increased the number of female-headed households, have caused a substantial and broad-based deterioration in the economic position of this age group. The decline in income cuts across race, gender, and educational attainment, but it is especially pronounced among the less educated—those with a high school diploma or less—and is almost as significant for high school graduates who do not obtain a 4-year college degree.

As shown in Table 2-1, the average real earnings for young adults declined significantly from 1979 to 1988, and this decline occurred during a period of strong economic expansion. Those who worked year-round on a full-time basis experienced a 5.2 percent decline in real earnings in the 1980s. The least educated workers suffered most: white males without a high school diploma saw a drop of 18.8 percent in real earnings; white females without a high school diploma, 14 percent. College graduates, especially women, enjoyed a slight increase in earnings, but high school graduates generally experienced sharp declines.

Table 2-2 illustrates changes in labor market participation during the 1980s for the various demographic groups, by level of education. (Labor market participation rates measure the proportion of persons working or looking for work in a specified population.) The unchanged employment-to-population rates for white men gives a somewhat misleading picture of the economic opportunities available to the less educated. The employment rates of dropouts and high school graduates had fallen sharply in the 1970s (Blackburn et al., 1990), and the rough stability of the 1980s simply reflects the earlier timing of that loss of employment. For young black males, however, employment rates dropped sharply during the 1980s, especially among high school dropouts.

---

[1] The real impact of stagnant or declining incomes among families with children is difficult to gauge because of problems in estimating the effects of declining family size over the last two decades. Smaller families mean that family income is shared among fewer children, and thus the impact of the declines may not be as severe as they appear.

TABLE **2-1**   Average Earnings of Workers Aged 25-34, 1979 and 1988

Demographic Group and Highest Educational Attainment	Average Earnings (1988 dollars)		Changes in Earnings, 1979-1988 (percent)
	1979	1988	
All Workers	21,823	20,678	–5.2
White Males			
Dropouts[a]	19,848	16,108	–18.8
High school graduates[b]	24,889	21,776	–12.5
College graduates[c]	29,288	29,780	+1.7
Black Males			
Dropouts	14,596	14,594	0
High school graduates	19,449	16,638	–14.5
College graduates	26,830	24,348	–9.3
White Females			
Dropouts	12,623	10,852	–14.0
High school graduates	15,403	15,348	0
College graduates	20,987	23,791	+13.4
Black Females			
Dropouts	11,749	11,169	–4.9
High school graduates	14,596	13,285	–9.0
College graduates	19,349	19,567	+1.1

NOTES: Whites include both the white and the "other" racial group.

[a]Completed schooling of less than 12 years.
[b]Schooling of 12 to 15 years.
[c]Schooling of 16 years or more.

SOURCE: These statistics were calculated using the March 1980 and 1989 Current Population Surveys. Earnings are defined as wage and salary income; only full-time, year-round workers were included in the sample for this table. The average earnings statistics are geometric means, reported in 1988 dollars.

The combination of a decline in the value of real earnings and rising levels of unemployment has thrust a very high proportion of families headed by an adult aged 25-34 into poverty. In 1991, 23.1 percent of all such families had incomes below the poverty level. For whites, the percentage living in poverty was 18.6; for blacks, 46.0; and for Hispanics, 38.0.

What explains the trends in employment opportunities and earnings

TABLE **2-2** Labor Market Participation by Race, Gender, and Education for Adults Aged 25-34, 1980 and 1989

Demographic Group	Employment-to-Population Ratio		
	Dropouts[a]	High School Graduates[b]	College Graduates[c]
White males			
1980	.80	.90	.94
1989	.80	.90	.94
Change, 1980-1989	0	0	0
Black males			
1980	.68	.80	.90
1989	.56	.75	.90
Change, 1980-1989	−.12	−.05	0
White females			
1980	.43	.59	.75
1989	.44	.67	.82
Change, 1980-1989	.01	.08	.07
Black females			
1980	.41	.64	.84
1989	.29	.64	.88
Change, 1980-1989	−.12	0	.04

[a]Completed schooling of less than 12 years.
[b]Schooling of 12 to 15 years.
[c]Schooling of 16 years or more.

SOURCE: The statistics were calculated using data from the March 1980 and March 1989 Current Population Surveys.

potential for young adults generally, and for less educated youths specifically? We discuss a number of economywide trends and institutional forces affecting young adult males. The analysis centers on young men because the majority of relevant studies do not include young women. Several economywide developments appear to have lowered demand for less educated young male workers.

JOB OPPORTUNITIES FOR YOUNG WORKERS

Sectoral Shifts in Employment

In recent decades, the number of blue-collar and skilled jobs has decreased and there has been a relative decline in the importance of the manufacturing sector. The total number of manufacturing jobs has remained relatively stable, which means that few opportunities are available for young workers entering the labor force. As a result, since 1970, the fraction of males employed in manufacturing has declined from 30 percent to 19 percent, while employment in the trade and service sectors has grown from 39 percent to 48 percent. The movement out of the manufacturing trades has been especially pronounced among young adult blacks, with a decrease from 46 percent of jobs held by blacks (male and female) in 1974 to 26 percent in 1984 (Bound and Johnson, 1992; Sum and Fogg, 1987).

The loss of manufacturing job opportunities has significantly affected the wages available to less educated workers since manufacturing has traditionally been a high-wage sector for blue-collar and skilled workers. Overall employment levels may also be affected, especially in situations where young, less skilled workers are unable to obtain service-sector jobs (due to the demand for higher skill levels) or unwilling to accept them (due to lower wages). For young blacks, the loss of manufacturing jobs is even more important because relative wages for black workers have been higher in this sector than in others (Berlin and Sum, 1988; Krueger and Summers, 1987; Sum and Fogg, 1987). These sectoral shifts account for an estimated 25 to 33 percent of the relative decline in the wages of young and less educated workers (Blackburn et al., 1990; Katz and Murphy, 1991; Bound and Johnson, 1992). Declining manufacturing employment accounted for 33 to 50 percent of the decline in the employment-to-population ratio of young black dropouts in the 1970s (Bound and Holzer, 1991).

Technological Change

Changes in production technology raise the overall education levels needed by industry, thereby diminishing employment opportunities for less educated workers. Studies over time and across industries have found positive associations between various measures of technological progress (e.g., capital spending, R&D spending, employment of technical personnel) and wage differentials among education levels. The evidence supports the notion that, on average, technological change tends to increase inequality between skill groups (Hamermesh, 1986; Bartel and Lichtenberg, 1987; Mincer, 1991; Allen, 1991).

Rising Unemployment

The average rate of unemployment has risen steadily over the past several decades (Murphy and Topel, 1987). After adjusting for cyclical changes, unemployment rates of 4 percent or less were common in the 1950s and 1960s, but unemployment seldom fell below 6 percent in the 1970s and 1980s. While there was improvement in overall unemployment in the late 1980s, even the lowest rate (5.2 percent) was well above the rates of earlier decades, and particularly tight labor markets were limited to a small number of metropolitan areas (Freeman, 1991). The higher average unemployment rates of the past 20 years appear to have contributed to the lower employment and earnings of young workers, especially among the less educated and blacks—populations that are particularly sensitive to aggregate changes in unemployment (Clark and Summers, 1982; Freeman, 1991). These workers are the first to be laid off during recessions and the last to be rehired during periods of recovery; their wages also appear to be sensitive to the tightness or looseness of the labor market (Freeman, 1991).

Immigration

During the past two decades, an estimated 750,000 legal and illegal immigrants entered the United States annually (Warren and Passel, 1987; Borjas et al., 1991b). Immigrant workers have increased the workforce of high school dropouts by approximately 25 percent, the workforce of high school graduates by 6 or 7 percent, and the workforce of college graduates by 10 to 11 percent (Borjas et al., 1991a). In the aggregate, this influx of foreign-born workers does not seem to have had a statistically significant impact on the employment and earnings of natives in cities such as New York or Los Angeles, cities that have many immigrants in comparison with cities like Kansas City or Cleveland, which have relatively few immigrants (Borjas, 1986; Altonji and Card, 1989; LaLonde and Topel, 1989). However, it does appear that the immigration of less educated workers affects the earnings and employment of natives with similar skill levels in the population as a whole as "spillover" from immigrant-intensive cities to other parts of the country. Perhaps 20 percent of the deterioration in the market for high school dropouts is due to the influx of less educated immigrants (Borjas et al., 1991a).

INSTITUTIONAL FACTORS INFLUENCING
JOB AVAILABILITY AND EARNINGS

Minimum Wage and Unions

Unionization and the minimum wage have often protected young workers, whose market position is generally weak. In recent years, these protections have been less effective. The federal minimum wage rose by only 109 percent between 1972 and 1990 (from $1.60 to $3.25), well short of the 191 percent inflation rate over the same period. Even the current statutory rate of $4.25 leaves a family of four that has one full-time earner at less than two-thirds of the federal poverty level. Although a lower minimum wage has the beneficial effect of stimulating job creation, particularly for teenagers, there are also costs. A lower minimum wage also constrains the wages paid to unskilled workers, jobs that are held by blacks, high school dropouts and young, less educated black women (Bound and Freeman, 1991; Blackburn et al., 1990). The small gains in employment that these groups have experienced as a result of low minimum-wage levels are not adequate to offset the declining real value of the wages that they earned, thus causing the overall earnings and income of the working poor to decline (Mincy, 1990).

Union membership brings less educated workers a premium in wages and fringe benefits relative to those earned by nonunion workers. Membership rates have fallen since the mid-1950s, however, and the decline has been especially steep in recent years. Between 1970 and 1990, union membership in the private sector fell from about 30 percent to only 12 percent. Approximately one-quarter of the falling relative position of less skilled young men is attributable to falling rates of unionization (Blackburn et al., 1990; Card, 1992; Freeman, 1993).

Isolation from Jobs

Worker demand is not always geographically matched to worker supply. Manufacturing employment, over half of which is already suburbanized, has increasingly deserted central cities. This reflects a broader movement of firms and middle-class families away from central cities, particularly from poor neighborhoods in northeastern and midwestern cities, to more affluent suburban areas. One consequence is that manufacturing jobs (and those in other sectors that require less education) have become more suburbanized in the past two decades, while financial and service-sector jobs (which require more education) have become more concentrated in inner cities. These trends are of greater significance to minority workers, who are disproportionately represented in central cities (Holzer, 1991; Wilson, 1987; Kasarda, 1989; see also Chapter 3).

Discrimination

Employment discrimination—generally defined as unequal treatment of individuals who possess equal productive characteristics—occurs as a direct consequence of employers' preferences for certain types of workers. Discrimination occurs in the "candidate" and "entry" and "promotion" stages of the employment process (Braddock and McPartland, 1987; Pettigrew and Martin, 1987). For example, among Chicago area employers interviewed in one study, 47 percent stated that blacks lack basic skills and the work experience necessary to fill "customer service" occupations; accordingly, recruitment was most often done through high schools and newspapers that reached white middle-class neighborhoods, rather than through those associated with large black populations (Kirschenman and Neckerman, 1990). Other studies have matched pairs of black and white or white and Hispanic men with similar resumes and trained them to behave comparably in interviews. Whites generally received about 50 percent more offers than blacks or Hispanics (Turner et al., 1991; Cross et al., 1989).

The extent to which discrimination has diminished over the past two decades is unclear. Most evidence suggests that racial discrimination against nonwhite men continues, and that women of all races suffer considerable discrimination in comparison with men (Jaynes and Williams, 1989). The previously cited study of Chicago-area businesses found strong prejudices against inner-city black men, who were viewed by employers as "unstable, uncooperative, dishonest and uneducated." Employers screened out job candidates based on class characteristics and were particularly wary of hiring men or women who exhibited speech and dress patterns associated with ghetto culture (Kirschenman and Neckerman, 1990). Although small-scale studies increase understanding of employer attitudes and hiring practices, it is impossible to extrapolate from the results to quantify the effects of this type of discrimination. Available methods are likely to underestimate discrimination, in part because the character of racial discrimination has become more subtle than in previous decades (Bielby and Baron,

1986). This factor may explain the inability of researchers to identify the reasons that blacks are less likely to advance to the "top rungs" of organizations (Braddock and McPartland, 1987; Davis and Watson, 1985; Hacker, 1992). Further, discrimination varies depending on the tightness of the labor market and has been shown to increase when overall unemployment rates are high (Tobin, 1965).

CHANGES IN THE SUPPLY AND QUALIFICATIONS OF YOUNG WORKERS

Supply of Young Workers

The large number of "baby boomers" entering the labor market in the 1970s depressed their wages relative to those of older groups, though there has been at least some evidence of "catching up" as this group has aged (Welch, 1979; Bloom et al., 1987). The "baby bust" of the 1960s and early 1970s reduced the number of young people entering the labor market, which might have been expected to raise the relative wages of younger workers across the board. However, this failed to occur, except in a small number of tight labor markets (Freeman, 1991; Mishel and Teixeira, 1991). One explanation may have been a decline in college enrollments, which increased the relative supply of less educated workers. The slowdown in the growth of college graduates in the workforce appears to be a major factor in the falling position of the less educated male workers (Blackburn et al., 1990; Katz and Murphy, 1991).

Adequacy of Basic Skills

Another explanation for decreased earnings among less educated workers is a decline in basic reading and math skills. According to the National Assessment of Educational Progress, 30 percent of adolescents and young adults lack basic literacy skills and are consequently unable to absorb and synthesize written information essential to carrying out an unfamiliar task (Venezky et al., 1987). Declining achievement and test scores in the late 1960s and 1970s have been linked to declining productivity and earnings at both the aggregate and individual levels (Bishop, 1989a,b). Individual scores on basic skills have significant effects on earnings, and the racial gap in scores can explain much of the racial differential in earnings at a given educational level (O'Neill, 1990; Ferguson, 1990). This might explain why blacks—dropouts, high school graduates, and college graduates alike—have substantially less success in the labor market than their white counterparts. Yet the test scores (as well as graduation rates) of young blacks have risen even while their relative and absolute earnings were falling (Bound and Freeman, 1991). Moreover, the relative earnings of less educated workers fell in the 1980s as the cohort aged (Blackburn et al., 1990). Since the schooling and basic skills of a cohort are relatively constant, the declining earnings of the less educated may be explained by higher demands for literacy skills related to the increased complexity of manufacturing processes. Thus higher paying jobs are increasingly less accessible to illiterate or marginally literate workers (Bailey, 1988).

Trends in basic skills cannot explain the declining economic position of less educated young adults. The demand for basic academic skills (due to technological changes and other factors) rose more rapidly over the past 15 years than the supply of young workers with such skills, but other forces are also at work.

Crime

Crime has become an attractive alternative to working for many poor, less educated young men. Among this group, particularly black high school dropouts, criminal involvement has become so common that it must be considered a major determinant in evaluating their rates of participation in legal labor markets. At any time, as many as 18 percent of *all* 18 to 24-year-old dropouts and 30 percent of 25- to 34-year-old dropouts are under supervision of the criminal justice system. Among blacks the figures are much higher: 41 percent of 18- to 24-year-old dropouts and over three-quarters of 25- to 34-year-old dropouts (Freeman, 1991). It is estimated that some 20 percent of all young black men are involved with the criminal justice system (Freeman, 1991).

Although it is difficult to estimate earnings from illegal activities, studies suggests that men with limited skills and few legal earnings opportunities net substantially more from criminal activities with rates of pay as much as 2 to 4 times higher than those from legitimate work. This estimate is consistent with ethnographic studies of youths involved in the drug trade (Taylor, 1989; Williams, 1989; Bourgois, 1989). Reuter et al. (1990) estimated median earnings in 1985-1987 for street-level crack dealing in Washington, D.C., at $30 per hour.

The substantial and increasing concentration of crime among high school dropouts suggests that the problem is linked to lack of skills—to functional illiteracy and the inability to perform in a modern technological and service-oriented economy—and to the decline in legitimate employment and earnings opportunities available to the less educated. The financial rewards of criminal activity have also increased with the growth in drug markets, and this may make the attractiveness of participation in illegal markets stronger for young men today than in recent periods.

DEMOGRAPHIC CHANGES

Demographic changes have also exerted a powerful influence in increasing the number of young adult households that are poor or on the margins of poverty. There has been an almost 40 percent increase since 1970 in the number of female-headed households with children under age 18. In that year, 2,858,000 families were headed by single mothers; in 1991, the number had increased to 6,823,000, or 9.9 percent of all families in 1970, contrasted with 21 percent of all families in 1991 (Bureau of the Census, 1991). The increase results from women marrying at a later age or remaining single throughout their lives and also from higher rates of divorce and separation (Mare and Winship, 1991). The trend has occurred across racial, ethnic, and income groups. However, the decline in the proportion of black women who are married and living with their husband has been especially dramatic.

Among black women aged 24-29, the percentage that had never married increased from 16.9 percent in 1960 to 53.2 percent in 1987 (Mare and Winship, 1991). Comparable percentages for white women were 12.4 and 26.3. The authors conclude that the decline in marriage rates among black women and the concomitant increase in black babies born to unmarried women has been a major cause of the persistently large gap between family incomes of blacks and whites. Although the illegitimacy ratio (proportion of births to unmarried women to all births) has increased across all race and income groups over the last 20 years, the greatest absolute increase has been among blacks. In 1989, 57 percent of all births to blacks were to unmarried women, compared with 17 percent among white women and 23 percent among Hispanic women (Bureau of the Census, 1990).

The incidence of poverty among female-headed families has stayed consistently 7 to 8 times higher than poverty among married-couple families. In 1990, 57.8 percent of female-headed households in the prime-age group had incomes below poverty. For whites, the percentage was 52.0; for blacks 67.8 and Hispanics

72.0. More than half (51.2 percent) of all black children lived in female-headed households in 1990, compared with 16.2 percent of white children and 27.1 percent of Hispanic children. The increase in female-headed households is a more powerful explanatory factor in describing the increase in poverty among prime-age adults than either the decline in the value of real earnings or increases in unemployment. However, the trends are interactive in complex ways and therefore need to be considered simultaneously.

Wilson (1987) has hypothesized that the diminished economic position of young black males is the primary contributing factor to the increasing proportion of black women who have children outside of marriage. Espenshade (1985), Farley and Bianchi (1987), and Farley (1988) have hypothesized that the improved economic position of women has reduced their need to rely upon husbands for income, and thus decreased their incentives to marry, and others have considered the effects of increased years of schooling on age at marriage and lifetime probability of marriage. Mare and Winship's analysis based on census and Current Population Survey data suggest that the changes in employment of young black men may account for about 20 percent of the decline in marriage rates for black women, and that increased earnings and school enrollment have very small effects. The explanation for this remarkable change in family composition is complex, and appears to involve the interaction of social and economic trends over the last several decades that has created a changed climate of expectation about marriage and childrearing.

CONCLUSIONS

Whether measured by earnings or employment, the economic position of prime-age young adults has diminished substantially in the past 20 years, especially among males and those with a high school education or less. The causes include several concurrent economywide trends in labor demand, labor supply, and institutional factors. Demographic changes, particularly the exceptional increase in female-headed households, have strongly influenced the economic position of families headed by young adults. However, the declining economic position of families with children is not confined to female-headed households. Although the demographic trends discussed are important in understanding poverty among children and adolescents, they should not obscure the reality that two-parent families have also experienced a decline in their standard of living. The decline has simply been less precipitous than for female-headed households. Over the last two decades, among families with children, only the top income quintile of two-parent families has experienced a substantial increase in real incomes.

However, the majority of children today rely upon the incomes of parents who have not obtained a 4-year college degree, and it is therefore the earnings and employment outlook for non-college-educated adults that will be critical. What are the economic prospects for future cohorts of less educated young workers? Is it possible that self-correcting mechanisms may work to ameliorate the trends that we have summarized? For example, the rising returns to a college diploma should encourage more young people to enroll in college; the deteriorating wages and employment of dropouts relative to high school graduates should further diminish dropout rates over time. Even if these changes occur, their impact is not likely to change the basic outlook we have described.

The same occupational and industrial shifts that reduced demand for less skilled workers are projected to continue through the 1990s (Personick, 1989). Employment and earnings in manufacturing and in high-wage, blue-collar occupations appear likely to continue to decline, while employment will grow most in areas requiring higher education or in low-wage service jobs. Employment discrimination continues. In poor urban neighborhoods, the social environment compounds the lack of employment opportunities for young people (see Chapter 3). Furthermore, the fact that criminal involvement has become so common among young disadvantaged men is producing a large criminal underclass that is difficult to integrate into the legitimate economy.

Although there is no single reason why young adults had diminishing success in the labor market over the past two decades, and why families headed by prime-age adults suffered a decline in living standards, the trends are persistent. We have described the most plausible explanatory factors to establish why a large and increasing percentage of American children and adolescents are likely to spend significant portions of their lives in or near poverty. The causes of declining family incomes are rooted in complex economic and sociological changes that are only partially understood, and that will therefore be difficult to alter. In the chapters that follow, we examine the major settings that shape the lives of adolescents, consider how these are influenced by family income, and assess how settings influence adolescent behavior and life opportunities.

REFERENCES

Allen, S.
1991   Technology and the wage structure. Mimeo, North Carolina State University, Raleigh.

Altonji, J., and D. Card
1989   The effects of immigration on the labor market outcomes of natives. In J. Abowd and R. Freeman, eds., *Immigration, Trade, and the Labor Market.* Chicago: University of Chicago Press.

Bailey, T.
1988   Education and Transformation of Markets and Technology in the Textile Industry. Technical paper 2, Conversion of Human Resources Projects, Columbia University.

Bartel, A., and F. Lichtenberg
1987   The comparative advantage of educated workers in implementing new technology. *Review of Economics and Statistics* 69(1):1-11.

Berlin, G., and A. Sum
1988   Toward a More Perfect Union: Basic Skills, Poor Families, and Our Economic Future. Occasional paper no. 3, Ford Foundation, New York.

Bielby, W.T., and J.N. Baron
1986   Men and women at work: sex segregation and statistical discrimination. *American Journal of Sociology* 91:759-799.

Bishop, J.
1989a   Incentives for learning: why American high school students compare so poorly to their overseas counterparts. In *Investing in People: Background Papers*, Vol. I. Commission on Workforce Quality and Labor Market Efficiency. Washington, D.C.: U.S. Department of Labor.
1989b   Is the test score decline responsible for the productivity growth decline? *American Economic Review* 79(1):178-197.

Blackburn, K., D. Bloom, and R. Freeman
1990   The declining economic position of less skilled American men. In G. Burtless, ed., *A Future of Lousy Jobs?* Washington, D.C.: Brookings Institution.

Bloom, D., R. Freeman, and S. Korenman
1987   The labor market consequences of generational crowding. *European Journal of Population* 3:131-176.

Borjas, G.
1986   The demographic determinants of the demand for black labor. In R.B. Freeman and H.J. Holzer, eds., *The Black Youth Employment Crisis.* Chicago: University of Chicago Press.

Borjas, G., R. Freeman, and L. Katz
1991a   On the Labor Market Effects of Immigration and Trade. Working paper, Russell Sage Foundation, New York.

Borjas, G., R. Freeman, and K. Lang
1991b   Undocumented Mexican-born workers in the U.S.: how many, how permanent? In J. Abowd and R. Freeman, eds., *Immigration, Trade, and the Labor Market.* Chicago: University of Chicago Press.

Bound, J., and R. Freeman
1991   What went wrong: the erosion of earnings and employment of young Black men in the 1980s. *Quarterly Journal of Economics* 107(1):201-232.

Bound, J., and H. Holzer
1991   Industrial Shifts, Skill Levels, and the Labor Market for White and Black
        Males. Mimeo, Michigan State University, Lansing.
Bound, J., and G. Johnson
1992   Changes in the structure of wages during the 1980s: an evaluation of
        alternative explanations. *American Economic Review* 82(3):371-392.
Bourgois, P.
1989   In search of Horatio Alger: culture and ideology in the crack economy.
        Contemporary Drug Problems 16(4):619-649.
Braddock, J.H., II, and J.M. McPartland
1987   How minorities continue to be excluded from equal opportunities: re-
        search on labor market and institutional barriers. *Journal of Social
        Issues* 43(1):5-40.
Bureau of the Census
1990   *Fertility of American Women: June 1990.* Population Characteristics
        Series P-20, No. 454. Washington, D.C.: U.S. Department of Com-
        merce.
1991   *Household and Family Characteristics.* Current Population Reports, P-
        20, No. 458. Washington, D.C.: U.S. Department of Commerce.
Card, D.
1992   Effect of Unions on the Distribution of Wages: Redistribution or Rela-
        beling. Working paper no. 4195, National Bureau of Economic Research,
        Cambridge, Mass.
Centers for Disease Control
1991   Advance report of final natality statistics. *Monthly Vital Statistics
        Report* 40(8):1-56.
Clark, K., and L. Summers
1982   The dynamics of youth unemployment. In R. Freeman and D. Wise,
        eds., *The Youth Labor Market Problem.* Chicago: University of Chi-
        cago Press.
Cross, H., G. Kenney, J. Mell, and W. Zimmermann
1989   Employee Hiring Practices: Differential Treatment of Hispanic and Anglo
        Job Seekers. Mimeo, Urban Institute, Washington, D.C.
Danzinger, S.H., and D.H. Weinberg
1992   The Historical Record: Trends in Family Income, Inequality, and Pov-
        erty. Paper prepared for the Panel on Poverty and Family Statistics,
        Committee on National Statistics, National Research Council, Wash-
        ington, D.C.
Davis, G., and G. Watson
1985   *Black Life in Corporate America.* New York: Anchor Press/Doubleday.
Espenshade, T.J.
1985   Marriage trends in America: estimates, implications, and underlying
        causes. *Population and Development Review* II(2):193-245.
Farley, R.
1988   After the starting line: blacks and women in an uphill race. *Demography*
        25(4):477-495.
Farley, R., and S. Bianchi
1987   The Growing Racial Difference in Marriage and Family Patterns. Re-
        search report 87-107, Population Studies Center, University of Michi-
        gan.
Ferguson, R.
1990   Racial Patterns in How School and Teacher Quality Affect Achieve-

ment and Earnings. Mimeo, John F. Kennedy School of Government, Harvard University, Cambridge, Mass.

Freeman, R.
1991   Employment and earnings of disadvantaged youth in a labor shortage economy. In C. Jencks and P. Peterson, eds., *The Urban Underclass.* Washington, D.C.: Brookings Institution.
1993   How much has de-unionization contributed to the rise in male earnings inequality? Chapter 4 in S. Danzinger and P. Gottschalk, eds., *Uneven Tides: Rising Inequality in America.* New York: Russell Sage Foundation.

Hacker, A.
1992   *Two Nations: Black and White, Separate, Hostile, Unequal.* New York: Scribners.

Hamermesh, D.
1986   The demand for labor in the long run. In O. Ashenfelter and R. Layard, eds., *Handbook of Labor Economics.* New York: North-Holland.

Holzer, H.
1991   The spatial mismatch hypothesis: what has the evidence shown? *Urban Studies* 28(1):105-122.

Jaynes, G.D., and R.M. Williams, Jr.
1989   *A Common Destiny: Blacks and American Society.* Committee on the Status of Black Americans, Commission on Behavioral and Social Sciences and Education, National Research Council. Washington, D.C.: National Academy Press.

John, C.-L., K. Murphy, and B. Pierce
1989   Accounting for the Slowdown in Black-White Wage Convergence. Unpublished manuscript, University of Chicago.

Kasarda, J.
1989   Urban industrial transition and the underclass. *The Annals of the American Academy of Political and Social Science* 501(Jan.):26-47.

Katz, L.F., and K. Murphy
1991   Changes in relative wages, 1963-1987: the role of supply and demand factors. *Quarterly Journal of Economics* 107(1):35-78.

Kirschenman, J., and K. Neckerman
1990   Hiring Strategies, Racial Bias, and Inner-City Workers. Mimeo, University of Chicago.

Krueger, A., and L. Summers
1987   Reflections of the interindustry wage structure. Pp. 17-47 in K. Lang and J. Leonard, eds., *Unemployment and the Structure of Labor Markets.* New York: Basil Blackwell.

LaLonde, R., and R. Topel
1989   Labor market adjustments to increased immigration. In J. Abowd and R. Freeman, eds., *Immigration, Trade, and the Labor Market.* Chicago: University of Chicago Press.

Mare, R., and C. Winship
1991   Socioeconomic change and the decline of marriage for blacks and whites. In C. Jencks and P.E. Peterson, eds., *The Urban Underclass.* Washington, D.C.: Brookings Institution.

Mincer, J.
1991   Human Capital, Technology, and the Wage Structure: What Do Time Series Show? Working paper no. 3581, National Bureau of Economic Research, Cambridge, Mass.

Mincy, R.
1990   Raising the minimum wage: effects on family poverty. *Monthly Labor Review* 113(7):18-24.

Mishel, L., and R. Teixeira
1991   The Myth of the Coming Labor Shortage. Mimeo, Economic Policy Institute, Washington, D.C.

Murphy, K., and R. Topel
1987   The evolution of unemployment in the United States: 1968-1985. In S. Fischer, ed., *NBER Macroeconomics Annual*. Cambridge, Mass.: MIT Press.

O'Neill, J.
1990   The role of human capital in earnings differences between White and Black men. *Journal of Economic Perspectives* 4(4):25-46.

Personick, V.
1989   Industry output and employment: a slower trend for the nineties. *Monthly Labor Review* 112(11):25-41.

Pettigrew, T.F., and J. Martin
1987   Shaping the organizational context for Black American inclusion. *Journal of Social Issues* 43(1):41-78.

Reuter, P., R. MacCoun, and P. Murphy
1990   *Money from Crime: A Study of the Economics of Drug Dealing in Washington, D.C.*. Santa Monica, Calif.: The RAND Corporation.

Sum, A.M., and W.N. Fogg
1987   The adolescent poor and the transition to early adulthood. In P. Edelman and J. Ladner, eds., *Adolescence & Poverty: Challenge for the 1990s*. Washington, D.C.: Center for National Policy Press.

Taylor, C.C.
1989   *The Dangerous Society*. East Lansing: Michigan State University.

Tobin, J.
1965   On improving the economic status of the negro. *Daedalus* 94:878-898.

Turner, M.A., M. Fix, and R.J. Struyk
1991   *Opportunities Denied, Opportunities Diminished: Discrimination in Hiring*. Washington, D.C.: Urban Institute.

Venezky, R.L., C.F. Kaestle, and A. Sum
1987   *The Subtle Danger: Reflections on the Literacy Abilities of America's Young Adults*. Princeton, N.J.: Educational Testing Service.

Warren, R., and J.S. Passel
1987   A count of the uncountable: estimates of undocumented aliens counted in the 1980 census. *Demography* 24:375-393.

Welch, F.
1979   The baby boom babies' financial bust. *Journal of Political Economy* 87(4):S65-S97.

Williams, T.
1989   *The Cocaine Kids*. Reading, Mass.: Addison-Wesley.

Wilson, W.J.
1987   *The Truly Disadvantaged*. Chicago: University of Chicago Press.

3

Families

Families are the primary setting for nurturing children, and their ability to succeed in this responsibility has been weakened over the last two decades by changes in their economic security and by changes in family structure that have increased the proportion of children and adolescents living with only one parent. This chapter begins with an overview of changes in family economics and structure and discusses how those changes influence adolescent development.

FAMILY ECONOMICS AND FAMILY STRUCTURE

Chapter 2 reviewed the deteriorating economic position of prime-age young adults. This chapter begins by elaborating on the consequences of those trends for young families with children. Between 1973 and 1990 the median income of families with children headed by a parent under age 30 dropped 32 percent when adjusted for inflation. The decline has been even sharper for families headed by a person under age 25. Although demographic changes, especially the increase in single-parent households, has been an important factor in increasing the number of children living at or near poverty, two-parent households have also suffered. Most two-parent families have maintained their relative standard of living only by virtue of having two wage earners. Almost 39 percent of children had mothers in the workforce in 1970; by 1990 the proportion was 61 percent. Furthermore, working mothers have increased their hours of work. In the decade from 1979 to 1989, the average number of hours worked by wives increased 32 percent. Without the income provided by wives entering the workforce and increasing their number of hours worked, incomes for 60 percent of two-parent families would have been lower in 1989 than in 1979 (U.S. Congress, 1992). While increasing workforce participation by wives has been critical in maintaining family incomes, the additional effort that families must make to maintain their incomes creates stress for the family and problems in providing care and supervision for children.

For families who have not been able to increase their earnings sufficiently to stay out of poverty, the consequences are severe and are not confined to material deprivation. Low-income parents report a greater degree of worry about their financial futures and concern for their child's health and education than do more affluent parents, a difference that is most pronounced among central-city inhabitants (National Commission on Children, 1991b). Economic hardship—whether from low wages, sustained poverty, or unemployment—significantly diminishes the emotional well-being of parents, with direct and indirect effects on children's health and well-being (McCord, 1990; Elder, 1992). Economic hardships are linked to family disintegration and to the increase in single-parent households. Further, single parents and parents experiencing economic hardship are less likely to use the "good" parenting practices that can help some children overcome the risks associated with their domestic and economic circumstances (Dornbusch, 1989; Spivak and Weitzman, 1987; Dubow and Luster, 1990).

It should not be surprising, then, that the most consistent, and typically the most powerful, predictor of adolescent success and well-being is family income. Adolescents growing up in families experiencing economic hardship are at high risk for health and behavioral problems, for school failure, and for becoming involved in criminal activities.

• Adolescents from low-income families (incomes less than 150 percent of the poverty rate) experience higher rates of poor physical health, mental disorders, and depression (Brindis et al., 1992; Klerman with Parker, 1991; Institute of Medicine, 1989; Comer, 1985; Tuma, 1989).

• Adolescents from low-income families are more likely to engage in delinquent acts, have early sexual intercourse, experience adolescent pregnancy, be arrested, and drop out of school. They are also less likely to make a successful transition from school into postsecondary education or the labor market (Irwin and Shafer, 1991; Earls, 1991; Dryfoos, 1990; Sum and Fogg, 1991).

• Adolescents from low-income families show lower rates of achievement in school. For example, only 69 percent of whites, 65 percent of blacks, and 61 percent of Hispanic unmarried youth from families with low earnings will graduate from high school or earn a general equivalency diploma by age 24 (Mortenson and Wu, 1990). The high failure rates among low income students reflect, in substantial measure, the fact that many low-income students live in single-parent homes. Regardless of income, female household headship favors increased high school dropout (Hauser and Phang, 1992). More than half of black high school students are now from single-parent households (20 percent of whites and 30 percent of Hispanics).

Family Structure

Family formation has changed dramatically in the past 20 years. Adults are waiting longer to get married, divorcing more frequently, and waiting longer to remarry after a divorce. Between 1970 and 1988, the proportion of 20- to 24-year-olds who had never married rose by 70 percent for women and by more than 40 percent for men. Indeed, over the past 15 years, the percentage of young people still living with their parents has steadily increased to about 54 percent at age 24 and 30 percent at age 29 (Grant Foundation, 1988; Bureau of the Census, 1989a).

Consequently, the absolute number of married couples with children declined during the 1980s. Although the "married with children" household remains the dominant family structure, its character has changed because of maternal employment. By 1987, only 29 percent of children in two-parent households were being reared in the traditional "breadwinner-homemaker" family structure (Zill, 1990). "Nontraditional" families show the greatest growth rates during the past decade, continuing trends that began 30 years ago. Increasing numbers of households are without children, and more adults are unmarried and living alone. Table 3-1 shows the change in living arrangements of children under age 18 between 1970 and 1990. Over this period, the percentage of children living in two-parent households decreased by 16.7 percent.

As noted in Chapter 2, there has been significant growth in single-parent households. About half of all marriages now end in divorce, a rate twice that of 1960. About a quarter of all births are to unmarried women, a majority of whom are *over* the age of 20. The net result has been that about 25 percent of all children

TABLE 3-1 U.S. Households with Children Under 18 (in 1,000s)

Household Type	1970	1980	1990	Percent Change, 1970-1990
Married with children	58,939	48,624	46,503	−21.09
Single parent	8,199	12,466	15,867	+51.67
Single mother	7,452	11,406	13,874	+53.78
Single father	748	1,060	1,993	+37.53
Other	2,024	2,337	1,768	−12.64

SOURCE: U.S. Congress (1991:1080).

live with only one parent, usually the mother, a rate double that of 1970 (Bureau of the Census, 1991a). Overall, about 50 percent of all children will reside in a single-parent home before age 18, spending an average of 6 years with a single parent (Bumpass, 1984; Norton and Glick, 1986).

Adolescent mothers represent a special case of family structure. Birthrates for adolescent mothers are increasing and, increasingly, the mothers are unmarried. Adolescent birthrates, which had declined steadily since World War II, began rising again in 1985, and by 1989 were higher than they had been since the early 1970s (Figure 3-1). But while births to unmarried women represented only 15 percent of all births to adolescents in 1960, and 30 percent in 1970, by 1989 over 67 percent of teenage mothers were unmarried, including 92 percent of black teenage mothers (Moore, 1992).

Single-Parent Households

Single-parent families are likely to live in or near poverty. Families with two wage earners have, on average, three times the family income of families with one wage earner. Poverty rates are almost six times higher for single-parent families than for two-parent families (Table 3-2). About 73 percent of children in single-parent families experience poverty at some point in their lives, and a substantial proportion (20 percent) spend 7 or more years in poverty. And since 87 percent of single parents are women, the

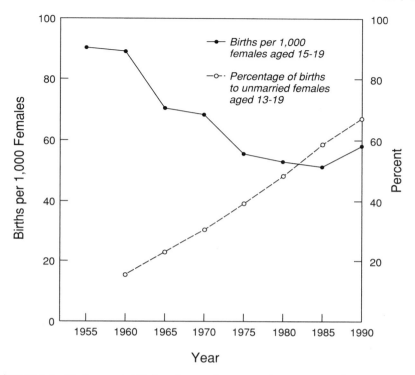

FIGURE 3-1 Births per 1,000 females aged 15-19 and percentage of teenage mothers who were unmarried. SOURCE: Moore (1992).

problems of single parenthood are often compounded by those of gender discrimination in employment and social welfare (Ellwood, 1988; Garfinkel and McLanahan, 1986; Handler and Hasenfeld, 1991; Hodgkinson, 1991; Bureau of the Census, 1989b). It is hardly surprising that single parents are twice as likely as married couples to be worried about "making ends meet" and concerned that their children will "get beat up," "get pregnant," "not get a job," or "drop out of school" (National Commission on Children, 1991b).

Divorce reduces the economic security of women and their children even if they are not thrust into poverty. One year after divorce, women's income averaged only 67 percent of their predivorce income compared with 90 percent for divorced men (Duncan and Hoffman, 1985). The data in Table 3-3 show that, despite increased maternal participation in the labor market, the economic security of children substantially declines after divorce. More-

TABLE **3-2** Child and Household Poverty, 1974-1990

Demographic groups	Rate of Poverty		
	Lowest (year)	Highest (year)	1990
All children under 18	15.4 (1974)	22.3 (1983)	20.6
White	11.2 (1974)	17.5 (1983)	15.9
Black	39.8 (1974)	47.6 (1982)	44.8
Hispanic	27.6 (1978)	40.3 (1985)	38.4
All married-couple families (with children under 18)	5.9 (1978)	10.1 (1983)	7.8
White	5.2 (1978)	9.2 (1983)	7.1
Black	12.0 (1978)	18.0 (1983)	14.3
Hispanic	N/A	N/A	20.8
All female heads of household (with children under 18)	39.6 (1979)	47.8 (1982)	44.5
White	31.3 (1979)	39.8 (1983, 1986)	37.9
Black	53.9 (1989)	63.7 (1982)	56.1
Hispanic	N/A	N/A	58.2

NOTE: N/A, not available.

SOURCE: Bureau of the Census (1991a:Tables 3 and 4).

over, only about 25 percent of mothers who are owed child support payments from fathers actually receive full payment; 24 percent receive no payment at all. Less educated and minority mothers are less likely to receive child support payments than are educated and nonminority mothers (U.S. Congress, 1991:666; Garfinkel and McLanahan, 1986).

Two-Parent Households

Even for two-parent households, working does not guarantee an escape from poverty if both parents have earnings at or near the minimum wage. In 1990, more than 59 percent of all poor families had one worker, but 18 percent had two or more workers and still remained poor (Bureau of the Census, 1991a). Table 3-4 shows characteristics of working poor households. The next group, those partially employed or unemployed, constitute 35 percent of poor

TABLE **3-3** Economic Status of Children Under 15
Years of Age, 4 Months Before and 4 Months
After Parental Separation

Measurement of Well-Being	Before	After
Average monthly per capita income	$ 549	$ 436
Average monthly family income[a]	$2,435	$1,543
Average monthly household income[a]	$2,461	$1,546
Mother worked full time, all weeks	33%	41%
Mother did not work at all	43%	31%
Worked	60%	72%
Average weekly hours of some work	34	37
In poverty	19%	36%
Receiving child support	16%	44%
Receiving AFDC	9%	18%
Receiving food stamps	10%	27%

[a]Household income aggregates income of all persons residing
with the child in a given month. Family income excludes income
from persons unrelated to the child.

SOURCE: Bureau of the Census (1991b).

two-parent families; involuntary unemployment was the primary
cause of poverty for the vast majority of these families (Ellwood,
1988; see also Shapiro, 1990; Bane and Ellwood, 1989).

Increases in the earned income tax credit and the extension of
certain Aid to Families with Dependent Children (AFDC) benefits
to two-parent families suffering from unemployment have improved
the safety net for poor and low-income families. However, it is
far from complete or adequate. In addition, these families are less
able to secure other types of temporary income support—such as
unemployment insurance—than are middle-income families. Less
than half of unemployed workers receive unemployment compensation, and those who either fail to qualify for benefits or exhaust
benefits before finding new work are concentrated in the low-
wage workforce. Furthermore, on average, jobs found after a period of unemployment pay about one-third less than the previous
job (Danziger and Gottschalk, 1988; U.S. Congress, 1991; Children's
Defense Fund and Northeastern University Center for Labor Market Studies, 1992).

The cumulative result is that full-time working poor families
may actually be the poorest of the poor after taking into account
the income transfer payments that are available to the nonwork-
ing poor but not to those who are employed (Ellwood, 1988). Two-

TABLE **3-4** Number of Families with Children
Who Work and Yet Remain Poor, 1980-1990
(in 1,000s)

Family type	1980	1985	1990
All families with children	5,004	5,803	6,001
No work	1,789	2,100	2,206
Some work	3,215	3,704	3,795
Up to 0.75 FTWE	1,572	1,765	1,713
0.75 FTWE or more	1,643	1,938	2,082
Married-couple families	1,977	2,262	2,012
No work	304	348	304
Some work	1,674	1,914	1,708
Up to 0.75 FTWE	335	574	424
0.75 FTWE or more	1,142	1,340	1,284

NOTE: FTWE, full-time worker equivalent: 35 hours a
week for 50-week period or 40 hours a week for 52-week period.

SOURCE: U.S. Congress (1991:1285).

parent working poor families in rural areas face perhaps the greatest degree of hardship because rural areas generally offer fewer
social services and benefits than urban areas (Shapiro, 1990).

FAMILY STRUCTURE, PARENTING STYLES, AND ADOLESCENT OUTCOMES

There is a broad literature on the relationships among family
structure, family processes, and adolescent outcomes. (By "outcomes" we mean the overall well-being and achievements of the
adolescent, including physical and mental health status, school
achievement, and the development of social skills that lead to
success in employment and common life.) From this literature,
family income clearly stands out as the strongest "predictor" of
outcomes. For example, it accounts for between 30 and 50 percent of the difference in high school graduation and school achievement among children from single- and two-parent households (Astone
and McLanahan, 1989; Zajonc, 1976; Milne et al., 1986). Economic disparities do not account for all of the difference in adolescent outcomes, however. Several other factors—family structure, home environment, childrearing practices, and child-parent

relationships—independently contribute to adolescent health and behavior and often account for a meaningful variation in those outcomes (see Marjoribanks, 1972; Walberg and Marjoribanks, 1973; Dornbusch, 1989).

For example, even after controlling for socioeconomic status, single-parent families and stepfamilies are far more likely to have adolescent children exhibiting deviant behavior (smoking, early dating, truancy, running away from home, contacts with police, and arrests) than are two-parent families (Dornbusch et al., 1985).

Children of Single-Parent Families

Adolescents growing up in single-parent families are disadvantaged in a number of ways that compromise their future, and the consequences have been shown to persist over multiple generations (McLanahan, 1986). Although the strong correlation between single-parent households and poverty makes it difficult to entirely distinguish the effects of poverty from those of single parenting, studies demonstrate that growing up in a single-parent household often has damaging effects regardless of income. Controlling for socioeconomic status, studies indicate that adolescents from single-parent families are more likely than their peers from two-parent families to engage in health-compromising behaviors, such as drug and alcohol use, unprotected sex, and cigarette smoking. They are also more likely to drop out of school, suffer from mental illness, and commit suicide. Overall, these risks appear to be more pronounced for sons than for daughters of single parents (Dornbusch et al., 1985; Kellam et al., 1977; Astone and McLanahan, 1989; Dornbusch and Gray, 1988; Hauser and Phang, 1992).

Despite best parental efforts, the data suggest that single-parent households constitute a high-risk setting for young people. Again, however, it is difficult to distinguish some effects of living with only one parent from the effects of poverty or low income since the correlations between the two are so high. As Bronfenbrenner (1991:4) summarizes:

> The developmental risks associated with a one-parent family structure are relatively small . . . in comparison with those involved in two other types of environmental contexts. The first and most destructive of these is poverty. Because many single-parent families are also poor, parents and their children are in double jeopardy. But even when two parents are present, research in both developed and developing countries reveals that in households living under stressful economic

and social conditions, processes of parent-child interaction and environmentally oriented child activity are more difficult to initiate and to sustain.

To be sure, research also indicates that when the mother, or some other adult committed to the child's well-being, does manage to establish and maintain a pattern of progressive reciprocal interaction, the disruptive impact of poverty on development is significantly reduced. But, among the poor, the proportion of parents who, despite their stressful life circumstances, are able to provide quality care is, under present conditions, not very large. And even for this minority, the parents' buffering power begins to decline sharply by the time children are five or six years old and exposed to impoverished and disruptive settings outside the home.

Across all social classes, giving too early autonomy to adolescents appears to have an unfortunate consequence—an increased probability that the youth will engage in deviant acts. A major factor in the early granting of autonomy involves family decision making. A major part of the explanation for this high rate of adolescent deviance in single-parent families is their propensity to permit adolescents to have early control over their own behavior. In such decision-making areas as choice of friends, choice of clothes, ways of spending money, and time they must come home, permitting such early decision making by the youth alone is an understandable response by an overloaded single parent (Dornbusch et al., 1985).

In a similar fashion, a national sample of American youth found that adolescents from single-parent families were performing less well in school than youth from two-parent households (Dornbusch and Wood, 1988). Once again, this relationship persisted across social classes. The children from single-parent households were not doing worse on IQ nor on achievement tests, yet their teachers rated them lower on intellectual ability and performance. Lower ratings from teachers were associated with high levels of adolescent deviance. A different sample of adolescents was used to replicate the key findings: single-parent households were more likely to give early autonomy, and that early autonomy was associated with higher levels of deviance and lower school performance (Dornbusch and Gray, 1988).

An analysis by Hauser and Phang of some 115,000 youths aged 15 to 24 covered in the October *Current Population Surveys* (1973 to 1989) confirms the finding that living in a female-headed household with no spouse present increases the probability that an adolescent will drop out of school. Controlling for social and economic characteristics of students and their households, the drop-out rates for adolescents in female-headed households are 61 percent higher among whites, 26 percent among blacks, and 23 percent among Hispanics.

Children of Divorce

Children from divorced families must confront the emotional stress of a breakup—the often prolonged time preceding and subsequent to divorce proceedings—in addition to conditions associated with single parenthood. Many of these children experience elevated levels of depression and anger, and declining school performance and self-esteem. Children of divorce experience a range of stresses of greater magnitude than children in two-parent households, and these stresses are directly associated with indices of adolescent maladjustment (Siegel and Griffin, 1984). Adolescents who experienced divorce at an early age may be at particularly high risk of school failure and emotional adjustment problems (Wallerstein, 1985; Heatherington and Camara, 1984).

The effects of divorce can be mediated by family practices, of course. Parents who maintain strong emotional relationships with their children, display supportive attitudes, and practice authoritative parenting (see below) can help their children and adolescents escape some of the risks of divorce (Heatherington and Camara, 1984; Montemayor, 1984; Buchanan et al., 1991). When custodial parents remarry, however, children experience another stressful transition, which appears especially difficult for girls. Adolescents who grow up in stepfamilies show disproportionately high levels of adolescent deviance and poor school performance. This effect is diminished when separated parents maintain collegial relations and engage in cooperative parenting (Dornbusch et al., 1985; Kellam et al., 1977; Astone and McLanahan, 1989).

Better outcomes for adolescent children can, nevertheless, occur despite overt hostility between parents. Buchanan et al. (1991) found that conflict between parents has negative effects by drawing the child into the conflict. Stress between the parents is often diverted to the parent-child relationships. But adolescents need not necessarily be caught between battling parents. If adolescents are not used as message carriers or informers, their adjustment is not harmed despite high levels of parental conflict. Thus, high-conflict parents who do not ask their adolescents to serve as messenger, informant, or spy can reduce the impact of their hostility upon adolescent children of divorce.

Adolescent Mothers and Their Children

Children born to adolescent mothers—usually a single parent who has yet to reach social maturity, who often has low earnings, and who is likely to be unmarried or divorced—face the highest risk of poor developmental outcomes. Not unexpectedly, children of adolescent mothers are at high risk for health, developmental, and academic problems (Luster and Mittelstaedt, 1991; Spivak and Weitzman, 1987; Hofferth, 1987). Adolescent children of adolescent mothers are far more likely than those of older mothers to do poorly in school and to engage in high-risk behaviors, including early sexual intercourse and adolescent pregnancy (Furstenberg et al., 1992).

Part of the reason for poor developmental outcomes is that households led by teenage parents often have very low family income. It is unclear whether the condition of teenage parenthood per se is responsible for the low future earnings of the mothers, or whether this outcome is best attributed to the low incomes of their own parents. However, it is clear that teenage mothers have low incomes and are at risk for future low earnings and not completing high school (Geronimous and Korenman, 1991). Recent research that examined the "alternative life courses" of adolescent parents illustrates the ways that young parents respond to the responsibilities of childrearing: for example, white mothers appear more likely to marry to legitimize their child; blacks are more likely to incorporate the mother and her infant into an extended household, with other adults—usually the adolescent's mother or maternal grandmother or both—assisting in child care (Furstenburg et al., 1992; Wilson, 1989; Luster and Dubow, 1990). Living with other adults appears to benefit adolescent mothers, who are more likely to complete high school and be employed than those who marry (Furstenberg and Crawford, 1978; Wilson, 1989; Hayes, 1987). Among adolescent mothers receiving AFDC, blacks were more likely than whites to remain in their parents' home after childbirth, continuing schooling and delaying marriage; they stayed longer on welfare, but were more likely to graduate from high school (Testa, 1992).

Parenting Style

Parenting style is a concept used by researchers to identify variations in the interactions and childrearing practices that characterize family life. Diana Baumrind has developed a generally accepted typology of parenting styles. Baumrind's parenting styles are based on interactions between the quality of affect and the quality of control. Authoritative parenting is highly demanding and controlling but is also supportive and responsive. Authoritarian parenting is also highly demanding and controlling but is also punitive. Authoritarian parents are not responsive to their children and project little warmth and supportiveness. In contrast, permissive parents are highly responsive and warm but not demanding. These households are characterized by a lack of rules and regulations. Disengaged parents (also referred to as rejecting-neglecting) are minimally demanding and for the most part unresponsive. Children are largely ignored except when they make demands, which are usually responded to with hostility and explosions (Baumrind, 1966, 1971, 1978, 1991a,b). Baumrind concludes that "authoritative" parenting—characterized by warmth, demandingness, and a willingness to discuss the application of rules to particular situations—is superior to "authoritarian" and "permissive" parenting (Baumrind, 1973; Baumrind and Black, 1967). While there are exceptions, a large body of research provides consistent support for this assertion. Authoritative parenting has been found to be associated with better psychosocial development, school grades, greater self-reliance, and lower levels of delinquent behavior among adolescents (Hill, 1980; Maccoby and Martin, 1983; Dornbusch et al., 1985; Clark, 1983; Steinberg et al., 1991). In contrast, authoritarian and permissive parenting, lack of nurturance, too little monitoring, and "too early autonomy" are consistently found to relate negatively to school achievement and positive social behaviors (Lepper and Greene, 1978; Dornbusch and Wood, 1988; Rumberger et al., 1990; Hayes, 1987).

Building on Baumrind's framework, other researchers have sought to identify the specific components of parenting style that are most powerful in affecting adolescent outcomes. For example, joint decision making between parents and adolescents contributes to positive adolescent outcomes (Epstein, 1991; Dornbusch and Gray, 1988). Consistent parenting and regularity of family events affect school achievement positively (Gigliotti and Brookover, 1975; Keith et al., 1986). Another powerful component is parental monitoring: parents who "keep track" of their adolescents and maintain high levels of supervision are more likely to have children with low levels of delinquency and drug use and better school performance (Patterson et al., 1989; Poole, 1978; Marjoribanks, 1983; Abrahamse et al., 1985; McCord, 1990). Some analysts believe that monitoring and joint decision making are effective because they shield the adolescent from the negative influence of peer groups (Fuligni and Eccles, 1992).

Parenting styles are not just a correlate of positive adolescent outcomes. Longitudinal studies indicate that authoritative parenting and parental involvement in school appear to cause later improved school performance. But there are ethnic differences in the power of parenting practices. A series of studies has found that parental behaviors have less influence on adolescent student achievement among blacks than among other ethnic groups (Steinberg et al., 1992b).

One possibility for the relative lack of influence of authoritative parenting among black adolescents is that they are especially influenced by their peers. It is possible that these peer influences are overwhelming and undermining the positive impact of good parenting. Unfortunately, there are no data to test this speculation (Steinberg et al., 1992a). On this issue, like many others, we have insufficient empirical information about adolescent development in different ethnic groups (Spencer and Dornbusch, 1990).

Finally, it is conceivable that community characteristics are overwhelming the impact of black family structures. High parental education and two-parent families are less predictive of high school grades for blacks than for non-Hispanic whites. It appears that the ethnic mix of the residential community affects the relation between family statuses and adolescent grades. Living in a census tract with a substantial proportion of minority residents affects non-Hispanic whites as well as blacks, reducing the influence of family statuses. That most blacks live in such census tracts, and fewer non-Hispanic whites do, helps to explain the ethnic differences in the influences of family statuses on adolescent school performance (Dornbusch and Ritter, 1991).

Violence in Families

Child abuse and neglect might be called the worst-case parenting style, and many children are also exposed to violence among other family members. Reports of maltreated children have increased substantially since 1976, when the first national figures for child maltreatment were generated. In 1976, approximately 670,000 children were reported to be maltreated. There were approximately 2.7 million children reported as abused or neglected in 1990; 1.25 million children reportedly died as a result of maltreatment in 1990 (79 percent of these deaths occurred in children under the age of 5) (U.S. Department of Health and Human Services, 1992; Daro and McCurdy, 1991). In 1990, 45 percent of maltreatment reports were for neglect, 25 percent for physical abuse, 16 percent for sexual abuse, and 6 percent for emotional abuse (U.S. Department of Health and Human Services, 1992). Unfortunately, these estimates of the incidence of maltreatment in the United States are based on official or unofficial reports which are problematic to interpret because of noncomparability of case definitions across states and the inclusion of duplicated cases. Studies of child maltreatment rates that employ standard survey techniques on nationally representative samples are rare (National Research Council, 1993).

Certain family structures and low income can increase the risk of abuse or neglect. The tensions surrounding family breakup may also increase the chance of witnessing or suffering abuse by an adult. Poor, unmarried, teenaged mothers having their first child are most likely to abuse or neglect that child (Olds et al., 1988). For children from families with incomes less than $15,000, the rate of physical abuse was 3-1/2 times greater, the rate of sexual abuse six times greater, and the rate of serious injury seven times greater than for the children of more affluent families (Sedlak, 1988).

Child abuse and neglect are strongly associated with negative adolescent outcomes. Adolescents who were physically abused or neglected as children are twice as likely to be arrested for a violent offense (Widom, 1989). Victims of child sexual abuse often display fear, immaturity, and neurotic behavior, as well as high levels of aggression and antisocial behavior (Finkelhor, 1991). Moreover, the experience of family violence appears to be transmitted from one generation to the next: one study found that, among adults who were abused as children, more than one-fifth later abused their own children (Straus et al., 1980).

CONCLUSIONS

Changes in family income and changes in family structure over the past two decades have made it more difficult for many parents to provide their children with the security and stability that are most conducive to physical and emotional health, success in school, and the avoidance of health- and life-compromising behaviors that jeopardize the successful transition to adulthood. Single parents and families living at or below the poverty level face the greatest challenges. However, even two-parent, middle-income families face problems. Raising a young person, especially an early adolescent, is a difficult experience under the best conditions, and the average parent now has 11 fewer hours to spend with the children each week as compared to parents in 1960 (Small et al., 1988; Fuchs, 1988). Moreover, less than 5 percent of all families have another adult (e.g., grandparent) living in the home, compared to 50 percent two generations ago. This reduces the backup support that might otherwise be available to working parents. As a result, children are increasingly on their own—an estimated 1.3 million children age 5 to 14 must care for themselves during the hours when they are not in school (National Commission on Children, 1991a).

The combination of financial insecurity for an increasing proportion of families, increased work effort by parents seeking to maintain their living standard, and the demographic changes that have so dramatically increased the number of children and adolescents living in single-parent households result in increasing numbers of adolescents who do not receive the nurturance necessary for positive development. The consequences are not inescapably negative. Indeed, the majority of adolescents—even those from poor and single-parent homes—do succeed despite the obstacles. However, the adverse outcomes—the failure rates—are unacceptably and unnecessarily high.

REFERENCES

Abrahamse, A.F., P.A. Morrison, and L.J. Waite
  1985   How Family Characteristics Deter Early Unwed Parenthood. Paper presented at the annual meeting of the Population Association of America, Boston.
Astone, N., and S. McLanahan
  1989   Family Structure and High School Completion: The Role of Parental Practices. Discussion paper no. 905-89, Institute for Research on Poverty, University of Wisconsin, Madison.
Bane, M.J., and D.T. Ellwood
  1989   One fifth of the nation's children: why are they poor? *Science* 245:1047-1053.
Baumrind, D.
  1966   Effects of authoritative parental control on child behavior. *Child Development* 37(4):887-907.
  1971   Current patterns of parental authority. *Developmental Psychology Monographs*, Part 2, 4(1):1-103.
  1973   The development of instrumental competence through socialization. Pp. 3-46 in A.D. Pick, ed., *Minnesota Sysmposium on Child Psychology*. Minneapolis: University of Minnesota Press.
  1978   Parental disciplinary patterns and social competence in children. *Youth and Society* 9(3):239-276.
  1991a   Parenting styles and adolescent development. Pp. 758-772 in R. Lerner, A.C. Petersen, and J. Brooks-Gunn, eds., *The Encyclopedia on Adolescence*. New York: Garland.

1991b   The influence of parenting style on adolescent competence and sub-
         stance abuse. *Journal of Early Adolescence* 11(1):56-94.
Baumrind, D., and A.E. Black
1967   Socialization practices associated with dimensions of competence in
         preschool boys and girls. *Child Development* 38:291-327.
Brindis, C.D., C.E. Irwin, Jr., and S.G. Millstein
1992   United States profile. Pp. 12-27 in E.R. McAnarney, R.E. Kreipe, D.P.
         Orr, and G.D. Commerci, eds., *Textbook of Adolescent Medicine*. Phila-
         delphia: W.B. Saunders.
Bronfenbrenner, U.
1991   What do families do? *Family Affairs* 4(1-2):1-6.
Buchanan, C., E.E. Maccoby, and S.M. Dornbusch
1991   Caught between parents: adolescents' experiences in divorced homes.
         Child Development 62:1008-1029.
Bumpass, L.
1984   Children and marital disruption: a replication and update. *Demography*
         21:71-82.
Bureau of the Census
1989a   *Singleness in America*. Statistical Brief SB-4-89, November. Washing-
         ton, D.C.: U.S. Department of Commerce.
1989b   *Single Parents and Their Children*. Statistical Brief SB-3-89, Novem-
         ber. Washington, D.C.: U.S. Department of Commerce.
1991a   *Poverty in the United States: 1990*. Current Population Reports, Series
         P-60, No. 175, August. Washington, D.C.: U.S. Department of Com-
         merce.
1991b   *The Economics of Family Disruption*. Statistical Brief SB-91-10, March.
         Washington, D.C.: U.S. Department of Commerce.
Children's Defense Fund and Northeastern University Center for Labor Market
         Studies
1992   *Vanishing Dreams: The Economic Plight of America's Young Families*.
         Washington, D.C.: Children's Defense Fund and Northeastern Univer-
         sity Center for Labor Market Studies.
Clark, R.
1983   *Family Life and School Achievement: Why Poor Black Children Suc-
         ceed or Fail*. Chicago: University of Chicago Press.
Comer, J.
1985   The Yale-New Haven primary prevention project: a follow-up study.
         Journal of the American Academy of Child Psychiatry 24(2):154-160.
Danziger, S., and T. Gottschalk
1988   Increasing inequality in the United States: what we know and what we
         don't. *Journal of Post-Keynesian Economics* 11(2):174-195.
Daro, D., and K. McCurdy
1991   *Current Trends in Child Abuse Reporting and Fatalities: The Results
         of the 1990 Annual Fifty State Survey*. Chicago: National Committee
         for the Prevention of Child Abuse.
Dornbusch, S.M.
1989   The sociology of adolescence. Pp. 223-259 in W.R. Scott and J. Blake,
         eds., *Annual Review of Sociology*. Palo Alto, Calif.: Annual Reviews.
Dornbusch, S.M., and K.D. Gray
1988   Single-parent families. Pp. 274-296 in S.M. Dornbusch and M.H. Strober,
         eds., *Feminism, Children, and the New Families*. New York: Guilford.

Dornbusch, S.M., and P.L. Ritter
  1991   Community influences on the relation of family statuses to adolescent
         school performance: differences between African-American and non-
         Hispanic whites. *American Journal of Education* 99(4):543-567.
Dornbusch, S.M., and K.D. Wood
  1988   Family Processes and Educational Achievement. Paper presented at
         Conference on Education and Family, Washington, D.C.
Dornbusch, S.M., J.M. Carlsmith, S.J. Bushwall, P.L. Ritter, H. Leiderman, A.H.,
         Hastorf, and R.T. Gross
  1985   Single parents, extended households, and the control of adolescents.
         Child Development 56:326-341.
Dubow, E., and T. Luster
  1990   Adjustment of children born to teenage mothers: the contribution of
         risk and protective factors. *Journal of Marriage and the Family* 52:393-
         404.
Duncan, G.J., and S.D. Hoffman
  1985   A reconsideration of the economic consequences of marital disruption.
         Demography 22(Nov.):485-989.
Dryfoos, J.
  1990   *Adolescents at Risk: Prevalence and Prevention.* New York: Oxford
         University Press.
Earls, F.
  1991   Not fear, nor quarantine, but science: preparation for a decade of re-
         search to advance knowledge about and control of violence in youths.
         In D.E. Rogers and E. Ginzberg, eds., *Adolescents at Risk: Medical and
         Social Perspectives.* Cornell University Medical College Seventh Con-
         ference on Health Policy. Boulder, Colo.: Westview Press.
Elder, G.
  1992   Family Stress in Rural America. Paper presented at the Society for
         Research on Adolescents, Washington, D.C.
Ellwood, D.T.
  1988   *Poor Support: Poverty in the American Family.* New York: Basic
         Books, Inc.
Epstein, J.L.
  1991   Family structures that promote student motivation and achievement: a
         developmental perspective. In C. Ames and R. Ames, eds., *Research on
         Motivation in Education*, Vol. 3. Orlando, Fla.: Academic Press.
Finkelhor, D.
  1991   Child sexual abuse. Pp. 77-94 in M.L. Rosenberg and M.A. Fenley, eds.,
         Violence in America. A Public Health Approach. New York: Oxford
         University Press.
Fuchs, V.R.
  1988   *Women's Quest for Economic Equality.* Cambridge, Mass.: Harvard
         University Press.
Fuligni, A.J., and J.S. Eccles
  1992   The Effects of Early Adolescent Peer Orientation on Academic Achieve-
         ment and Deviant Behavior in High School. Paper presented at the
         biennial meetings of the Society for Research on Adolescence, Washing-
         ton, D.C.
Furstenberg, F.F., and A.G. Crawford
  1978   Family support: helping teenage mothers to cope. *Family Planning
         Perspectives* 10:322-333.

Furstenberg, F.F., Jr., M.E. Hughes, and G. Brooks-Gunn
    1992   The next generation: the children of teenage mothers grow up. Pp. 113-135 in M.K. Rosenheim and M.F. Testa, eds., *Early Parenthood and Coming of Age in the 1990s.* New Brunswick, N.J.: Rutgers University.

Garfinkel, I., and S.S. McLanahan
    1986   Single mothers and their children. In J.L. Palmer and I.V. Sawhill, eds., *The Changing Domestic Priorities Series.* Washington, D.C.: The Urban Institute Press.

Geronimous, A., and S. Korenman
    1991   The Socioeconomic Consequences of Teen Childbearing Reconsidered. Working paper no. 3701, National Bureau of Economic Research, Cambridge, Mass.

Gigliotti, R.J., and W.B. Brookover
    1975   The learning environment: a comparison of high and low achieving elementary schools. *Urban Education* 10(3):245-261.

Grant Foundation (The William T.) on Work, Family and Citizenship
    1988   *The Forgotten Half: Non-College Youth in America.* Washington, D.C.: The William T. Grant Foundation on Work, Family and Citizenship.

Handler, J.F., and Y. Hasenfeld
    1991   *The Moral Construction of Poverty: Welfare of Reform in America.* New York: Sage Publications.

Hauser, R.M., and H.S. Phang
    1992   *Trends in High School Dropout Among White, Black, and Hispanic Youth, 1973 to 1989.* Madison: Institute for Research on Poverty, University of Wisconsin.

Hayes, C.D., ed.
    1987   *Risking the Future: Adolescent Sexuality, Pregnancy, and Childbearing.* Committee on Child Development, Commission on Behavioral and Social Sciences and Education, National Research Council. Washington, D.C.: National Academy Press.

Heatherington, E., and K. Camara
    1984   Families in transition: the processes of dissolution and reconstitution. Pp. 398-437 in R. Parke, ed., *Review of Child Development Research.* Chicago: University of Chicago Press.

Hill, J.P.
    1980   The family. Pp. 32-55 in M. Jonson, ed., *Toward Adolescence: The Middle School Years.* Seventy-ninth yearbook of the National Society for the Study of Education. Chicago: University of Chicago Press.

Hodgkinson, H.
    1991   Reform versus reality. *Phi Delta Kappan* 73(1):9-16.

Hofferth, S.L.
    1987   The children of teen child bearers. Pp. 174-206 in S.L. Hofferth and C.D. Hayes, eds., *Risking the Future: Adolescent Sexuality, Pregnancy, and Childbearing,* Vol. II. Committee on Child Development Research and Public Policy, Commission on Behavioral and Social Sciences and Education, National Research Council. Washington, D.C.: National Academy Press.

Institute of Medicine
    1989   *Research on Children and Adolescents with Mental, Behavioral, and Developmental Disorders: Mobilizing a National Initiative.* Washington, D.C.: National Academy Press.

Irwin, C.E., and M.A. Shafer
    1991   Adolescent sexuality: negative outcomes of a normative behavior. In D.E. Rogers and E. Ginzberg, eds., *Adolescents at Risk: Medical and Social Perspectives.* Cornell University Medical College Seventh Conference on Health Policy. Boulder, Colo.: Westview Press.

Keith, T.Z., T.M. Reimers, P.G. Febrmann, S.M. Pottebaum, and L.W. Aubew
    1986   Parental involvement, homework, and television time: direct and indirect effects on high school achievement. *Journal of Educational Psychology* 78(5):373-380.

Kellam, S.G., M.E. Ensminger, and J. Turner
    1977   Family structures and the mental health of children. *Archives of General Psychiatry* 34:1012-1022.

Klerman, L.V., with M.B. Parker
    1991   *Alive and Well? A Research and Policy Review of Health Programs for Poor Young Children.* New York: National Center for Children in Poverty, Columbia University.

Lepper, M.R., and D. Greene
    1978   *The Hidden Costs of Reward: New Perspectives on the Psychology of Motivation.* Hillsdale, N.J.: Lawrence Erlbaum Associates.

Luster, T., and E. Dubow
    1990   Predictors of the quality of the home environment that adolescent mothers provide for their school-aged children. *Journal of Youth & Adolescence* 19(5):475-494.

Luster, T., and G. Mittelstaedt
    1991   Adolescent mothers. In T. Luster and L. Okagaki, eds., *Parenting: An Ecological Perspective.* Hillsdale, N.J.: Lawrence Erlbaum Associates.

Maccoby, E., and S. Martin
    1983   Socialization in the context of the family: parent-child interaction. Pp. 1-101 in E.M. Heatherington, ed., *Handbook of Child Psychology.* New York: Wiley.

Marjoribanks, D.
    1972   Environment, social class, and mental abilities. *Journal of Educational Psychology* 63(2):103-109.
    1983   The evaluation of a family learning environment model. *Studies in Educational Evaluation* 9:343-351.

McCord, J.
    1990   Problem behaviors. In S.S. Feldman and G.R. Elliott, eds., *At the Threshold: The Developing Adolescent.* Cambridge, Mass.: Harvard University Press.

McLanahan, S.
    1986   The consequences of single parenthood for subsequent generations. *Focus* (Fall):16-21.

Milne, A.M., D.E. Myers, A. Rosenthal, and A. Ginsburg
    1986   Single parents, working mothers, and the educational achievement of school children. *Sociology of Education* 59(July):132.

Montemayor, R.
    1984   Picking up the pieces: the effects of parental divorce on adolescents with some suggestions for school-based intervention programs. *Journal of Early Adolescence* 4:289-314.

Moore, C.
    1992   Facts at a glance. Newsletter reporting U.S. data on teen fertility in 1989. Child Trends, Washington, D.C.

Mortenson, T.G., and Z. Wu
1990 *High School Graduation and College Participation of Young Adults by Family Income Backgrounds: 1970 to 1989.* Iowa City, Iowa: American College Testing.

National Commission on Children (U.S.)
1991a *Beyond Rhetoric: A New American Agenda for Children and Families.* Washington, D.C.: National Commission on Children.
1991b *Speaking of Kids: A National Survey of Children and Parents.* Washington, D.C.: National Commission on Children.

National Research Council
1993 *Understanding Child Abuse and Neglect.* Panel on Research on Child Abuse and Neglect, Commission on Behavioral and Social Sciences and Education. Washington, D.C.: National Academy Press, forthcoming.

Norton, A.J., and P.C. Glick
1986 One parent families: a social and economic profile. *Family Relations* 35(1):9-17.

Olds, D.L., C.R. Henderson, Jr., R. Tatelbaum, and R. Chamberlin
1988 Improving the life-course development of socially disadvantaged mothers: a randomized trial of nurse home visitation. *American Journal of Public Health* 78(11):1436-1445.

Patterson, G., B. DeBaryshe, and E. Ramsey
1989 A developmental perspective on antisocial behavior. *American Psychologist* 44:329-334.

Poole, M.E.
1978 Identifying early school leaving. *The Australian Journal of Education* 22(1):13-24.

Rumberger, R.W., G. Poulos, R. Ghatak, P.L. Ritter, and S.M. Dornbusch
1990 Family influences on dropout behavior in one California high school. *Sociology of Education* 63(4):283-299.

Sedlak, A.J.
1988 Study of National Incidence and Prevalence of Child Abuse and Neglect. National Center on Child Abuse and Neglect, Washington, D.C.

Shapiro, R.J.
1990 The family under economic stress. In *Putting Children First: A Progressive Family Policy for the 1990s.* Washington, D.C.: Progressive Policy Institute.

Siegel, R., and N. Griffin
1984 Correlates of depressive symptoms in adolescents. *Journal of Youth & Adolescence* 13:475-487.

Small, S., G. Eastman, and S. Cornleius
1988 Adolescent autonomy and parental stress. *Journal of Youth & Adolescence* 17:377-391.

Spencer, M.B., and S.M. Dornbusch
1990 Challenges in studying minority youth. Pp. 123-146 in S.S. Feldman and G.R. Elliott, eds., *At the Threshold: The Developing Adolescent.* Cambridge, Mass.: Harvard University Press.

Spivak, H., and M. Weitzman
1987 Social barriers faced by adolescent parents and their children. *Journal of the American Medical Association* 258(11):1500-1504.

Steinberg, I., N.S. Mounts, S.D. Lamborn, and S.M. Dornbusch
1991 Authoritative parenting and adolescent adjustment across varied ecological niches. *Journal of Research on Adolescence* 1:19-36.

Steinberg, L., S.M. Dornbusch, and B. Brown
  1992a Ethnic differences in adolescent achievement: an ecological perspective. *American Psychologist* 47(60):723-729.

Steinberg, L., S.D. Lamborn, S.M. Dornbusch, and N. Darling
  1992b Impact of parenting practices on adolescent achievement: authoritation parenting, school involvement and encouragement to succeed. *Child Development* 63:1266-1281.

Straus, M.A., R.J. Gelles, and S.K. Stinmetz
  1980 Physical violence in a nationally representative sample of American families. In J. Trost, ed., *The Family in Change.* Vasteras, Sweden: International Library.

Sum, A.M., and W.N. Fogg
  1991 The adolescent poor and the transition to early adulthood. In P. Edelman and J. Ladner, eds., *Adolescence & Poverty: Challenge for the 1990s.* Washington, D.C.: Center for National Policy Press.

Testa, M.F.
  1992 Racial variation in the early life course of adolescent welfare mothers. In M.K. Rosenheim and M.F. Testa, eds., *Early Parenthood and Coming of Age in the 1990s.* New Brunswick, N.J.: Rutgers University.

Tuma, J.M.
  1989 Mental health services for children: the state of the art. *American Psychologist* 44(2):188-199.

U.S. Congress
  1991 *1991 Green Book.* Committee on Ways and Means, House of Representatives. Washington, D.C.: U.S. Government Printing Office.
  1992 Families on a Treadmill: Work and Income of the 1980s. Unpublished manuscript, Joint Economic Committee, U.S. Congress, Washington, D.C.

U.S. Department of Health and Human Services
  1992 National Child Abuse and Neglect Data System. Working paper 1, 1990 summary data component. U.S. Department of Health and Human Services, Washington, D.C.

Walberg, H.J., and K. Marjoribanks
  1973 Differential mental abilities and home environment: a canonical analysis. *Developmental Psychology* 9(3):363-3689.

Wallerstein, J.
  1985 The over-burdened child: some long-term consequences of divorce. *Social Work* 30:116-123.

Widom, C.S.
  1989 Child abuse, neglect, and violent criminal behavior. *Criminology* 27(2):251-271.

Wilson, M.N.
  1989 Child development in the context of the Black extended family. *American Psychologist* 44(2):380-385.

Zajonc, R.B.
  1976 Family configuration and intelligence. *Science* 192:227-236.

Zill, N.
  1990 U.S. Children and Their Families: Current Conditions and Recent Trends, 1989. Unpublished report, Child Trends, Washington, D.C.

4

Neighborhoods

Most of social interactions of
families and adolescents are embedded within neighborhood settings. A "neighborhood" can be defined both spatially, as a geo-
graphic area, and functionally, as a set of social networks. Neighborhoods are spatial units in which face-to-face social interactions
and processes take place in relatively intimate, personal settings
and situations. They are a place for social interaction, a place for
education and human service—both formal and informal—and a
place for preparing for and engaging in employment. A "community" may differ from a neighborhood in size or in residents' or
outsiders' characterization (for example, a housing complex or a
large area defined by accepted landmarks). Moreover, a "community" may have a political orientation. But, generally speaking, it
is difficult for residents and social scientists to precisely distinguish the difference between social and political interactions and
between neighborhood and community. As a result, the terms are
often used interchangeably, as we do in this report.

However defined, a neighborhood is a key setting for adolescent
development. This chapter summarizes research about neighborhoods, with a focus on poverty concentration and racial and ethnic stratification, and then examines the effects of these neighborhoods on adolescent development. We note, however, that
there are both methodological and theoretical limitations to the
research on neighborhoods.

Methodologically, it is difficult to identify causal relationships between complex social settings and individual behavioral outcomes, and most results are open to more than one explanation (see Jencks and Mayer 1990a; Reiss and Roth, 1993). Also problematic is the definition of the areas under study: regions, standard metropolitan statistical areas (SMSAs), and cities are large, heterogeneous units with politically defined boundaries which are not coterminous with neighborhoods and may have no theoretical relevance for many research questions on adolescent outcomes; thus most researchers use intraurban units of analysis, usually census tracts, as proxies for "neighborhood," although they too do not necessarily correspond to neighborhoods. In addition, much research is based on decennial census data, but there is a significant time lag in the availability of those data for research. Thus, conclusions may be drawn for the period between 1970 and 1980, but one can only speculate from incomplete data regarding subsequent trends.

Almost all research examines metropolitan (i.e., urban and suburban) neighborhoods, with little attention to the unique characteristics and problems of rural areas. Moreover, the available research focuses almost exclusively on poor neighborhoods, and so there are few comparative data from affluent areas. Another limitation is that most research has focused on the structural features of neighborhoods, not on community-level interactions or processes. A theoretical bias toward consensual theories of community, rather than theories of a community-as-a-resource, has led researchers to look for internal sources of disorganization rather than external sources. As such, relatively few community studies attempt to analyze how private-sector actions, government policy, and regulatory law influence neighborhoods. There is also relatively little attention to a significant body of ethnographic research (see Anderson, 1991b; Skogan, 1990). In spite of the limitations, however, the available research on neighborhoods does provide significant insights into this setting for adolescents.

CHANGES IN METROPOLITAN NEIGHBORHOODS

Poverty Concentration and Racial and Ethnic Stratification

Household poverty and segregation by class and race are fundamental elements of metropolitan areas, and there is a clustering of poor people in many of these areas. By 1980, the 10 largest metropolitan areas accounted for almost half of all poor persons who live in the poorest neighborhoods—those census tracts in which at least 40 percent of all residents have poverty-level incomes. The numbers of such residents are increasing. The 1970s saw a 29.5 percent increase in the number of poor people living in these neighborhoods, to an estimated 2.45 million. This growth was not evenly distributed. A little over half of all SMSAs showed no change or a decrease in concentrated poverty; the others, especially large cities in the Northeast and Midwest, showed increases in this concentrated poverty (Jargowsky and Bane, 1990; Farley, 1990). An analysis of the neighborhood changes from the 1990 census is not yet available, but evidence suggests that trends seen in the 1970s have continued through the 1980s.

Poor neighborhoods are also racially and ethnically stratified despite declines in stratification during the 1970s (Farley, 1990; Wilson, 1987; Massey and Denton, 1987). The average black family, for example, lives in a census tract in which 30 percent of families are poor; for the average Hispanic family, the figure is 23 percent; the average Asian family, 20 percent; and the average non-Hispanic white family, 14 percent (Massey and Eggers, 1990). However, there are regional and metropolitan characteristics that affect these differences. For example, trends during the 1970s toward racial integration were strongest in the smaller metropolitan areas and weakest in SMSAs with the largest black populations. For Hispanics, stratification was most pronounced in large metropolitan areas with low rates of population growth, in areas with large Hispanic populations, and in areas with high rates of Hispanic immigration (Massey and Denton, 1989). Nonetheless, the poorest neighborhoods remain the most highly stratified: an estimated 87 percent of all residents in such neighborhoods are members of racial or ethnic minority groups (Jargowsky and Bane, 1990).

Racial stratification is not limited to the core cities within SMSAs. Although suburban stratification is about 12 percent lower than in central cities, it is still high, especially for blacks in the Northeast and Midwest (Massey and Denton, 1988). In 1980, 86 percent of suburban whites still lived in census tracts with less than 1 percent black residents. In other words, black suburbanization seems to represent not integration, but an extension of racially segregated living patterns into neighborhoods adjacent to or near central cities (Judd, 1992; Logan and Schneider, 1984; Massey and Denton, 1988).

Social Composition of Poor Neighborhoods

Adults in poor neighborhoods differ in important ways from those in more affluent areas. For example, high poverty neighborhoods have much higher proportions of unmarried mothers, single-parent families, and unemployed young men (Jargowsky and Bane, 1990).

Ricketts and Mincy (1990) argue that the social composition of an increasing number of neighborhoods has deteriorated during the 1970s, resulting in an increase in "underclass neighborhoods." They define "underclass" neighborhoods as census tracts with high values (at least one standard deviation above the national mean) for each of four indicators: working-age males not attached to the labor force, households headed by a woman with children, households receiving welfare, and dropouts among the school-age population. They use the term "concentrated poverty neighborhoods" to define those with 40 percent or more residents having poverty-level incomes. Although the poverty rate remained fairly constant from 1970 to 1980, there was a 75 percent increase in the number of census tracts with concentrated poverty, and, significantly, a 331 percent increase in the number of underclass neighborhoods (see Table 4-1). That is, over the course of the decade, the number of Americans living in neighborhoods with high concentrations of poverty had more than tripled.

Concentrated poverty goes hand-in-hand with many social problems, and the increases in both concentrated poverty and underclass

TABLE **4-1** Poor and Underclass Areas, by Census Tracts, 1970-1980

Type of Area	1970		1980		Growth (percent)
	Number	Percent	Number	Percent	
Population (thousands)					
Underclass	752	0.5	2,484	1.4	230
Concentrated poverty	3,775	2.5	5,569	3.1	48
United States	148,456	100.0	181,171	100.0	22
Number of tracts					
Underclass	204	0.6	880	2.1	331
Concentrated poverty	1,080	3.1	1,887	3.9	75
United States	34,498	100.0	42,865	100.0	24

SOURCE: Ricketts and Mincy (1990). Reprinted by permission.

TABLE **4-2**   Social Problems, by Type of Area, 1970-1980

Area and Social Problem	Population (thousands)		Growth 1970-1980 (percent)
	1970	1980	
Underclass areas			
Number of household heads with public assistance income	46	292	535
Number of adult males not attached to the labor force	100	250	150
Number of able-bodied, working-age adults with no regular attachment to the labor force (excluding students and women with children)	98	446	355
Concentrated poverty areas			
Number of household heads with public assistance income	179	585	227
Number of adult males not attached to the labor force	433	1,023	136
Number of able-bodied, working-age adults with no regular attachment to the labor force (excluding students and women with children)	457	785	72
United States			
Number of household heads with public assistance income	1,791	5,026	185
Number of adult males not attached to the labor force	12,896	20,240	57
Number of able-bodied, working-age adults with no regular attachment to the labor force (excluding students and women with children)	16,459	19,273	17

SOURCE: Ricketts and Mincy (1990). Reprinted by permission.

census tracts far surpass changes in other neighborhoods. For example, the underclass neighborhoods had a 355 percent increase in the measure of "idleness" (i.e., people with no regular attachment to the labor force or education), 5 times the increase in poor neighborhoods, and 20 times the increase for the overall U.S. population (see Table 4-2). By 1980, more than half of all poor neighborhoods had become underclass neighborhoods.

The growth in crack and cocaine markets since the early 1980s has placed additional stress on poor neighborhoods. The highly visible, lucrative, and violent drug markets have simultaneously accelerated the exodus of stable families and undermined the authority of long-term community leaders. The operation of drug markets and the violence associated with them has weakened inhibitions against violence in all neighborhood contexts. The large amounts of money that can be made in the drug trade act as a magnet to draw children and adolescents into criminal activity (Reiss and Roth, 1993). Adolescents who are not involved as participants in drug markets are still influenced by their presence; some are victims of drug-related violence, while many more are unable to engage in normal neighborhood activities because of the dangers associated with drug markets.

Racial and Ethnic Composition of Schools

Because the vast majority of students attend neighborhood schools and because school funding is related directly to family and neighborhood wealth, public schools tend to be stratified by class, race, and ethnicity. About 90 percent of all students attend public schools, and less than 5 percent of those students attend schools with substantial bussing programs (Mayer, 1991). Therefore, student bodies reflect the composition of the neighborhood.

As a result, poor children are concentrated in some schools and are largely absent from others. Almost half of all black children and almost 40 percent of Hispanic children live in poverty. About half of children in public schools in central cities are black or Hispanic, and most are poor. In 1989, 51.8 percent of public school students in central cities were black or Hispanic, a percentage that has increased steadily since the 1970s (Alsalem et al., 1992). Concentrations within individual schools are even more pronounced. According to analyses by Orfield and colleagues (1983, 1989, 1992:v), "school segregation of Hispanics has increased dramatically," while segregation has "remained relatively stable for Blacks" over the past 20 years. Consequently, many students in the public education system continue to attend segregated schools. As seen in Table 4-3, for example, 80 percent of all Hispanic students in the South attend schools with at least 50 percent minority population. Thirty-eight percent of these Hispanic students are in "intensely segregated" schools with 90 to 100 percent minority populations. Comparable concentrations exist for black students. In the Northeast, for example, over three-quarters of all black students attend "predominately minority" schools, with almost half attending intensely segregated schools.

Minority students are also most likely to attend the nation's poorest schools. Analyses of national data indicate that about 75

TABLE **4-3** Students in Predominantly Minority and Intensely Segregated Schools, 1988 (in percent)

Minority Group and Area	Minority	Intensely Segregated
Hispanic		
South	80.2	37.9
Northeast	70.7	44.2
Midwest	52.3	24.9
West	71.3	27.5
Black		
South	56.5	24.0
Border	59.6	34.5
Northeast	77.3	48.0
Midwest	70.1	41.8
West	67.1	28.6

SOURCE: Orfield and Monfort (1992). Reprinted by permission

percent of black students and 46 percent of Hispanic students attend schools ranked in the bottom 20 percent by socioeconomic status (SES). By contrast, less than 7 percent of black and Hispanic students attend high-SES schools (Mayer, 1991).

Regional Differences

Metropolitan areas in the Northeast and Midwest were hit especially hard by the economic downturn during the 1970s. The greatest deterioration in metropolitan neighborhoods, as measured by increased concentration of poverty, was also in the Northeast, followed by the Midwest. In addition, the number of underclass neighborhoods grew fastest in the Northeast (Jargowsky and Bane, 1990:Ch. 2; Ricketts and Mincy, 1990). On a regional level, therefore, it would be expected that the greatest increase (or least decrease) in social problems would also be in the Northeast and perhaps the Midwest.

Analyses of regional trends by Mayer (1991) from 1970 to 1980 support these expectations. As seen in Table 4-4, the Northeast had the smallest decrease in public assistance recipients and teenage births, the smallest increase in labor force participation rates, and the biggest increases in single-parent families (overwhelmingly female) and poverty rates. The Northeast also had the sec-

TABLE **4-4**   Social Problems, by Census Bureau Region, 1970-1980

Social Problem	United States	Census Region			
		Northeast	Midwest	South	West
Population receiving public assistance (percent)					
1975	7.1	7.7	6.4	7.1	7.4
1980	6.5	7.4	6.0	6.0	6.7
Change	− 0.6	− 0.3	− 0.4	−1.1	− 0.7
Female-headed families (percent)					
1970	10.8	11.8	9.3	11.6	10.3
1980	14.3	16.1	13.0	14.6	13.6
Change	3.5	4.3	3.7	3.0	3.3
Population with less than 4 years of high school (percent)					
1970	47.7	47.1	46.3	54.9	37.7
1980	33.5	32.9	32.0	39.8	24.5
Change	−14.2	−14.2	−14.3	−15.1	−12.2
Families below poverty level (percent)					
1969	10.7	7.6	8.3	16.2	8.9
1979	9.6	8.7	8.0	11.9	8.5
Change	−1.1	1.1	− 0.3	− 4.3	− 0.4
Murder rate (per 1,000)					
1970-1971	8.2	6.3	6.8	11.7	6.7
1980-1981	10.0	8.1	7.6	12.8	10.8
Change	1.9	1.8	0.9	1.1	4.1

SOURCE: Data compiled by Mayer (1991).

ond-highest increase in the murder rate. The South, in contrast, had the greatest decreases in public assistance recipients and poverty rates, the smallest increase in female-headed families, the greatest increase in high school graduates, and the second-smallest increase in murder rates. Although analyses of 1980-1990 data have not yet been done, there is no general evidence to suggest that these regional differences would have changed.

There are multiple factors that contribute to, and maintain, poverty concentration and racial stratification. Public policy in the last two decades has not strongly aided urban areas, but there are other factors and difficult complexities in drawing conclusions about deteriorating neighborhoods. As highlighted by Massey and Eggers (1990:1186):

> In the final analysis . . . we have only linked patterns and trends in the concentration of poverty to two proximate causes—changes in the distributional structure of income and in patterns of residential segregation. The ultimate causes are more complex, relating to the functional transformations of American cities, the decline of manufacturing, the suburbanization of employment, the origins of discrimination of housing markets, and the persistence of racial prejudice in modern society.

Once a neighborhood begins to substantially lose its economic base, however, other factors come into play. Adults and young people become socially isolated, losing the kind of networks and self- or group identifications that support customary behavior and prevent deviant behavior (Wilson, 1987; Fernandez and Harris, 1990; Harrell and Peterson, 1992; Crane, 1991b). Social institutions— schools, the social welfare system, and the criminal justice system—tend to anticipate and facilitate failure, shame, and hopelessness (Williams and Kornblum, 1985; Chapter 8). Parents also lose some degree of hope and have fears for the well-being of themselves and their children (National Commission on Children, 1991). Employers also respond: people living in underclass neighborhoods are less likely to be hired for a job than those in better-off neighborhoods, even with the same background and skills; and one study of Chicago-area employers found screening of prospective employees by address to be a surrogate for racial and socioeconomic status of neighborhoods (Kirschenman and Neckerman, 1991).

As their economic and social systems break down, the poorest of neighborhoods seem increasingly unable to restrain criminal or deviant behaviors (Wilson, 1987, Anderson, 1991a; Reiss and Roth, 1993). These disorganized areas are vulnerable to the processes that "hollow out" urban neighborhoods: fires in abandoned buildings, housing deterioration, fires in occupied buildings, housing abandonment, reduction of fire services, and accelerating outmigration by stable members of the community, leaving behind an isolated subgroup of residents who are unable or unwilling to move into accepted adult roles (Wilson, 1987; Rainwater, 1970, 1987). Not surprisingly, the result is that economically poor neighborhoods differ from more affluent neighborhoods in terms of diminished private economic activity, the types of public and social services available, limited recreational and youth development programs, and higher levels of crime (Littell and Wynn, 1989; Schneider and

Logan, 1982; Reiss and Roth, 1993). Adolescents themselves lose hope and have a diminished ability to use the few opportunities that are available (Sullivan, 1990; Eisenhower Foundation, 1990).

POOR NEIGHBORHOODS AND ADOLESCENT DEVELOPMENT

There is little reason to expect that the conditions summarized above are favorable for adolescent development. In recent years, researchers have examined potential influences from two perspectives. Ethnographic research has examined community-level processes and interactions, with an emphasis on identifying the ways in which adolescents respond to deteriorating neighborhood conditions. Quantitative research has examined the structural features of neighborhoods, such as concentrated poverty and the characteristics of adult residents, and their estimated effects on adolescents.

Educational Attainment

Neighborhood effects appear to work through the social milieu or settings in which adolescents live and act and can be considered as responses to a lack of legitimate economic opportunity. Taylor (1991), for example, reports that black males in poor neighborhoods often relinquish their belief in the possibility of conventional achievement and mobility in mainstream society. And, as documented by Ogbu (1984) and Farrel (1990), this perceived lack of opportunity, and the weight of discrimination, leads to diminished academic performance.

Studies on the structural influences of neighborhoods provide some support for this view. There is strong evidence, for example, that growing up in a high-SES neighborhood raises a teenager's educational attainment (i.e., promotion and graduation), independent of family characteristics (Jencks and Mayer, 1990a). Controlling for family education, income, and other variables, one 10-year study of urban adolescent males found that, overall, the higher the mean family income in a neighborhood (defined by ZIP codes), the greater the number of years of school completed. Moreover, the data suggest that black males stay in school longer if they have white neighbors, but drop out sooner if they are racially segregated (Datcher, 1982). A later study, using a different methodology, replicated these findings for young women (Corcoran et al., 1987).

Two recent studies, building on these investigations, have found that adolescents living in low-SES neighborhoods are more likely to drop out of high school than adolescents with similar family backgrounds who live in advantaged neighborhoods. One study found that dropout rates were lowest in census tracts with a high percentage of adult workers in professional and managerial jobs and highest in neighborhoods in which fewer than 10 percent of workers were in "high-status" occupations, especially among black adolescents. The other study, controlling for family background (e.g., mother's education, family structure, income-to-needs ratio) estimated that on average, a teenage girl's chance of dropping out of high school increases from 10.8 percent to 14.9 percent when the proportion of families in her ZIP code with incomes over $30,000 decreases by one standard deviation. An increase in the proportion of families that are headed by female single parents also increased the dropout rate among both blacks and other minority ethnic groups (Brooks-Gunn et al., 1993).

Teenage Pregnancy

There is strong evidence that poor neighborhoods increase the likelihood of early pregnancy and childbearing. For example, researchers have found that many young women in poverty recognize the risks of early parenthood, but opt for this choice because it provides proof that they are attractive and successful. It also provides adult status more immediately than hoping for a job that may not come. Other teenage mothers lack the strong and sustained relationships with adults that are necessary to resolve basic identity issues. In this context, babies are a real and meaningful source of love in a setting with insufficient positive sanctions and caring attachments (Anderson, 1990; Musick, 1991).

Holding race and family background constant, births to unmarried adolescents are more likely in poor neighborhoods than in more affluent ones (Jencks and Mayer, 1990b). However, this effect is apparently modified by both race and family background. For example, higher numbers of high-status workers in a census tract reduce the chance that black, but not white, adolescents will have a baby. The number of black teenage girls having a baby increased from 7.4 percent to 19.8 percent as the proportion of high-status workers decreased from 31.2 percent to 3.5 percent (Crane, 1991b). On average, the chance of having a baby decreases from 10.6 percent to 6.9 percent as the average proportion of households with incomes over $30,000 increases by one standard deviation; among black girls, the decline is from 32.4 percent to 26.7 percent. A higher proportion of families headed by females increases the likelihood of becoming pregnant for all teenage girls (Brooks-Gunn et al., 1993).

Employment

It is likely that poor neighborhoods also affect adolescent employment prospects. Not only are employers less likely to hire young people from such neighborhoods, but adolescents often believe it more profitable to enter underground or illegitimate employment markets, such as drug dealing or gambling, than formal labor markets (Williams, 1989; Reiss and Roth, 1993). And since many adolescents are unemployed, peer influences, especially those other youths of the same sex, offer significant barriers to gainful employment. Several studies show that growing up in an urban neighborhood that either is predominantly black or has a high rate of welfare dependency reduces young men's chances of finding well-paid jobs in adulthood. However, the median income of a neighborhood does not appear to affect young people's economic prospects independent of its racial mix or welfare recipient rate (Jencks and Mayer, 1990b). More recent analysis shows that, in the 50 largest cities in the United States, the higher the poverty rate of a census track, the more likely teenage males are to be idle (i.e., not in school, employed, or in the military). For example, a 16- to 19-year-old male is eight times more likely to be idle if he lives in a census tract with a poverty rate of at least 50 percent than if he lives in a tract with a poverty rate of 10 to 19 percent (Massey et al., 1991). Other studies have confirmed that the most highly distressed neighborhoods appear to have a stronger negative effect on employment opportunities than neighborhoods in a "middle range" (Crane, 1991a; Brooks-Gunn et al., 1993).

Delinquency and Violent Crime

There is a relatively large body of research on neighborhoods, crime, and victimization (see Chapter 8), but few studies specifically examine adolescents or young adults (but see Sampson and Lauritsen, 1991; Reiss and Roth, 1993). However, age is one of the strongest individual-level correlates of offending: arrests for violent crimes peak around age 18 and decline gradually thereafter (Visher and Roth, 1986). We thus assume that most of the following discussion of research findings is generally applicable to young persons.

Urban areas have the highest rates of crime, and within urban areas the rates for both offending and victimization are highest in neighborhoods with concentrated poverty. Violent crime rates are also higher in neighborhoods with high percentages of people in the 12- to 20-year-old age group and large concentrations of single-parent households. And although concentrations of blacks, poor families, and single-parent households are also associated with homicide rates, the level of income disparity within neighborhoods is the strongest predictor (Reiss and Roth, 1993; Block, 1979; Sampson, 1985; Smith and Jarjoura, 1988).

Population density is often found to correlate with higher rates of violent crime, independent of neighborhood composition (Smith and Jarjoura, 1988; Beasely and Antunes, 1974; Sampson and Lauritsen, 1991). However, it is unclear whether it is neighborhood density per se or the density of residential structures that has the strongest influences. One study, for example, found that rates of crime victimization were 2 to 3 times higher in high-density neighborhoods, regardless of compositional factors such as age, race, and gender, but the analysis also revealed a strong positive association between rates of robbery and assault victimization and the percentage of housing with structures of five or more units (Sampson, 1983). Other studies have confirmed that the percentage of multiple-unit dwellings and renter-occupied housing are major predictors of crime rates in urban neighborhoods (Roneck, 1981; Scheurman and Kotrin, 1986).

Overall, these available studies suggest that a mix of neighborhood characteristics contribute to criminal offending. However, covariation among predictor variables and the use of cross-sectional designs in most studies limits the conclusions that can be drawn regarding causality. Two recent studies have sought to overcome these barriers. The first investigated changes in community structure and violent crime in Baltimore neighborhoods from 1970 to 1980 (Taylor and Covington, 1988). It found that neighborhoods with increasing concentrations of poor persons also experienced increasing violence rates. Less expected was an increased level of violence in gentrifying neighborhoods—those with increasing proportions of affluent persons (measured by owner-occupied housing and family income). The authors conclude that violence is associated with neighborhood change but that the underlying mechanisms are different for disparate neighborhoods. In increasingly poor neighborhoods, violence appears to be related to increased relative deprivation; in gentrifying neighborhoods, violence may be related to increased social disorganization.

The second study examined variation in homicide rates among SMSAs and cities over a 30-year period (Land et al., 1990), using common structural and demographic predictors discussed above. The analysts found that resource deprivation (a composite measure of poverty concentration and income stratification) had the largest effect on the homicide rate. All else being equal, cities with a large poor population and a high percentage of blacks, in conjunction with a high percentage of single-parent families and high divorce rates, had disproportionately high homicide rates. These predictors were more powerful for the 1970-1980 period, suggesting that increasing the concentration of disadvantaged persons within stratified neighborhoods has contributed to the recent increase in violent crime (Land et al., 1990).

CONCLUSIONS

Metropolitan neighborhoods in the United States, in both central cities and suburban areas, are characterized by a high degree of stratification by family income, race, and ethnicity. During the 1970s, there was an increase in the number of very poor neighborhoods and a substantial growth in underclass neighborhoods. Consequently, more children and adolescents are growing up in neighborhoods in which high proportions of adults are poor, unemployed, on welfare programs, or single parents. Blacks are most likely to be living in these neighborhoods, followed by Hispanics, Asians, and whites. In general economic and social integration is occurring in smaller metropolitan areas outside the Northeast and Midwest and in areas in which there are relatively small minority populations, but high levels of stratification still exist throughout the country.

Until analyses of 1990 census data are completed, trends during the 1980s cannot be confirmed. However, with overall trends toward higher poverty and unemployment, combined with the deteriorating labor market for young workers, it is likely that levels of concentrated poverty and residential segregation by class and race remained, at best, at 1980 levels.

Relatively few studies rigorously examine the hypothesis that variation in neighborhood composition is a causal factor in adolescent development. However, those few studies confirm that stratified neighborhoods independently contribute to dropping out of school, teenage parenthood, violent crime, and victimization. The economic and occupational mix of neighborhoods appears to have a stronger influence on adolescent development than racial composition. However, it also appears that economic factors affect black and white adolescents in different ways and affect blacks more strongly. The data also suggest that adolescents may be differentially affected by different levels of neighborhood poverty: very poor neighborhoods differ both economically and socially from other neighborhoods, and these differences are likely to affect adolescent behavior.

Some youth do prosper in such disadvantaged settings, "superkids" who were sheltered from the influence of street life by parents and community institutions or were able to establish important relationships with other neighborhood adults (Williams and Kornblum, 1985). But in far too many cases, adolescents are overwhelmed by the worst aspects of their neighborhood settings.

REFERENCES

Alsalem, N., L.T. Ogle, G.R. Rogers, and T.M. Smith
  1992   *The Condition of Education.* Washington, D.C.: U.S. Department of Education.
Anderson, E.
  1990   Neighborhood effects on teenage pregnancy. Pp. 375-398 in C. Jencks and P.E. Peterson, eds., *The Urban Underclass.* Washington, D.C.: The Brookings Institution.
  1991a Alienation and Crime Among the Ghetto Poor. Unpublished manuscript, Department of Sociology, University of Pennsylvania.
  1991b *Streetwise: Race, Class and Change in an Urban Community.* Chicago: University of Chicago Press.
Beasely, R.W., and G. Antunes
  1974   The etiology of urban crime: an ecological analysis. *Criminology* 11:439-461.
Block, R.
  1979   Community, environment, and violent crime. *Criminology* 17:46-57.
Brooks-Gunn, J., G. Duncan, P. Kato, and N. Sealand
  1993   Do neighborhoods influence child and adolescent behavior. *American Journal of Sociology,* in press.
Corcoran, M., R. Gordon, D. Laren, and G. Solon
  1987   Intergenerational transmission of education, income and earnings. Unpublished manuscript, University of Michigan, Ann Arbor.
Crane, J.
  1991a Effects of neighborhoods on dropping out of school and teenage childbearing. In C. Jencks and P.E. Peterson, eds., *The Urban Underclass.* Washington, D.C.: The Brookings Institution.
  1991b The epidemic theory of ghettos and neighborhood effects on dropping out and teenage childbearing. *American Journal of Sociology* 5:1226-1259.
Datcher, L.
  1982   Effects of community and family background on achievement. *Review of Economics and Statistics* 64:32-41.

Eisenhower Foundation (Milton S.)
1990   *Youth Investment and Community Reconstruction: Street Lessons on Drugs and Crime for the Nineties.* Washington, D.C.: Milton S. Eisenhower Foundation.

Farley, R.
1990   Residential segregation of social and economic groups among blacks, 1970-89. In C. Jencks and P.E. Peterson, eds., *The Urban Underclass.* Washington, D.C.: The Brookings Institution.

Farrel, E.
1990   *Hanging In and Dropping Out: Voices of At-Risk High School Students.* New York: Teachers College Press.

Fernandez, R.M., and D. Harris
1990   Social Isolation and the Underclass. Unpublished manuscript, Center for Urban Affairs and Policy Research, Northwestern University.

Harrell, A.V., and G.E. Peterson, eds.
1992   *Drugs, Crime, and Social Isolation: Barriers to Urban Opportunities.* Washington, D.C.: Urban Institute Press.

Jargowsky, P., and M.J. Bane
1990   Ghetto poverty in the United States, 1970-1980. Pp. 235-273 in C. Jencks and P.E. Peterson, eds., *The Urban Underclass.* Washington, D.C.: The Brookings Institution.

Jencks, C., and S.E. Mayer
1990a   The social consequences of growing up in a poor neighborhood. In L.E. Lynn and M. McGeary, eds., *Concentrated Urban Poverty in America.* Washington, D.C.: National Academy Press.
1990b   Residential segregation, job proximity, and black job opportunities. In L.E. Lynn and M. McGeary, eds., *Inner-City Poverty in the United States.* Washington, D.C.: National Academy Press.

Judd, D.R.
1992   Segregation forever? *The Nation* 253(20):740-744.

Kirschenman, J., and K.M. Neckerman
1991   "We'd love to hire them, but . . .": the meaning of race for employers. Pp. 203-232 in C. Jencks and P.E. Peterson, eds., *The Urban Underclass.* Washington, D.C.: The Brookings Institution.

Land, K., P. McCall, and L. Cohen
1990   Structural covariates of homicide rates: are there any invariances across time and space? *American Journal of Sociology* 95:922-963.

Littell, J., and J. Wynn
1989   *The Availability and Use of Community Resources for Young Adolescents in an Inner-City and a Suburban Community.* Chicago: Chapin Hall Center for Children, University of Chicago.

Logan, J.R., and M. Schneider
1984   Racial segregation and racial change in American suburbs. *American Journal of Sociology* 89:874-878.

Massey, D., and N. Denton
1987   Trends in the residential segregation of Blacks, Hispanics and Asians: 1970-1980. *American Sociological Review* 52:802-825.
1988   Suburbanization and segregation in U.S. metropolitan areas. *American Journal of Sociology* 94(3):592-626.
1989   Hypersegregation in U.S. metropolitan areas: Black and Hispanic segregation along five dimensions. *Demography* 26(3):373-391.

Massey, D., and M. Eggers
1990   The ecology of inequality: minorities and the concentration of poverty. *American Journal of Sociology* 95:1153-1188.

Mayer, S.E.
1991   The Effect of School and Neighborhood Social Mix on Adolescents' Transitions to Adulthood. Commissioned paper prepared for the Panel on High-Risk Youth, Commission on Behavioral and Social Sciences and Education, National Research Council, Washington, D.C.

Musick, J.S.
1991   The high-stakes challenge of programs for adolescent mothers. Pp. 111-138 in P.B. Edelman and J. Ladner, eds., *Adolescence and Poverty: Challenge for the 1990s*. Washington, D.C.: Center for National Policy Press.

National Commission on Children
1991   *Speaking of Kids: A National Survey of Children and Parents*. Washington, D.C.: National Commission on Children.

Ogbu, J.U.
1984   *The Next Generation: An Ethnography of Education in an Urban Setting*. New York: Academic Press.

Orfield, G.
1983   *Public School Desegregation in the United States, 1968-1980*. Washington, D.C.: Joint Center for Political Studies.

Orfield, G., and F. Monfort
1992   *The Status of School Desegregation: The Next Generation*. Alexandria, Va.: National School Boards Association.

Orfield, G., F. Monfort, and M. Aaron
1989   Status of school desegregation 1968-1986. In *Segregation, Integration, and Public Policy: National, State, and Metropolitan Trends in Public Schools*. Chicago: University of Chicago.

Rainwater, L.
1970   *Behind Ghetto Walls: Black Families in a Federal Slum*. Chicago: Aldine Press.
1987   Class, Culture, Poverty, and Welfare. Unpublished manuscript, Department of Sociology, Harvard University.

Reiss, A.J., and J.A. Roth, eds.
1993   *Understanding and Preventing Violence*. Panel on the Understanding and Control of Violent Behavior, Committee on Law and Justice, National Research Council. Washington, D.C.: National Academy Press.

Ricketts, E., and R. Mincy
1990   Growth of the underclass: 1970-1980. *Journal of Human Resources* 25(2):137-145.

Roneck, D.
1981   Dangerous places: crime and residential environment. *Social Forces* 60:74-96.

Sampson, R.J.
1983   Structural density and criminal victimization. *Criminology* 21:276-293.
1985   Neighborhood and crime: the structural determinants of personal victimization. *Journal of Research in Crime and Delinquency* 22:7-40.

Sampson, R.J., and J.L. Lauritsen
1991   Violent Victimization and Offending: Individual, Situational, and Community-Level Risk Factors. Unpublished manuscript, Panel on the Understanding and Control of Violent Behavior, University of Chicago.

Scheurman, L., and S. Kotrin
   1986   Community careers in crime. Pp. 67-100 in A.J. Reiss, Jr. and M. Tonry, eds., *Communities and Crime.* Chicago: University of Chicago Press.
Schneider, M., and J.R. Logan
   1982   Suburban racial segregation and black access to local public resources. *Social Science Quarterly* 63:762-770.
Skogan, W.G.
   1990   *Disorder and Decline: Crime and the Spiral of Decay in American Neighborhoods.* New York: The Free Press.
Smith, D.R., and G.R. Jarjoura
   1988   Social structure and criminal victimization. *Journal of Research in Crime and Delinquency* 25:27-52.
Sullivan, M.
   1990   *Getting Paid: Economy, Culture, and Youth Crime in the Inner City.* Ithaca, N.Y.: Cornell University Press.
Taylor, R.L.
   1991   Poverty and adolescent black males: the subculture of disengagement. Pp. 139-162 in P. Edelman and J. Ladner, eds., *Adolescence and Poverty: Challenge for the 1990s.* Washington, D.C.: Center for Public Policy Press.
Taylor, R., and J. Covington
   1988   Neighborhood changes in ecology and violence. *Criminology* 26:553-590.
Visher, C., and J. Roth
   1986   Participation in criminal careers. Pp. 211-291 in A. Blumstein et al., eds., *Criminal Careers and Career Criminals.* Washington, D.C.: National Academy Press.
Williams, T.
   1989   *The Cocaine Kids: The Inside Story of a Teenage Drug Ring.* Menlo Park, Calif.: Addison-Wesley.
Williams, T., and W. Kornblum
   1985   *Growing Up Poor.* Lexington, Mass.: Lexington Books.
Wilson, W.J.
   1987   *The Truly Disadvantaged: The Inner City, The Underclass, and Public Policy.* Chicago: University of Chicago Press.

5

Health and Health Care

Adolescent health has become an identified concern for policy makers and researchers only in the past decade (U.S. Office of Technology Assessment, 1991a). This attention stems from changing conceptions of illness and disease prevention and awareness that adolescent health issues are often different from those of children or adults. It also stems from the recognition that conventional concepts of medical care, rooted in the biological determinants of disease, are not directly applicable to the serious health problems manifested by adolescents, many of which are related to patterns of behavior adopted by adolescents in response to their environments. There is also concern that the health status of adolescents has failed to improve over the past two decades. Since the early 1980s, for example, adolescent deaths from homicide, suicide, and HIV/AIDS have increased. Furthermore, the rates of teenage pregnancy, sexually transmitted diseases, and drug use have either increased or remained at high levels relative to that observed in other countries. Finally, it has become apparent that many adolescents who have one type of problem often have others; approximately 25 percent are considered at high risk for a poor transition into adulthood (Osgood, 1989; Millstein et al., 1992; Dryfoos, 1990).

These findings have led to a broad consensus among health care workers and researchers that most of the salient causes of adolescent mortality and morbidity are preventable. For example, poverty is consistently the strongest sociodemographic predictor of poor health (Gans et al., 1990), but poverty can be reduced by employment or income transfers. Similarly, using seat belts can reduce the harm of accidents, and using condoms can prevent pregnancy as well as sexually transmitted diseases. Moreover, evaluations of health service programs indicates that they can reduce the frequency of many conditions and ameliorate the severity of others, even when social factors weigh heavily in the genesis of the conditions (Starfield, 1985).

The extent of overlap and preventability of many types of health problems provides a focus for adolescent health care that is consistent with the World Health Organization (WHO) definition of health as "the complete physical, mental, and social well-being" of the individual (*Health Promotion*, 1987). Indeed, one recent study concludes (U.S. Office of Technology Assessment, 1991a:4):

> This broader view of health—emphasizing mental and social, as well as physical, aspects and a sense of well-being as well as the absence of problems—can be said to fit the period of adolescence much better than does a narrow focus on the absence of physical health problems.

HEALTH STATUS OF ADOLESCENTS

In many respects, the United States has made progress in ensuring good physical health for its citizens. People in all groups (except black males) live about 7 years longer than they did in 1967. However, violence and intentional injury remain serious health problems in this country. Compared with 30 other industrialized countries, the United States has the highest rates of sexual assault and assault with force, and is third in homicide. Concurrently, the United States is becoming a "melancholy" society: since the early 1900s, successive birth cohorts have shown increased rates and earlier onset of depression and suicide (van Dijk et al., 1990; Murphy and Wetzel, 1980).

These trends are particularly pronounced among adolescents (see Table 5-1). Fifty years ago, most adolescents died from natural causes, but there has since been a steady decrease in adolescent deaths by cancer, heart disease, and cardiovascular disease. Unfortunately, those declines have been offset in part by steady increases in death through accidental and intentional injuries (including suicide), which now account for 75 percent of the 20,000 adolescent deaths each year. Indeed, mortality rates for adolescents have increased since the mid-1980s. And, because of high injury and violence rates, youth in the United States are far more likely to die during adolescence than their age-mates in other

TABLE **5-1** Deaths of People Aged 15 to 24, by Age and Cause of Death, 1965-1988 (number per 1,000)

Cause of Death	1965	1980	1988
15 to 19 years old			
All causes	95.1	97.9	88.0
Motor vehicle accidents	40.2	43.0	37.3
All other accidents	16.5	14.9	9.4
Suicide	4.0	8.5	11.3
Males, white	6.3	15.0	19.6
Females, white	1.8	3.3	19.6
Males, all other races	5.2	7.5	4.8
Females, all other races	2.4	1.8	2.6
Homicide	4.3	10.6	11.7
Males, white	3.0	10.9	8.1
Females, white	1.3	3.9	3.0
Males, all other races	30.6	47.9	506.4
Females, all other races	7.1	10.1	10.2
Cancer	7.6	5.4	4.4
Heart disease	5.3	2.3	2.2
Pneumonia/influenza	2.1	0.6	0.5
20 to 24 years old			
All causes	127.3	132.7	115.4
Motor vehicle accidents	49.3	46.8	39.7
All other accidents	18.7	18.8	12.4
Suicide	8.9	16.1	15.0
Males, white	13.9	27.8	27.0
Females, white	4.3	5.9	4.4
Males, all other races	13.1	20.9	20.0
Females, all other races	4.0	3.6	3.0
Homicide	10.0	20.6	19.0
Males, white	7.4	19.9	14.8
Females, white	2.3	5.4	4.7
Males, all other races	80.5	109.4	105.6
Females, all other races	17.3	23.3	19.7
Cancer	9.0	7.2	5.7
Heart disease	9.3	3.5	3.6
Pneumonia/influenza	2.3	1.0	0.9

SOURCE: Office of Education Research and Improvement (1991).

industrialized countries (Irwin et al., 1991; Fingerhut and Kleinman, 1989; Eisenberg, 1984).

Adolescent suicide rates have nearly tripled since 1960 and are now second only to those for people over age 65. More than 5,000 adolescents kill themselves each year, and an estimated 400,000 attempt suicide. Males are disproportionately represented in the first group and females in the second. Teenage deaths by violence are directly related to economic and social conditions in low-income neighborhoods (see Chapter 8) and to the availability of guns in American society. Age-adjusted rates of suicide by means of firearms increased 45 percent in a decade, while the rate for other means remained the same (Eisenberg, 1984). In 1987 firearms accounted for 68 percent of all adolescents who were murdered and 83 percent of all suicides.

The rise in teenage homicide and suicide suggests an increasingly high level of hopelessness, grief, and anger among adolescents. Another indication of such feelings is the rise in the proportion of children and adolescents receiving professional psychological assistance, which increased by 50 percent from 1981 to 1988 (Zill and Schoenbom, 1990). Between 15 and 19 percent of all children and adolescents suffer an emotional or psychiatric problem that warrants mental health treatment, and rates may have increased in recent years to between 17 and 22 percent (Institute of Medicine, 1989; Tuma, 1989). The occurrence of such a problem increases with age and varies by gender: for adolescents aged 12-17, for example, 20.4 percent of older adolescent males and 16.5 of their female counterparts have experienced an emotional or behavioral disorder (Zill and Schoenbom, 1990). The Institute of Medicine (1989:33) notes:

> [The] fact that so many children are affected should not suggest that these mental disorders are trivial or transient; on the contrary, childhood mental disorders are serious, persistent, and lead to suffering for the children and their families.

Over the past decade, drug, alcohol, and cigarette use and unprotected sexual intercourse have come to be seen as significant health problems. One-third of all high school seniors report having drunk at least five drinks in a row at least once during a 2-week period, 17 percent report monthly use of marijuana, and about 19 percent smoke cigarettes on a daily basis (Bachman et al., 1991; National Institute on Drug Abuse, 1990). Among young women aged 15-17, the proportion who are sexually active has risen steadily over the past 20 years and was 38 percent in 1988. Boys at all ages report having sexual intercourse more frequently than girls and at an earlier age. Contraceptive use, especially use of condoms, seems to be increasing, but about one-half of sexually active teenagers have unprotected sexual intercourse. About 2.5 million adolescents contract a sexually transmitted disease each year, and prevalence rates have increased over the past decade—especially for syphilis—to levels that were last seen in the 1940s (Sonenstein et al., 1990; Irwin et al., 1991).

Unprotected sexual intercourse also contributes significantly to the risk of AIDS. AIDS is the fastest-growing cause of death among adolescents and young adults: within 5 years it is projected to be the leading cause of death among men aged 25-44. Given the time lag between viral infection and diagnosis, the number of undiagnosed cases of HIV infection among 13- to 29-year-olds is approximately 4.5 times greater than the total number of reported cases (about 8,000 as of April 1991). Those most at risk are runaways, youths engaged in prostitution, incarcerated youths, youths with homosexual experiences, and intravenous drug users. However, the spread of the epidemic makes such risk factors increasingly less useful in predicting individual or community risk (Joseph, 1992).

THE HEALTH CARE SYSTEM AND ADOLESCENT HEALTH

The provision of health care services to adolescents is the result of four intertwined characteristics of the structure of the U.S. health system. First is the medical model of care: that is, adolescent health is the domain of physicians and other medical professionals operating out of hospitals, clinics, and offices. Second, many if not most adolescents lack a consistent source of basic care over time. Third is the tangle of health insurance arrangements that define who can afford care and what services are eligible for reimbursement. Fourth, a large majority of adolescents have no financial access to care independent of their family, and access to appropriate service remains a large barrier; however, adolescents' health needs may sometimes be best addressed independently, outside the context of their families (U.S. Office of Technology Assistance, 1991a).

Another important characteristic of the U.S. health system is that it is becoming more specialty-oriented. The proportion of young physicians who are choosing to train in a specialty rather than in primary care is increasing, and the availability of primary care physicians to the population is declining (Starfield, 1992).

The dearth of primary care is particularly problematic for children and youth, and especially for teenagers, since their major problems are not in the realm of medical or surgical subspecialties. Adolescents have a special need for the readily available, first-contact care that is the hallmark of primary care. Four other features of primary care are also urgently needed by adolescents (Starfield, 1992):

1. Comprehensiveness of care, which involves a broad range of services, is critical; the social as well as biological components of their problems require multidisciplinary approaches.

2. A long-term perspective on care is especially important for adolescents because many of their problems are not amenable to prevention, diagnosis, and management in only a few visits.

3. Consistent provision of services over time by professionals who know the adolescent also fosters a trusting relationship, so that adolescents feel comfortable in seeking advice for incipient problems, presenting their existing problems, and accepting care and advice about the prevention and management of problems.

4. Coordinated care is needed to integrate all aspects of services, including those that have to be provided by various specialists and other health professionals, into a person-centered system is also essential.

The services that do exist for adolescents are fragmented and oriented toward specific problems rather than toward the constellations of problems that characterize adolescents. Existing services for substance abuse, mental health, trauma (e.g., emergency care), and reproductive and maternal health have developed largely in isolation from each other. In fact, the entire field of adolescent heath is new; the current U.S. health care system does not yet have a strategy for dealing with adolescents or for dealing with the broad concept of health embodied in the WHO definitions.

Evolution of Adolescent Health Care

The medical community became aware of the special health needs of adolescents only very recently. Most research on adolescent health during the first half of the twentieth century was concerned with the effects of various infectious diseases (Gallagher, 1982). Subsequently, conceptions of illness broadened, but adolescent health problems were still viewed in a biomedical context, as distinct disease entities, and psychosocial disorders, such as truancy, teenage pregnancy, and suicide, were seen as social deviancy. The first real professional attention came in the early

1940s, when the morbidity and mortality burden of infectious diseases had diminished and other types of health problems were taking their place. However, the first textbook of adolescent medicine was not published until 1960 (Gallagher, 1960). And a major pediatric text published in 1975 reflected the medical community's neglect of the totality of adolescent health needs: sections on adolescent health included only growth and development, sexual maturation, nutrition, and psychological development rooted in Freudian theory (Vaughan et al., 1975). The American Medical Association (AMA) officially recognized adolescent medicine as a subspecialty in the 1970s, and the first subspecialty examination will be administered in 1994 for board-certified pediatricians and internists who aspire to certification in adolescent medicine.

By the early 1990s the concept of adolescent health had become broader. Indeed, almost all aspects of adolescent development can now be viewed within the purview of "health." For example, *The Health of Adolescents*, a text sponsored by the AMA, has chapters on substance abuse, sexually transmitted diseases, pregnancy and its outcomes, chronic illness and disability, injuries, disorders of self-image, depression, suicide, and maltreatment of adolescents (Hendee, 1991). Other recent works add delinquency and school failure to the list of health-related problems (Dryfoos, 1990; Strasburger and Greydanus, 1990). A major review by the U.S. Office of Technology Assessment (1991a) also reviewed data on family problems, nutrition and fitness problems, parenting, mental health, and homelessness. Two comprehensive textbooks on adolescent health published in 1992 provide authoritative surveys of the field (McAnarney et al., 1992; Friedman et al., 1992).

By 1980 there were 35 fellowship training programs for adolescent medicine, 9 of which were federally funded; there are currently 44 such programs, 6 of which are federally supported. The number of physicians trained in adolescent medicine remains very small. It is estimated that there are about seven adolescent medicine specialists per 100,000 individuals between 14 and 20 years old. This small number of specialists is not even adequate to provide backup for the referrals and consultations made by a much larger number of primary care providers who are not trained in adolescent medicine (Starfield, 1992).

Health Services Organization and Delivery

Insufficient training of practitioners is a major barrier to managing adolescent health problems (Blum, 1987). Physicians often fail to recognize patients' health problems and are much more likely to respond to physical symptoms than to psychosocial ones, even when the latter reflect serious psychosocial morbidity (see, e.g., Starfield and Borkowf, 1969). Another barrier is the general tendency of medical education to stress the diagnosis and management of problems rather than their prevention. Since adolescents comprise a small percentage of the practices of most physicians, there is little opportunity to gain on-the-job experience in dealing with adolescent concerns. Rates of visits to office-based physicians are 1.7 and 0.9 visits per person per year for white and black adolescents, respectively, compared with 2.7 visits per year for the population as a whole (Blum, 1990). These rates remained unchanged between 1980 and 1985 (DuRant, 1991). In fact, teenagers are less likely to have a regular source of care than are younger children (Blum, 1988).

Among office-based physicians, teenagers have most of their contacts with general practitioners, family physicians, or pediatricians. The remainder, about 45 percent of all visits, are distributed among a variety of other specialists, including obstetricians and gynecologists, orthopedic surgeons, dermatologists, internists, ophthalmologists, and general surgeons. Among young adolescents aged 10-14, about one-third of visits are to family physicians and one-third to pediatricians. For older adolescents (aged 15-19), family practitioners account for 35 percent of visits and pediatricians for only 8 percent; but obstetricians and gynecologists receive more visits than pediatricians, 12 and 15 percent, respectively (Nelson, 1991). The extent to which these specialists are equipped for or interested in dealing with the full constellation of adolescent problems is unknown, but it is likely to be minimal. (Similar data are not available for adolescents who do not receive their care from office-based practitioners.)

What is clear, however, is that few physicians are dealing specifically with the problems prevalent among adolescents. Substance use and abuse, sexually transmitted diseases, disorders of self-image, depression, suicide, and maltreatment of adolescents are highlighted in studies of adolescent health, yet they do not appear among the most common diagnoses, problems, procedures, or therapies associated with office-based visits. The 10-minute average length of visits by adolescents in physician offices hardly provides the time to elicit and deal with problems of such complexity (Irwin, 1986). In addition, many of the health issues of adolescents, such as drug use or sexual intercourse, are socially stigmatizing or difficult to discuss. Such issues make physician-patient relationships particularly difficult; adolescents may be unwilling to present, discuss, or deal with these problems when physicians provide care (DuRant, 1991; Waitzkin, 1991). In addition, since many adolescents with these problems are seen in settings (categorical programs, neighborhood clinics, hospital-based adolescent clinics) that are not part of the national ambulatory care surveys, the incidence of these diagnoses is underreported in office-based practice data.

As a result, adolescents—and especially adolescents who engage in high-risk behavior—have no apparent home in the U.S. medical system. They have relatively low visit rates in office-based practice, and their problems are poorly represented in standard medical data. The problem is exacerbated by a system of health services that is designed to provide specialty services rather than primary care. Most other industrialized countries have highly developed general practitioner services that serve as portals of entry into other services. The mode of payment and organization in the U.S. system permits and even encourages patients to seek care from specialists rather than generalists. No aspiring new specialty, including adolescent medicine, is required to specify whether its practitioners function as generalists for its target population or, rather, as a secondary (consultative) or tertiary (referral) resource for generalists (i.e., family physicians, general pediatricians, or general internists). As a result, it has been impossible to determine how many such specialists would be needed to serve the target population or to begin planning and organizing a health service system to meet adolescent needs.

There is a growing consensus that the present health care system is too restricted and too fragmented, and that funds are not made available to respond effectively to the major health problems of adolescents. As a result, many have concluded that adolescent health services should be provided in alternative settings in the community. The defining features of these systems are an emphasis on prevention and outreach, consistent with a public health perspective on illness and health. The most frequently described option is school-based services. Currently only 1 percent of adolescents are served by clinics in schools. Although there have been some notable successes with school-based clinics, there is concern about the extent of their impact on health, the stability of their long-term funding, the commitment of school systems to maintain clinics when educational programs themselves are threatened by reductions in funding, and the fact that many clinics restrict the provision of family planning services by not offering contraceptives as an option for young people (Earls et al., 1989; Millstein, 1988). Other alternatives include the provision of health and mental health services through "street-based" clinics and community-based youth development programs (see Chapter 10). Unfortunately, exposure of adolescents to these new services is often a matter of chance, social class, or area of residence, rather than need.

Mental Health Services

Approximately 25 percent of all adolescents are diagnosed with significant forms of emotional distress. Yet, as with the health system generally, it is misleading to speak of a mental health "system" for adolescents. Services are provided through special education in schools, community mental health centers, and inpatient facilities, but these components are poorly integrated and often unavailable to many youths who need them. Consequently, the mental health system meets the needs of a minority of adolescents, with some estimates indicating that up to three-quarters of adolescents with a diagnosable mental disorder do not have any contact with a mental health provider (Joint Commission on Mental Health of Children, 1969; President's Commission on Mental Health, 1978; Knitzer, 1982; U.S. Office of Technology Assessment, 1991b). Moreover, low-income and minority adolescents are the most likely to be denied access or to receive low-quality services (U.S. Office of Technology Assessment, 1991a; Cross et al., 1989; Berlin, 1983; Padilla et al., 1975).

Mental health services have traditionally focused on treatment rather than prevention of illness or the promotion of emotional stability. The difficulties of this approach are well known. Affordability and access are both problems. Even for those young people for whom insurance is available, mental health treatment is offered only on a short-term basis, and often in restrictive inpatient settings. For example, anorexia nervosa, a growing problem among adolescent girls, is rarely covered by insurance programs, and the limit on payments for emotional illness is so low that institutions often cannot afford to deal with adolescents with these problems (see below). Within schools, less than one-third of all students in special education receive psychological, social work, or counseling services. There is only one school psychologist per 2,500 students nationwide, and only about 2 percent of all adolescents receive service from school psychologists (Meyers, 1989; Tremper, 1991). When preventive services are offered, they have been focused on the behavioral problems seen as being reflective of poor mental health—substance abuse, violence, delinquency—rather than on the emotional well-being of young people themselves (U.S. Office of Technology Assessment, 1991b).

HEALTH INSURANCE

A comprehensive review of adolescent health insurance in 1979 and 1986 documented an estimated 25 percent increase in the proportion of adolescents (aged 10 to 18) without health insurance (U.S. Office of Technology Assessment, 1991b). By 1986, slightly more than 20 percent of all adolescents did not have public (Medicaid) or private health coverage, and young adults (aged 19 to 24) were even less likely to be covered (Newacheck and McManus, 1989). Near-poor adolescents are much less likely than their poor or nonpoor counterparts to be insured: fully one-third of near-poor youths completely lack coverage for their health care. By far the leading reason is that health insurance is too expensive (70 percent); an additional 11 percent report that they lost health insurance as a result of job loss in the family; only 6 percent lack insurance because they feel they do not need it or want it (Newacheck and McManus, 1989). The 1981 Omnibus Budget Reconciliation Act, through federal and state actions, limited eligibility for Aid to Families with Dependent Children, which in turn decreased eligibility for coverage by Medicaid. Lack of insurance coverage is not limited to those reared in poverty; about two-thirds of uninsured adolescents live in families with incomes above the poverty level.

Private Coverage

Even where it is available, insurance is inadequate for many adolescent problems. Treatment-oriented services dominate private health insurance plans (U.S. Office of Technology Assessment, 1991b). For example, virtually all employment-based private health insurance plans (which cover about 90 percent of individuals with private health insurance) cover diagnostic X-ray and laboratory tests, hospital room and board, inpatient and outpatient surgery, physician visits in the hospital and office, and inpatient mental health care. Such plans also generally provide coverage for outpatient mental health services (95 percent), prescription drugs (93 percent), substance abuse treatment (90 percent), home health care (86 percent), and extended care (79 percent). But preventive services are generally not covered by private health insurance. For example, a minority of private health plans provide coverage for general dental care (37 percent), vision care (35 percent), immunizations (29 percent), routine physical exams (28 percent), hearing problems (27 percent), and orthodontia (27 percent) (U.S. Office of Technology Assessment, 1991b). These restrictions are especially important for adolescent well-being since they correspond directly to important acute and preventive needs of youth. Adolescents in low-income families that do not have private insurance, who are not eligible for Medicaid, and whose families are unable to pay out-of-pocket for preventive services are especially unlikely to receive such services.

Thus, coverage by private health insurance does not guarantee access to all services that may be needed. Restrictions on payment (e.g., maximum amount, coinsurance, or deductibles) can be a deterrent to receiving services, especially for adolescents, for example (U.S. Office of Technology Assessment, 1991b):

- Limitations on the number of hospital days for treatment of mental illness and substance abuse place adolescents at a special disadvantage because their stays in the hospital are longer than those of adults.
- Preventive services for affective or behavioral disorders, such as depressed mood, conduct problems, or drug use, are often not covered.
- About one-third of privately insured adolescents are not covered for maternity-related services.
- At least eight states restrict private health insurance coverage of abortion services, and four others require it to be optional and at additional cost to the receiver. The extent of coverage for contraceptive services is unknown, as is coverage for diagnostic procedures related to pregnancy itself.
- Waiting periods and exclusion of preexisting conditions disproportionately affect employed adolescents because their duration of employment tends to be shorter than that for older employees. (Only 24 percent of employed adolescents receive health insurance through their employment.)

Access to health care services may become even more restricted in the future. Health insurance coverage for dependents has been declining, requirements for cost-sharing have been increasing, and employers are eliminating many benefits such as coverage for substance abuse treatment (U.S. Office of Technology Assessment, 1991a). In addition, the rapid growth of self-insurance among the nation's employers appears likely to decrease the comprehensiveness of services to those covered by the insurance, because self-insured plans are exempt from most state laws mandating that insurance plans include specified benefits.

Medicaid Coverage

For the 12 percent of insured adolescents who are covered by Medicaid, coverage is generally more complete than private insurance (Newacheck and McManus, 1989). There are no copayments or deductibles, and teenage mothers may establish eligibility on their own rather than through a parent. Federal regulations mandate minimum Medicaid benefits, but the 50 states vary widely in the extent to which they insure optional services. States can limit the frequency and number of covered services, decree certain services as not medically necessary, or restrict the sites where services are provided. Furthermore, like private health insurance, coverage of mental health services and substance abuse services is more extensive for inpatient than outpatient services, thus discouraging early or preventive care of these types of problems (U.S. Office of Technology Assessment, 1991b).

The nature of the differences among states may be illustrated by comparing states at the extremes of their coverage. California provides Medicaid coverage for children of families with incomes up to 75 percent of the federal poverty level and up to 85 percent for pregnant women and infants. The state covers the full range of pregnancy-related services and also covers poor children in intact families up to age 21. In contrast, Alabama sets eligibility at 13 percent of the poverty level even for pregnant women, and it does not offer Medicaid to medically needy families or to poor children in intact families (Children's Defense Fund, 1991).

Legislation in 1989 added Medicaid requirements that should have helped to address adolescent health needs. Coverage must now include a comprehensive history and physical examination, appropriate immunizations, laboratory tests, health education, and dental, vision, and hearing services. This legislation also permitted payment to medical practitioners to diagnose and treat any health condition discovered on screening, even though the services go beyond what the state would cover if the patient had presented the health problem. In practice, the states have concentrated almost three-quarters of these expenditures on pre-school-age children. Only 22 state programs covered five or more visits in adolescence, and patients aged 12-20 represent only 3.4 percent of all children served by the program (McManus et al., 1993).

The Medicaid expansion mandated by the Congress in 1990 will make all poor adolescents eligible for standard Medicaid by the year 2002. However, the limitations inherent in Medicaid will still restrict certain services. Access will continue to be through the family, so that teenagers will not be able to receive care on their own initiative. And even for adolescents who have their own Medicaid card, access to services is often only for certain conditions, such as family planning, sexually transmitted diseases, and pregnancy services. That is, the adolescent must have a defined health problem in order to receive services. Moreover, Medicaid does not reimburse costs for many of the services needed such as social work and nutrition, and the reimbursement for other services is so low that youths are essentially disenfranchised: for example, reimbursement for the treatment of substance abuse is so low as to be a disincentive to treatment (U.S. General Accounting Office, 1991). New developments in the Medicaid program hold promise of improving access to services for the poorest children over the next few years. The Medicaid eligibility reforms of 1990 required states to provide Medicaid coverage to children born after September 30, 1983, with family incomes up to 100 percent of the federal poverty level. Earlier legislation had made this provision optional, and there was wide variability among the states in the extent to which it was adopted. Thus, by the turn of the century, most of the poorest adolescents will be covered by Medicaid. State Medicaid coverage must now include periodic screening at intervals consistent with professionally set guidelines, must include health education and anticipatory guidance, and must cover treatment for all services identified at screening, as long as they are within federal guidelines. The improvement of services themselves may follow from other anticipated reforms, including those concerning the payment of physicians and those requiring states to monitor adolescent health.

Consequences for Adolescent Health

The service gaps that result from inadequate insurance are precisely for the types of health services most needed by adolescents who are at risk for unsuccessful transitions to adulthood. Specifically, coverage restrictions and reimbursement schedules ensure that relatively few adolescents receive preventive services, such as reproductive health or the necessary intervention for problems stemming from affective disorders or substance use. For example, gonorrhea and syphilis are sexually transmitted diseases whose serious manifestations are preventable by good medical care, yet the prevalence of gonorrhea in 1988 was 65.1 per 100,000 adolescents aged 10-14, 1,072.9 per 100,000 age 15-19, and 1,241.5 per 100,000 aged 20-24. In the same year, the prevalence of syphilis (primary and secondary) was 1.0, 21.9, and 53.3 per 100,000, respectively, for the same age groups. The rates of syphilis increased by 25 percent, 46 percent, and 60 percent, respectively, between 1985 and 1990. Measles and mumps are completely preventable with immunization, yet adolescents constituted fully 48 percent and 62 percent of the reported cases of these two diseases in 1987 (Irwin et al., 1991).

Predictably, uninsured adolescents are also less likely to receive medical care. They are less likely to have contacts with physicians (Newacheck and McManus, 1989); when they do have a regular source of care, it is less likely to be a physician and more likely to be a hospital clinic, a walk-in facility, or an emergency room (Blum, 1990).

Although there is little research concerning the impact on adolescent health of access to care or a regular source of care, there is ample evidence for the population as a whole (see, for example, Starfield, 1992). Patients who have a regular source of care are more likely to be recognized as needing services, and existing mental and behavioral problems (such as those common in adolescents) are far more likely to be recognized if the regular source of care is a person rather than a place. People with a regular source of care have fewer emergency hospitalizations and shorter hospitalizations. They are less likely to contract preventable illnesses and more likely to comply with prescribed treatments and to keep follow-up appointments. When patients visit the same doctor over time rather than different doctors, care is more effective and less costly. Furthermore, interventions that involve sustained interactions between health professionals and families are more successful than those provided by a variety of separate sources. These interventions are even more effective when the service includes teams of professionals, especially home visitors, and when they include interactions with other services, in addition to the health care.

SPECIAL PROBLEMS: CONFIDENTIALITY AND CONSENT

Laws concerning parental consent and confidentiality of service pose additional barriers to adolescent health care (Bensinger and Natenshon, 1991). Under public law, parental consent is generally required for the care of a minor child, on the assumption that such individuals lack the competence required to receive care and carry out the recommendations resulting from care. Other rationales for parental consent include the state's interest in involving the family in a child's care and the providers' interests in assuring that reimbursement will be received for the service care (U.S. Office of Technology Assessment, 1991b).

The requirement for parental consent is generally waived under certain circumstances: when the adolescent can demonstrate his or her "independence" (e.g., marriage, maintenance of a separate domicile, or service in the armed forces) or for crisis situations (e.g., medical emergencies or when the adolescent is a victim of child abuse). Most states also allow minors to receive care for sexually transmitted diseases without the consent of a parent. Just under one-half of all states allow the provision of family planning services to minors without parental consent, although there are often considerable restrictions on what may be provided and to whom. About one-half of all states permit pregnant adolescents to receive care without parental consent. About one-fourth of all states require parental consent for abortions, a number that may soon increase. Just under one-fourth require parental notification of a minor's abortion decision, and about the same number provide for parental notification of pregnancy-related health services at the provider's discretion. Almost all states allow services to be provided without consent for substance abuse, but some include either drug-abuse or alcohol-related services but not both. A few states require parental notification of services related to substance abuse, and a few require it for mental health treatment. Slightly more than one-half of the states require parental consent for outpatient mental health services (U.S. Office of Technology Assessment, 1991b); somewhat fewer require such consent for inpatient mental health care, but generally adolescents can be committed without their consent to inpatient mental health care.

Requirements for parental consent or notification interfere with the acceptability and receipt of needed health services in several ways. First, the widely discrepant and highly nuanced rules and regulations are confusing to recipients of services, who are unlikely to know to what they are entitled. Rather than facing possible rejection for services, they often find it easier to avoid seeking care. Second, the deterrent effect of parental notification in the case of family planning and abortion services may be extrapolated to other types of adolescent health services.

Problems of confidentiality and consent affect both conventional and community-based medical services for adolescents. Society as a whole has yet to reach consensus on the extent to which adolescents should be granted the freedom to make their own decisions about seeking and obtaining health services and the conditions under which such freedom might be granted. Since the adequate provision of medically appropriate services to adolescents may conflict with decision making in some families, a more consistent societal approach to resolving the inevitable conflicts would be needed to improve the situation regarding health care for adolescents.

CONCLUSIONS

The U.S. health system is woefully inadequate in dealing with the health of adolescents. Existing services do not address the most serious health risks facing adolescents, nor are they organized in a systematic or structured way, nor are they available or accessible to many of those with the greatest need for service. As a result, the adolescent health system not only fails to reduce the effects of other high-risk settings, but fails to protect adolescents from further risk to their health. Indeed, it is no exaggeration to say that "there is no adolescent health care system in the United States." Yet adolescents face a higher risk of death from injury, homicide, and suicide than any other age group, and this risk appears to be rising. Other prevalent health problems include substance abuse, chronic illness and disability, sexually transmitted diseases, pregnancy and its outcomes, mental disorders (e.g., disorders of self-image, depression, suicide), and physical or sexual abuse. At the same time, however, adolescents are far less likely to visit a doctor's office or to have any regular source of medical care than are either younger children or adults.

The current structure of the U.S. health system fails to address these needs. Few physicians specialize in adolescent health, and other practitioners are poorly trained in recognizing adolescent health problems, particularly when the symptoms are psychosocial rather than physical. The overall U.S. health care system is fragmented, especially for adolescents because of the diversity of their needs. Adolescents are unlikely to know where to go and are likely to be referred often before finding an appropriate setting. The adolescent health system lacks all of the essential elements of primary care: a consistent point of entry into the system, a locus of ongoing responsibility, adequate backup for consultation and referral services by adolescent specialists, and comprehensiveness. Adolescents from low-income families—precisely those who are at highest risk for health problems—are also those least likely to be covered by health insurance. Moreover, even when available, insurance may be inadequate to the many needs of adolescents. Most private plans stress treatment rather than prevention or outreach, and payment restrictions (maximums, coinsurance, deductibles) further reduce the range of services available. Only 12 percent of low-income adolescents are currently covered by Medicaid, although for them the coverage is generally more complete than private insurance. However, the amounts and services covered by Medicaid can vary widely from state to state, and complicated regulations may discourage adolescents from seeking care. Rules regarding parental notification, which have a deterrent effect in the case of family planning and abortion, may also deter adolescents from seeking other health care services, and inadequate reimbursement schedules may cause providers to limit the number of Medicaid patients that they will serve.

Current trends do not bode well for adolescent health services. With few exceptions, new health policies will compound the problems that adolescents are now experiencing. Families, communities, and the society at large are generally reluctant to accept adolescent values that diverge sharply from community norms; to the extent that adolescent health problems stem from generally unaccepted behavior, health services have not been adapted to respond to the needs of adolescents. And access to existing, though inadequate, health services may become more restricted as private insurance coverage decreases. Even the movement of the U.S. health system into managed care, with tight controls on the number and extent of services that may be provided, may further place adolescents in jeopardy because of the dearth of research on the effectiveness of treatment for adolescent health problems. This should be a major area of research interest in health care services research.

REFERENCES

Bachman, J., D. Johnston, and P. O'Malley
    1991   Press Release: Summary of 1990 Senior Drug Use. University of Michigan News and Information Services, Ann Arbor.
Bensinger, J., and A. Natenshon
    1991   Difficulties in recognizing adolescent health issues. Pp. 381-410 in W. Hendee, ed., *The Health of Adolescents*. San Francisco: Jossey-Bass Publishers.

Berlin, I.
1983   Anglo adoptions of Native Americans: repercussions in adolescence. *Journal of the American Academy of Child Psychiatry* 17:387-388.

Blum, R.
1987   Physicians' assessment of deficiencies and desire for training in adolescent care. *Journal of Medical Education* 62(5):401-407.
1988   Health insurance and medical care; health of our nation's children, United States. *Advance Data from Vital and Health Statistics*, No. 188. Hyattsville, Md.: National Center for Health Statistics.
1990   Adolescent medicine. *Journal of the American Medical Association* 263(19):2621-2623.

Children's Defense Fund
1991   *The State of America's Children*. Washington, D.C.: Children's Defense Fund.

Cross, T., B. Bazron, K. Dennis, et al.
1989   *Towards a Culturally Competent System of Care: A Monograph on Effective Services for Minority Children Who are Severely Emotionally Disturbed*. Washington, D.C.: Georgetown University.

Dryfoos, J.
1990   *Adolescents at Risk: Prevalence and Prevention*. New York: Oxford University Press.

DuRant, R.
1991   Overcoming barriers to health care access. Pp. 431-52 in W. Hendee, ed., *The Health of Adolescents*. San Francisco: Jossey-Bass Publishers.

Earls, F., L. Robins, A. Stiffman, and J. Powell
1989   Comprehensive health care for high-risk adolescents: an evaluation study. *American Journal of Public Health* 79:999-1005.

Eisenberg, L.
1984   The epidemiology of suicide in adolescents. *Pediatric Annals* 13(1):47-54.

Fingerhut, I.A., and J.C. Kleinman
1989   Trends and current status in childhood mortality. U.S. 1900-85. *Vital and Health Statistics*, Series 3, No. 26, DHHS Pub. No. PHS 89-1410. Hyattsville, Md.: National Center for Health Statistics.

Friedman, S.B., M. Fisher, and S.K. Schonberg
1992   *Comprehensive Adolescent Health Care*. St. Louis, Mo.: Quality Medical Publishers.

Gallagher, J.R.
1960   *Medical Care of the Adolescent*. New York: Appleton-Century-Crofts, Inc.
1982   The origins, development, and goals of adolescent medicine. *Journal of Adolescent Health Care* 3:57-63.

Gans, J.E., with D. Blyth, A. Elster, and L.L. Gaveras
1990   *America's Adolescents: How Healthy Are They?* Chicago: American Medical Association.

Health Promotion
1987   Ottawa Charter for Health Promotion. *Health Promotion* 1(4):iii-v.

Hendee W., ed.
1991   *The Health of Adolescents*. San Francisco: Jossey-Bass Publishers.

Institute of Medicine
1989   *Research on Children and Adolescents with Mental, Behavioral, and Developmental Disorders*. Washington, D.C.: National Academy Press.

Irwin, C.
  1986   Why adolescent medicine? *Journal of Adolescent Health Care* 7(suppl):2S-
          12S.
Irwin, C., C. Brindis, S. Brodt, T. Bennett, and R. Rodriguez
  1991   *The Health of America's Youth: Current Trends in Health Status and
          Utilization of Health Service.* San Francisco: University of California.
Joint Commission on Mental Health of Children
  1969   *Crisis in Child Mental Health.* New York: Harper and Row.
Joseph, S.C.
  1992   AIDS and adolescence: a challenge to both treatment and prevention.
          Pp. 96-103 in D.E. Rogers and E. Ginzberg, eds., *Adolescents at Risk:
          Medical and Social Perspectives.* San Francisco: Westview Press.
Knitzer, J.
  1982   *Unclaimed Children.* Washington, D.C.: Children's Defense Fund.
McAnarney, E., R. Kreipe, D. Orr, and G. Commerci
  1992   *Textbook of Adolescent Medicine.* Philadelphia: W.B. Saunders.
McManus, M., R. Kelly, P. Newacheck, and J. Gephart
  1993   The Role of Title V Maternal and Child Health Programs in Assuring
          Access to Health Services for Adolescents. National Center for Educa-
          tion in Maternal and Child Health, Arlington, Va.
Meyers, J.
  1989   The practice of psychology in the schools for the primary prevention of
          learning and adjustment problems in children: a perspective from the
          field of education. In L.A. Bond and B.E. Compas, eds., *Primary Preven-
          tion and Promotion in the Schools.* Newbury Park, Calif.: Sage Publi-
          cations.
Millstein, S.G.
  1988   The Potential of School-Linked Centers to Promote Adolescent Health
          and Development. Carnegie Council on Adolescent Development working
          paper, New York.
Millstein, S., C. Irwin, N. Adler, L. Cohn, S. Kegeles, and M. Dolcini
  1992   Health-risk behaviors and health concerns among young adolescents.
          Pediatrics 89:422-428.
Murphy, G.E., and R.D. Wetzel
  1980   Suicide risk by birth cohort in the United States, 1949-1974. *Archives
          of General Psychiatry* 37:519-523.
National Institute on Drug Abuse
  1990   *National Household Survey on Drug Abuse: Main Findings, 1988.* Rockville,
          Md.: National Institute on Drug Abuse.
Nelson, C.
  1991   Office visits by adolescents. *Advance Data from Vital and Health
          Statistics,* No. 196. Hyattsville, Md.: National Center for Health Sta-
          tistics.
Newacheck, P., and M. McManus
  1989   Health insurance status of adolescents in the United States. *Pediatrics*
          84:699-708.
Office of Education Research and Improvement
  1991   Youth indicators 1991. *Trends on the Well-Being of American Youth.*
          Washington, D.C.: U.S. Department of Education.
Osgood, D.W.
  1989   Covariation of Risk Behaviors During Adolescence. Background paper
          of the U.S. Office of Technology Assessment Study on Adolescent Health,
          U.S. Congress.

Padilla, A., R. Ruiz, and R. Alvarez
1975   Community mental health services for the Spanish-speaking/surnamed population. *American Psychologist* 30(9):892-905.
President's Commission on Mental Health
1978   *Report to the President,* Vols. I-IV. Washington, D.C.: U.S. Government Printing Office.
Sonenstein, F.L., J.H. Pleck, and L.C. Ku
1990   Patterns of Sexual Activity Among Adolescent Males. Paper prepared for the 1990 annual meeting of the Population Association of America, Toronto, Canada.
Starfield B.
1985   *The Effectiveness of Medical Care: Validating Clinical Wisdom.* Baltimore, Md.: Johns Hopkins University Press.
1992   *Primary Care: Concept Evaluation and Policy.* New York: Oxford University Press.
Starfield, B., and S. Borkowf
1969   Physicians' recognition of complaints made by parents about their children's health. *Pediatrics* 43:168-172.
Strasburger, V., and D. Greydanus, eds.
1990   The at-risk adolescent. *State of the Reviews 1990* 1(1). Philadelphia: Hanley and Belfus, Inc.
Tremper, C.R.
1991   The role of schools as mental health service providers and brokers. In American Psychological Association, *Economics and Regulation of Children's Services.* Lincoln: University of Nebraska Press.
Tuma, J.
1989   Mental health services for children: the state of the art. *American Psychologist* 44(2):188-99.
U.S. General Accounting Office
1991   *Substance Abuse Treatment: Medicaid Allows Some Services but Generally Limits Coverage.* GAO/HRD-91-92. Washington, D.C.: U.S. General Accounting Office.
U.S. Office of Technology Assessment
1991a   *Adolescent Health—Volume I: Summary and Policy Options.* OTA-H-468. Washington, D.C.: U.S. Government Printing Office.
1991b   *Adolescent Health—Volume III: Cross-Cutting Issues in the Delivery of Health and Related Services.* OTA-H-467. Washington, D.C.: U.S. Government Printing Office.
van Dijk, J., P. Mayhew, and M. Killias
1990   *Experiences of Crime Across the World: Key Findings from the 1989 International Crime Survey.* Deventer, Netherlands: Kluwer Law and Taxation Publishers.
Vaughan, V.C., R.J. McKay, and W.E. Nelson, eds.
1975   *Nelson Textbook of Pediatrics.* Philadelphia: W.B. Saunders Company.
Waitzkin, H.
1991   *The Politics of Medical Encounters: How Doctors and Patients Deal with Social Problems.* New Haven, Conn.: Yale University Press.
Zill, N., and C. Schoenbom
1990   Developmental, learning, and emotional problems. *Advance Data.* National Center for Health Statistics, No. 190. Washington, D.C.: U.S. Department of Health and Human Services.

6

Academic Schooling

Education is widely viewed in the United States as the means by which individuals from economically or socially disadvantaged backgrounds can build the skills and credentials needed for successful adult roles in mainstream American life. For many students, however, schools do not now work this way, despite two decades of public debate and reform. This chapter focuses on academic schooling, particularly on those schools that are the educational setting for students from low-income families and neighborhoods, and those who are labeled "low achievers." Adolescents from low-income families and neighborhoods are at much higher risk of educational failure than their more affluent suburban counterparts.[1] Because of residential stratification, most of these adolescents attend schools with the fewest material resources and the least well-trained teachers. Their schools use instructional methods that are not conducive to learning challenging tasks. Compounding these disadvantages are generally lower expectations for student achievement. "The *low* expectations in our suburban high schools are *high* in comparison to

---

[1]Given the focus of this report on "settings," this chapter does not discuss students with identified physical or mental handicaps: such special education students are at the highest risk for school failure, with prevalence rates varying by disability and measure. We note, however, that special education is sometimes used inappropriately as a "placement" for students with behavioral problems that do not warrant special education.

expectations in urban schools and rural schools with concentrations of children in poverty . . . this absence of challenge, of rigor, is dulling the minds and dashing the hopes of millions of America's children" (Commission on Chapter 1, 1992:1).

The income stratification that concentrates large numbers of low-income students into poorly funded schools is followed by instructional stratification, most often on the basis of prior performance. Low-achieving students are likely to be exposed to instructional practices—tracking and grade retention—that deny them educational opportunities, stigmatize them, and contribute to their sense of uncertainty and alienation. Many disadvantaged adolescents are unable to overcome these conditions. Students from low-income families are far more likely to receive bad grades or be held back, and as much as three times more likely to drop out before completing high school, than the children of more affluent families: "consigning them to lives without the knowledge and skills they need to exist anywhere but on the margins of our society, and consigning the rest of us to forever bear the burden of their support" (Commission on Chapter 1, 1992:1).

The educational system has not adequately addressed the conditions of schools in low-income neighborhoods, which face special challenges. Not only are their students more likely to have significant academic deficits and behavioral problems, but the schools in low-income neighborhoods face challenges for which they have not been prepared and receive little public understanding or support (see Chapter 4). Moreover, recent reforms generally ignore the organizational and instructional practices that might promote better academic achievement (Braddock and McPartland, 1992), and existing compensatory programs are deeply flawed from an instructional perspective. The net result is that many students continue to find education boring, instruction lacking in relevance, and schools inhospitable places for learning.

STUDENT ACHIEVEMENT

The school performance of adolescents is typically assessed through measures of individual achievement and grade attainment. Studies have produced a wealth of data on national trends in individual achievement. Over a range of measures, adolescents in 1990 generally performed at about the same level as adolescents in 1970. This stability, however, is at relatively low levels of demonstrated ability. For example, only 42 percent of all 17-year-olds (still in school) can be considered "adept" readers, and a majority are performing at only an eighth grade level in math. In contrast, graduation rates have shown a slow increase (about 3.5 percent) increase since 1970. In 1990, 82.3 percent of all 18- to 24-year-olds had earned a high school diploma or a general equivalency diploma (GED) (Carter and Wilson, 1991; Mullis and Jenkins, 1990; Mortenson and Wu, 1990; Bean and Tienda, 1987; De La Rosa and Maw, 1990).

Trends in achievement show differences among racial and ethnic groups. For whites, achievement test scores have remained virtually unchanged for 20 years. In contrast, the performance of black adolescents has steadily improved, as has that of Hispanics (to a lesser degree), thereby narrowing the achievement gap between whites and blacks. Nonetheless, the average achievement scores of blacks tend to be two to three grade levels lower than those of whites, and the difference in graduation rates is approximately 5 percent. Despite the average gains in achievement on National Assessment of Educational Progress assessments, questions about the distribution of those gains remain, especially in light of evidence from some urban school districts that show a widening race gap in student reading performance (Entwisle and Alexander, 1992). Average trends appear to mask continuing, perhaps worsening, problems at the lower end of the distribution and in large school districts with many poor children (Braddock and McPartland, 1992).

Graduation rates similarly show differences among racial and ethnic groups. For whites, they have remained constant over the past 20 years. Blacks have made substantial gains in completing high school (by diploma or GED), rising from 59.5 percent of 18- to 24-year-olds in 1970 to 77 percent in 1990. Relatively few Latinos complete high school: over the past 10 years, the proportion of 18- to 24-year-olds who had a diploma or GED has fluctuated from a low of 54.1 percent in 1980, to a high of 62.9 percent in 1985, and back to 54.5 percent in 1990 (Carter and Wilson, 1991).

Family income and occupational background are the strongest predictors of school performance. From early adolescence, it is evident that schools are unable to capture the interest or facilitate the achievement of many low-income students. For example, fully 11 percent of eighth graders from low-socioeconomic-status (SES) backgrounds were absent more than one-quarter of the 1989 school year, a rate double that of high-SES students. Low SES is strongly and consistently associated with poor academic performance, and children from low-income families are three times more likely to drop out of school than are children from middle-income families and nine times more likely than students from high-income families (Barro and Kolstad, 1987; Smith and O'Day, 1991; National Center for Education Statistics, 1990, 1991). Graduation rates also vary by income: in 1989, 65 percent of unmarried young adults from the lowest quartile of family income had earned a diploma or GED, compared with 93 percent of those from the highest quartile. The detrimental effects of low income are most powerful for racial and ethnic minorities: among Hispanics, for example, only 39.6 percent of young adults from the lowest income quartile had a diploma or GED, compared with 85 percent from the highest quartile (Mortenson and Wu, 1990).

These trends, which are based on individual scores, mask other differences. For example, although the national dropout rate is estimated at 11.2 percent, the average for cities is substantially higher, with many cities losing more than 15 percent of their students (U.S. Department of Education, 1992). Another measure of the system is the frequency of "worst cases" among schools: 25 percent of all poor urban high schools have dropout rates of 50 percent or higher (Braddock and McPartland, 1992). By comparison, less than 1 percent of all other high schools have such extremely high dropout rates. Truancy is another issue for city schools. Data for Maryland, for example, show that more than 67 percent of students in urban high schools are absent for more than 20 days each year, a rate more than twice the state average (Maryland School Performance Program, 1991).

More important, few studies examine the distribution of student performance for individual schools. Thus, little is known about the frequency and location of worst cases or about schools that may be effective in helping students from minority or disadvantaged backgrounds catch up in achievement.

DIFFERENCES BETWEEN LOW-INCOME AND MORE AFFLUENT SCHOOLS

Economic and social stratification influence many key aspects of the educational system. The homogeneous composition of many schools stems directly from neighborhood stratification on the basis of family income, race, and ethnicity. Public expenditures for education, when dependent largely on local wealth, serve to further stratify the educational experiences of adolescents simply on the basis of their family background. Consequently, as noted above, students from low-income families usually attend schools in poor neighborhoods where they confront conditions not experienced by students from more advantaged backgrounds. These conditions, such as a relative lack of safety and the lowest level curriculum and performance expectations, have independent effects on school achievement. As a result, many students whose lives are rooted in family or neighborhood poverty simply do not have the kind of day-to-day experiences that would stimulate their intellectual development and complement the mission of schools. This web of disadvantage also confronts schools as they seek to improve student achievement, and schools in poor neighborhoods confront these challenges with fewer resources than schools in more affluent neighborhoods.

Financial Resources

There are large disparities in expenditures among schools in different states, schools in different districts within states, and schools within individual districts. The amount of available funding is largely dependent on the distribution of wealth in the form of property (Educational Testing Service, 1991). One result is that property-poor districts usually have low expenditures per pupil, even with high tax rates, while property-rich districts usually have high expenditures per pupil, even with relatively low tax rates (Odden, 1991). In Maryland, for instance, the one inner-city district (Baltimore) and five rural districts each spend less than $4,500 per student, compared with three suburban districts that spend $6,000-$7,500 per student. Thus, schools in the poorer Maryland districts have about $45,000-$60,000 less each year for each classroom of 30 students than schools in affluent districts.

In 1991, per pupil expenditures in the 47 largest urban school districts averaged $5,200; in suburban school districts, they were $6,073; in rural districts $5,476. When estimates take into account other measures of student need (such as the number of poor, limited-English-proficient, and disabled students), urban school per pupil expenditures are about 7 percent below the national average, although in a number of urban districts per pupil expenditures exceed the state average (Council of the Great City Schools, 1992). Although an $873 per pupil funding gap may not appear significant, in an average class of 25 students the difference is $21,825—enough to employ a teacher's aide, pay higher salaries, offer special instructional assistance, or improve dilapidated classrooms. Differences in funding of this magnitude could make a clear qualitative difference in the total educational experience.

Despite increases in inflation-adjusted educational spending per pupil during the 1970s and 1980s, inequalities in per pupil expenditures did not change much across the country from the mid-1970s to the mid-1980s. This is because the mechanisms of school finance did not change substantially, and in some cases efforts to equalize disparities were overcome by recessionary and inflationary trends (Odden, 1991; Berne, 1988). The issue is currently being addressed by courts in several states, including California, New Jersey, Texas, and Virginia (Briffault, 1990). Compensatory education funds from federal and state sources are targeted toward low-achieving students, and sometimes to poor schools, but these resources are very limited in comparison with the overall financial disparities (Braddock and McPartland, 1992).

Resource Availability and Instruction

Differences in funding levels may translate into differences in the educational experiences offered to students in low-income and more affluent schools. Per pupil expenditures directly affect the availability of textbooks, laboratory equipment, resource rooms, library books, and a range of other educational resources (Mayer, 1991; Kozol, 1991). In one national survey, for example, in districts with more than one-third of the students from families below the poverty line, 59 percent of fourth grade teachers reported a lack of resources, compared with 16 percent in districts with no students below the poverty line. For eighth grade, the comparable results for math teachers were 40 percent in disadvantaged urban districts and 10 percent in more affluent urban districts (Braddock and McPartland, 1992). These assessments reflect in part the greater demands on urban school districts. A recent analysis, for example, indicated that urban and suburban schools spend about equal percentages (62 percent of the funds available to them) on classroom instruction, but the urban schools spend more per pupil on health care, nutrition, and central office administration, while the suburban schools spend more on student extracurricular activities and maintenance and repair of buildings (Council of the Great City Schools, 1992).

Students in low-income schools tend to have less contact with the best qualified math and science teachers, although this finding holds for many, but not all, measures (Oakes, 1990). Many of the most experienced and qualified teachers use seniority rights to secure assignments in schools with fewer poor or minority students. Salary differences also matter. A recent study of over

900 school districts in Texas showed that the better paying districts were able to attract more qualified (higher test scores) and more experienced teachers. Teacher qualifications and experience, in turn, were the most powerful predictors of differences in student test performance after controlling for family and neighborhood factors (Ferguson, 1991).

Schools also differ on the extent to which parents are involved in school decision making, conferences with teachers, and home-school instructional programs. Over the past decade, studies consistently demonstrate the positive effects of such programs on student achievement, yet parents from low-income neighborhoods, especially racial and ethnic minorities, are least likely to participate. The reasons for this lack of participation include not only the lack of funds, but also different levels of school commitment, cultural and language barriers, and time constraints and stress on working poor families. Even in programs under Chapter 1 of the Elementary and Secondary Education Act (which provides funds to schools with low-income students), which requires poor schools to implement parent-participation programs, the level of involvement remains low (see below). By high school, few low-income or minority parents participate either through traditional or Chapter 1 programs, and school staff often do not encourage them to become involved (Epstein, 1992; Swap, 1990; Comer, 1988).

Differences in financial resources, instructional materials, staff qualifications, and parent involvement ultimately produce marked differences between the climate, norms, and instruction of poor schools and those of more affluent schools (Maeroff, 1988; Kozol, 1991). For example, one study of four urban elementary schools found that pupils in middle-income schools were more likely to be encouraged to be independent and otherwise "take initiative," while students in low-income schools were rewarded for more passive or deferential behaviors. Academically, the more affluent schools encouraged students to explore ideas, often verbally, while the low-income schools emphasized the retention of facts, often through written drill and practice (Leacock, 1969). Moreover, tracking (discussed later in the chapter) is most rigid in low-income schools, especially those with high proportions of racial and ethnic minorities. Differences also exist in the quality of vocational education between relatively poor and affluent schools (Oakes, 1990; see Chapter 7).

However, evidence regarding the links between per pupil expenditures and student achievement is mixed. In the aggregate, data show little relationship between expenditures and outcomes.

A recent review of 187 past studies concluded that variations in school expenditures are not systematically related to student performance (Hanushek, 1990). Hanushek's review demonstrates the need to conduct studies that focus on the connections between the ways in which funds are expended in a school and student outcomes. If, for example, increased funds simply raise existing teachers' salaries without improving other aspects of the educational environment, such as large class size, or providing better instructional materials, little improvement may be visible. Or it may take time for existing staff to retire before good pay attracts the more highly qualified teachers who would otherwise head for suburban districts (Smith and O'Day, 1991). The Hanushek analysis did not differentiate the results of the small number of studies that examine how increased funding is used from the larger body of studies that do not. This considerably weakens the conclusions we can draw from the analysis, because no distinction is made between schools where higher levels of funding reach the classroom compared with schools where increased levels of spending are absorbed in administration and other nonclassroom expenditures (Slavin, 1987a; Smith and O'Day, 1991; Rosenbaum, 1980).

ORGANIZATIONAL AND
INSTRUCTIONAL STRATIFICATION

Students face two major transitions during adolescence—moving from elementary school to a middle grade building and, 2 or 3 years later, moving to a high school. Each transition dramatically changes the education experiences (Boyer, 1983). As they move through the education system, students are faced with many "increases": the size of the school and of the student body, use of competitive motivational strategies, rigor in grading and a focus on normative grading standards, teacher control, and whole-class instruction. These changes can be stressful for adolescents, and data indicate that the experience of transition itself may have an independent negative effect on student attitudes and achievement, especially in large urban schools (Eccles and Midgley, 1989). Transcripts from one urban school district revealed that, among students who ultimately dropped out (35 percent), the most significant declines in performance occurred during the first year of middle school and the first year of high school (Roderick, 1991).

With each transition into a new school, more stratification occurs. Different subject matter is taught by different teachers, and within subject matter, students are often grouped by ability level.

Students placed in the lower "tracks" are at the greatest risk for being retained in grade and vice versa. Both practices are grounded in tradition, and are intended to ensure that instruction is paced at students' ability to learn, and that subjects are mastered before the student advances. An unintended consequence is that students feel stigmatized. They are separated from many of their peers and develop a sense of uncertainty and alienation toward school (Carnegie Council on Adolescent Development, 1989). More significant, both practices involve substantial risks for students' academic achievement.

Ability Grouping ("Tracking")

Ability grouping takes different forms. Usually, students are assigned to one class by ability and move together from subject to subject. Less rigid methods occur when students are assigned by ability to each subject separately. Although it is presumed that different forms of tracking will affect students differently, the little research that has been conducted has not detected consistent differences, and in this discussion, we do not distinguish among them (see Slavin, 1990). Students enter each grade level with a range of competencies, social skills, and behavioral styles. Given this diversity, educators have long questioned the merits of grouping students for instruction on the basis of one or more selected attributes (Dewey, 1938). Traditionally, educators have tended to instruct students in homogeneous groups, though the practice recently has been a focus of much research and debate. Proponents generally assume that low achievers will learn more effectively, and instruction will be more efficient, with students of similar ability. Opponents see tracking as stigmatizing and assert that both social and academic development will be diminished (see Slavin, 1990).[2]

Ability grouping for academic instruction begins informally during kindergarten and the early elementary years. Grouping decisions, typically for reading and math, are based on teachers' judgments, although research shows that low-income and minority students are often inappropriately tracked to the slower groups (Rist, 1970;

---

[2]Those who believe that homogeneous instruction has potential as an instructional tool use the phrase "ability grouping." Others use the phrase "tracking," in part due to concerns that "ability" is a misnomer given that current assessments have questionable validity for the purpose of grouping students. We use the terms interchangeably.

McPartland et al., 1987). In middle and high schools, ability grouping becomes more formalized, based largely on achievement test scores and other measures of prior preparation (see Braddock, 1990a; Slavin, 1990). Tracking is used most rigidly in poorer middle and high schools and in those with sizable proportions of black and Hispanic students (more than 20 percent). Black and Hispanic students are disproportionately represented in remedial tracks both because the schools they attend use tracking systems extensively and because they are likely to score lower on academic achievement tests (Goodlad, 1984; Braddock, 1990b; Oakes, 1990).

Research into the effects of ability grouping on achievement is usually based on one of two approaches, and they produce different results. Comparisons among students in homogeneous and heterogeneous classes have consistently found that ability grouping has little or no impact on overall student achievement (Good and Marshall, 1984; Kulik and Kulik, 1987). In contrast, comparisons between students in different tracks have found that high-track assignment tends to accelerate achievement somewhat while low-track assignment significantly reduces achievement, even controlling for factors such as socioeconomic status (Alexander et al., 1978; Gamoran and Maré, 1989; Oakes, 1982). A recent best-evidence synthesis of the broad literature of ability grouping and student achievement concurs with these assessments, although there may be some differential effects for middle and high schools, and in some classes, such as social studies. The author concludes that "decisions about whether or not to group by ability must be made on bases other than likely impacts on achievement" (Slavin, 1990:17).

Ability grouping has not been shown to improve learning among low-achieving students. Further, the social consequences for students placed in low-achievement tracks are unambiguously negative (Rosenbaum, 1980; Good and Marshall, 1984; Oakes, 1990). Research shows that sorting mechanisms may not substantially change student academic performance per se, but rather reinforce, compound, or exacerbate preexisting differences among students in competency and self-perception. Students placed in lower tracks rarely move into higher tracks (Wheelock, 1992; Dreeben, 1968; Oakes, 1990). The inferior quality of instruction and learning environments in the lower tracks is the principal reason why students seldom emerge from lower tracks into more advanced programs. In addition, instruction in those tracks emphasizes basic skills rather than higher-order learning, and students are less likely to be on-task. In higher grades, as tracks become more fixed and students more clearly labeled, tracking effectively sorts students according to their future educational and career options. Students become keenly aware of their reduced opportunities, thus contributing to their loss of academic interest and motivation (Braddock, 1990a,b; Gamoran, 1987; Slavin, 1987b; Oakes, 1985; Oakes, 1990; Trimble and Sinclair, 1987).

Grade Retention

Grade retention has traditionally been used to ensure that students do not advance unless they have specific skills and basic competencies (such as reading comprehension) to function at the next grade level. The objectives of grade retention are to ensure the integrity of the academic process and to protect students from compounding failure by advancing without mastering prerequisite skills for sequential subjects such as mathematics. However, grade retention has not been uniformly applied, and during the 1960s and 1970s "social promotions" were relatively common. During the 1980s, however, schools responded to calls for higher standards by establishing core curriculums and by requiring students to enroll in more core academic courses.

Although there is little disagreement among educators and others on the need for higher standards, there is concern that higher standards will result in the increasing use of grade retention, and that retention has not been shown to be effective in bringing low-achieving students up to a higher level of performance (Labaree, 1984; Hamilton, 1986). When social promotions fell into disfavor in the late 1970s, the academic competence of high school graduates may have improved, but the performance of low-achieving students did not. As a result, 35.3 percent of all 13-year-old males had been retained once in 1988, compared with 24.1 percent in 1976. Females are less likely to be retained, but by 1988 their rate was 24.8 percent. At all ages, the likelihood of grade retention is far greater for minorities. For example, by age 17, 14.3 percent of all black males have been retained *twice*, compared with 12.5 percent of Hispanics and 6.2 percent of whites. Among females, the proportions are 14.3 percent for Hispanics, 10.0 percent for blacks, and 3.8 percent for whites (Simons et al., 1991).

The fear of retention is highly stressful for pupils (Smith and Shepard, 1987). Students who are retained often show declines in social adjustment and smaller gains in academic achievement than comparable students who were promoted (Holmes, 1983; Holmes and Matthews, 1984; Reynolds, 1992). Retention also increases the risks of dropping out of the system before completing high school, by as much as 40 to 50 percent. These findings do not support a return to social promotions as an appropriate response to low-achieving students. However, the policy of grade retention has not proved successful in motivating and assisting students so that they are not alienated from the educational process. Chapter 10 reviews approaches that appear to be more effective in raising student performance levels (Hess, 1987; Grissom and Shepard, 1989; Bachman et al., 1971).

PREVENTING SCHOOL FAILURE

Of the many federal, state, and local programs targeted to low-achieving students, this section discusses Chapter 1 of the Elementary and Secondary Education Act and a range of programs that fall under the rubric of dropout prevention. Both seek to prevent school failure. Chapter 1 programs concentrate on elementary and middle schools and provide funds for academic remediation on the assumption that acquiring basic skills will allow low-achieving students to move more successfully through the education system. Dropout prevention programs, in contrast, have traditionally focused on older students, and although academic remediation is one of many objectives, their main goal is simply to motivate at-risk students to stay in school and earn a diploma.

Chapter 1 Programs

Chapter 1 (previously Title I), which has existed since 1965, represents the federal government's largest commitment to education for low-achieving students who live in poor neighborhoods. Since 1988, funding has increased 24.7 percent to a level of $6.2 billion (Jennings, 1991). Nationally, the program serves about 14,000 schools. Chapter 1 is also the most extensively researched education program in the country (see Birman et al., 1987; Kennedy et al., 1986a; Turnbull et al., 1990; Stringfield, 1991).

Although its primary focus is low-income students, Chapter 1 serves a range of students of mixed family incomes. For example, about 70 percent of all school districts receive some Chapter 1 funding, and an estimated 58 percent of students who receive Chapter 1 services are not themselves from poor families (Kennedy et al., 1986b). About 23 percent of funds are directed to middle grade students and 10 percent to high school students, with the remainder being directed to elementary schools (Kennedy et al., 1986b; Birman et al., 1987). This pattern reflects an assumption that early intervention is the most beneficial and efficient way to assist disadvantaged students. Educators also hesitate to implement Chapter 1 in secondary schools because of scheduling difficulties, fear that older students will choose not to participate, and the belief that intervention is too late for high school students (Birman et al., 1987; Zeldin et al., 1991). In fact, the program is moving even further away from directly serving low-achieving adolescents: the current emphasis is on preschool and kindergarten students (LeTendre, 1991).

On a daily basis, Chapter 1 constitutes only a minor intervention designed to complement, not supplant, the regular curriculum. Among middle schools and high schools that offer Chapter 1 programs, 70 percent offer reading and math, in addition to language arts or English as a second language. The remaining schools offer either reading or math only. Approximately two-thirds of all secondary schools use a pull-out or tracking model, in which students leave their regular classroom to receive small-group instruction for 10 to 40 minutes (Birman et al., 1987). Thus, Chapter 1 students do not receive substantially more instructional time in each subject (approximately 10 minutes a day) than other students (LeTendre, 1991).

Evaluations of Chapter 1 programs are mixed. Through Chapter 1 and similar efforts, poor and minority children have made notable gains: school dropout rates have decreased, and graduation rates and mastery of rudimentary skills have substantially improved. National evaluations find improvement for students relative to other "needy" students, but the gains are unimpressive compared with other students in the regular curriculum (Kennedy et al., 1986a,b). The 50 percent reduction in the achievement gap between poor and minority children from other Americans over the past 15 years is thought to be the result of Chapter 1 programs (Commission on Chapter 1, 1992:3).

Chapter 1 is often criticized for its dependence on ability grouping and traditional forms of academic remediation. Other criticisms include the lack of integration with the regular curriculum and a lack of parent involvement (Birman et al., 1987; Commission on Chapter 1, 1992).

The 1988 amendments to Chapter 1 provide educators with new options for designing and implementing programs, including schoolwide programs and instructional approaches that allow for less homogeneous groupings of students. Yet, because of the structure of the program as well as the status quo orientation of most educators, districts and schools have been slow to implement these reforms or change the basic assumptions underlying the Chapter 1 program (LeTendre, 1991; Turnbull et al., 1990; Plunkett, 1991). The conclusions of a recent blue-ribbon panel review of Chapter 1 (Commission on Chapter 1, 1992:9) echos these assessments and observes that "the core problem with Chapter 1 is even more basic: its add on design, wherein eligible students get extra help to succeed in the regular school program, cannot work when the regular school program is seriously deficient . . . if Chapter 1 is to help children in poverty to attain both basic and high level knowledge and skills, it must become a vehicle for improving whole schools serving concentrations of poor children."

However, scholars note that changes will be difficult to achieve. As Slavin (1991:592) observes:

> The broad targeting of Chapter 1 helps maintain the political popularity of the program, but it is otherwise hard to justify. Congress has addressed this issue by setting aside funds for "concentration grants" to districts with large numbers of children in poverty, but there is still a need to target Chapter 1 funds far more on schools that serve students from poor communities.
>
> Chapter 1 is extremely important to our must vulnerable children. For 25 years it has focused attention and resources on low achieving students in disadvantaged schools. Yet Chapter 1 can be much more than it is today.

Dropout Prevention and Student Motivation

In the early 1980s, national attention focused on the problem of school dropouts and brought it to the fore of education policy concerns (Mann, 1986; Finn, 1989; Wehlage and Rutter, 1986). The response was a rapid increase in dropout prevention programs, many of which were enacted with categorical federal and state funds, often on a demonstration basis (Higgins and Mueller, 1988). Initially, the dropout problem was conceptualized as a risk facing older adolescents, and hence most programs were implemented in high schools; there were at least 1,000 programs by 1987, most of which had been in operation for less than 4 years (U.S. General Accounting Office, 1987). Currently, the dropout problem is considered a school issue, not an individual issue.

Studies of the characteristics of dropouts have found that they are more likely to be from poor families, living in single-parent households, have parents who do not participate in decision making for adolescent problems, and live in urban areas. Dropping out is also associated with having a handicapping condition, engaging in delinquent behaviors, being retained in grade, being truant from school, being pregnant or a parent, having poor grades, and working more than 15 hours per week. Students who reenter school after dropping out are most likely to be white and to have had better grades and test scores before dropping out than those who do not reenter and had dropped out later in their high school careers (Ekstrom et al., 1986; Kolstad and Owings, 1986; U.S. General Accounting Office, 1987).

The early dropout prevention programs were designed in a manner consistent with these findings. Almost all dropout prevention programs were designed to target specific students for special services aimed at improving academic performance, changing student attitudes, and reducing absenteeism (U.S. General Accounting Office, 1987). Unfortunately, few studies assess the overall effectiveness of dropout prevention models (Grant Foundation, 1991), and the research is inconclusive (Massachusetts Advocacy Center and Center for Early Adolescence, 1988:47):

> For the most part, the proliferation of new dropout prevention programs reflects good-faith efforts on the part of [our] schools and communities to meet the needs of vulnerable young people. But these efforts also represent a triumph of hope over experience. While [we] believe new approaches can help individual students, the lack of evidence leads us to be cautious about endorsing any one approach, even when it is rooted in common sense. Because [we] know all too well that practices such as grade retention and suspension also flourish because they "make sense," persisting despite research that indicates their ineffectiveness in improving the achievement or behavior of vulnerable students, [we] are also aware that common sense may not be the best guide to program effectiveness.

Educators and researchers have reexamined assumptions regarding dropout prevention. The current consensus is that dropout prevention needs to begin at least by middle school and, ideally, in elementary school or even preschool (see Higgins and Mueller, 1988), but the empirical basis for such judgments is not firm (Ramey and Campbell, 1987; Rohwer, 1971; Zigler and Berman, 1983). A second point of consensus is that effective dropout prevention does not occur through categorical or add-on services, but through the use of schoolwide alternatives to tracking, grade retention, suspension, and expulsion (see Massachusetts Advocacy Center and Center for Early Adolescence, 1988). Indeed, the strategy of preventing dropouts by improving schools has become a practical necessity: with an estimated one-fourth of all urban schools having dropout rates around 50 percent, it is no longer feasible to provide individualized service, and decisions for targeting those most in need become almost arbitrary.

According to this new consensus, a primary aim of dropout prevention programs should be to implement schoolwide practices that will reduce students' alienation from the educational process and facilitate their interest in the learning process (Wehlage et al., 1989). Some studies suggest that the choice to leave school is tied to the perceived need to move quickly into adult status. After poor grades, the most frequently cited reasons for withdrawing from school are that "school is not for [me]," or because students want to seek and obtain employment or become a parent (Grant Foundation, 1988; Bishop, 1989). Staying in school is even more difficult for minority adolescents who must overcome peer pressures not to excel, and overt or subtle messages communicated by the school curriculum and teachers that excellence is not expected (Felice, 1981; Fordham and Ogbu, 1986; Pine and Hilliard, 1990). Until schools address these perceptions and reduce alienation, it is unlikely that dropout prevention programs will be effective, or that high-risk students will be motivated to learn (Hamilton, 1990:123):

> Noncollege youth have solid grounds for skepticism. Many of them have been "exposed to" the same subject matter year after year for five or six years by the time they get to high school. While their more academically able classmates encounter some new material and are challenged by added depth, those in the lower tracks receive a blandly repetitive curriculum of "basic and applied" subjects. . . . School-weary American youth become dropouts or remain in school unwillingly and unproductively, psychological dropouts who waste their own time and that of their teachers. Moreover, most high school students have direct evidence to dispute their teachers' claims that learning lessons in school will pay off in the labor market. They are already working [in the secondary labor market]. . . . Many of their older friends, siblings, and workmates are working in the secondary labor market, further obscuring from their view the kinds of career jobs that require academic knowledge.

CONCLUSIONS

Because of class and residential stratification, students from poor families usually receive their education in the poorest schools. These schools have fewer financial and material resources, and they are often unable to retain the most skilled administrators and teachers. Student achievement levels in these schools are significantly lower on virtually all measures than for students in suburban schools.

Traditional educational practices negatively affect the schooling of low-achieving students. Historically, schools have addressed the diversity of student achievement by tracking students into homogeneous ability groups and by retaining students who fail courses because of poor attendance, grades, or test scores. These practices have not demonstrated the expected benefits for low-achieving adolescents, and a range of studies show negative academic and social consequences, such as exacerbating existing academic or behavioral problems.

Compensatory education funds from federal and state sources are targeted toward disadvantaged and low-achieving students, but they have shown limited success, particularly among older adolescents. Dropout prevention programs for older adolescents are less effective when implemented as remedial or vocational add-ons to the regular curriculum. It has become apparent that the roots of poor achievement lie not only in the condition of poverty or in individual differences, but also in the use of instructional practices such as tracking and grade retention, and the generally lower achievement expectations for adolescents in concentrated poverty schools.

Alternatives do exist, and a research base is gradually developing to identify promising approaches. However, there are few clear solutions to the problem of how to teach students who lack prerequisite knowledge in courses such as mathematics. Chapter 10 describes some of the approaches that appear promising. The application of these alternative approaches is, however, very limited. Consensus is building regarding the changes that are needed in Chapter 1; however, these are likely to be difficult to achieve politically.

REFERENCES

Alexander, K.L., M.A. Cook, and E.L. McDill
  1978   Curriculum tracking and educational stratification. *American Socio-logical Review* 43:47-66.
Bachman, J.G., S. Green, and I.D. Wirtanen
  1971   Dropping out—problem or symptom. In *Youth in Transition*, Vol. III. Ann Arbor: Institute for Social Research, University of Michigan.
Barro, S.M., and A. Kolstad
  1987   *Who Drops Out of High School? Findings from High School and Beyond.* Washington, D.C.: Center for Education Statistics, U.S. Department of Education.
Bean, F.D., and M. Tienda
  1987   *The Hispanic Population of the United States.* New York: Russell Sage Foundation.
Berne, R.
  1988   Equity issues in school finance. *Journal of Education Finance* 14:159-180.

Birman, B.F., M.E. Orland, R.K. Jung, et al.
1987   The Current Operation of the Chapter 1 Program. Final Report from the National Assessment of Chapter 1. Office of Educational Research and Improvement, U.S. Department of Education, Washington, D.C.

Bishop, J.H.
1989   Why the apathy in American high schools? *Educational Researcher* 18:6-10, 42.

Boyer, E.L.
1983   *High School: A Report on Secondary Education in America.* New York: Harper & Row.

Braddock, J.H.
1990a   Tracking the middle grades: national patterns of grouping for instruction. *Phi Delta Kappan* 71(6):445-449.
1990b   *Tracking: Implications for Student Race-Ethnic Subgroups.* Baltimore, Md.: Center for Research on Effective Schooling for Disadvantaged Students, Johns Hopkins University.

Braddock, J.H., and J. McPartland
1992   Education of At-Risk Youth: Recent Trends, Current Status, and Future Needs. Commissioned paper for the Panel on High-Risk Youth, Commission on Behavioral and Social Sciences and Education, National Research Council, Washington, D.C.

Briffault, R.
1990   Our localism. *Columbia Law Review* 90:1-115, 346-454.

Carnegie Council on Adolescent Development of the Carnegie Corporation
1989   *Turning Points: Preparing American Youth for the 21st Century.* New York: Carnegie Council on Adolescent Development of the Carnegie Corporation.

Carter, D.J., and R. Wilson
1991   *Minorities in Higher Education: Ninth Annual Status Report.* Washington, D.C.: American Council on Education.

Comer, J.
1988   Educating poor minority children. *Scientific American* 259(5):42-48.

Commission on Chapter 1
1992   *Making Schools Work for Children in Poverty: Summary.* Washington, D.C.: American Association for Higher Education.

Council of the Great City Schools
1992   *National Urban Education Goals: Baseline Indicators, 1990-91.* Washington, D.C.: Council of the Great City Schools.

De La Rosa, D., and C.E. Maw
1990   *Hispanic Education: A Statistical Portrait, 1990.* Washington, D.C.: National Council of La Raza.

Dewey, J.
1938   *Experience and Education.* New York: Collier.

Dreeben, R.
1968   *On What Is Learned in School.* Reading, Mass.: Addison-Wesley.

Eccles, J.S., and C. Midgley
1989   Stage—environment fit: developmentally appropriate classrooms for young adolescents. Pp. 139-186 in C. Ames and R. Ames, eds., *Research on Motivation in Education, Volume 3: Goals and Cognitions.* New York: Academic Press.

Educational Testing Service
1991   *The State of Inequality.* Princeton, N.J.: Policy Information Center, Educational Testing Service.

Ekstrom, R.B., M.E. Goertz, J.M. Pollack, and D.A. Rock
1986   Who drops out of high school and why? Findings from a national study. *Teachers College Record* 87(3):357-373.

Entwisle, D.R., and K.L. Alexander
1992   Summer setback: race, poverty, school composition, and mathematics achievement in the first two years of school. *American Sociological Review* 57:72-84.

Epstein, J.
1992   School and family partnerships. Pp. 1139-1151 in M. Alkin, ed., *Encyclopedia of Education Research,* 6th ed. New York: Macmillan.

Felice, L.G.
1981   Black student dropout behavior: disengagement from school, rejection, and racial discrimination. *Journal of Negro Education* 50(4):415-424.

Ferguson, R.F.
1991   Paying for public education: new evidence on how and why money matters. *Harvard Journal on Legislation* 28(2):465-498.

Finn, J.D.
1989   Withdrawing from school. *Review of Educational Research* 59(2):117-142.

Fordham, S., and J.U. Ogbu
1986   Black students school success: coping with the burden of "acting white." *Urban Review* 18(3):176-206.

Gamoran, A.
1987   The stratification of high school learning opportunities. *Sociology of Education* 60:135-155.

Gamoran, A., and R.D. Mare
1989   Secondary school tracking and educational inequality: compensation, reinforcement, or neutrality? *American Journal of Sociology* 94:1146-1183.

Good, T.L., and S. Marshall
1984   Do students learn more in heterogeneous or homogeneous groups? In P.L. Peterson, L.C. Wilkinson, and M. Hallinan, eds., *The Social Context of Instruction: Group Organization and Group Process.* New York: Academic Press.

Goodlad, J.I.
1984   *A Place Called School.* New York: McGraw-Hill.

Grant Foundation (The William T.), and the Institute for Educational Leadership
1988   *The Forgotten Half: Pathways to Success for America's Young and Young Families.* Washington, D.C.: William T. Grant Foundation and the Institute for Educational Leadership.
1991   *Voices from the Field: 30 Expert Opinions on America 2000, the Bush Administration Strategy to "Reinvent" America's Schools.* Washington, D.C.: William T. Grant Foundation, Commission on Work, Family and Citizenship and the Institute for Educational Leadership.

Grissom, J.B., and L.A. Shepard
1989   Repeating and dropping out of school. Pp. 334-363 in L.A. Shepard and M.L. Smith, eds., *Flunking Grades: Research and Policies on Retention.* Philadelphia: Falmer Press.

Hamilton, S.F.
1986   Raising standards and reducing dropout rates. *Teachers College Record* 87(3):411-429.
1990   *Apprenticeship for Adulthood: Preparing Youth for the Future.* New York: The Free Press.
Hanushek, E.A.
1990   *The Impact of Differential Expenditures on School Performance.* Washington, D.C.: Issue Analysis, American Legislative Exchange Council.
Hess, G.A.
1987   *Schools for Early Failure: The Elementary Years and Dropout Rates in Chicago.* Chicago: Chicago Panel on Public School Finances.
Higgins, P.S., and D.P. Mueller
1988   The Prevention of Poor School Performance and School Failure: A Literature Review. Unpublished manuscript, Amherst H. Wilder Foundation Prevention Planning Project, St. Paul, Minn.
Holmes, C.T.
1983   The fourth R: retention. *Journal of Research and Development in Education* 17(1):1-6.
Holmes, C.T., and K.M. Matthews
1984   The effects of nonpromotion on elementary and junior high school pupils: a meta analysis. *Review of Educational Research* 54(2):225-236.
Jennings, J.F.
1991   Chapter 1: a view from Congress. *Educational Evaluation and Policy Analysis* 13(4):335-338.
Kennedy, M.M., B.F. Birman, R.E. Demaline, et al.
1986a The Effectiveness of Chapter 1 Services: Second Interim Report from the National Assessment of Chapter 1. Office of Educational Research and Improvement, U.S. Department of Education, Washington, D.C.
Kennedy, M.M., R.K. Jung, and M.E. Orland
1986b Poverty, Achievement, and the Distribution of Compensatory Education Services. Office of Educational Research and Improvement, U.S. Department of Education, Washington, D.C.
Kolstad, A.J., and J.A. Owings
1986   High School Dropouts Who Change Their Minds About School. Paper presented at the American Educational Association, San Francisco, Calif.
Kozol, J.
1991   *Savage Inequalities: Children in America's Schools.* New York: Crown Publishers.
Kulik, J.A., and C.L. Kulik
1987   Effects of ability grouping on student achievement. *Equity and Excellence* 23:22-30.
Labaree, D.F.
1984   Setting the standard: alternative policies for student promotion. *Harvard Educational Review* 54(1):67-87.
Leacock, E.B.
1969   *Teaching and Learning in City Schools: A Comparative Study.* New York: Basic Books.
LeTendre, M.J.
1991   Improving Chapter 1 programs: we can do better. *Phi Delta Kappan* 72(8):576-580.

Maeroff, G.I.
1988   Withered hopes, stillborn dreams: the dismal panorama of urban schools. *Phi Delta Kappan* 69(9):632-638.

Mann, D.
1986   Can we help dropouts—thinking about the undoable. *Teachers College Record* 87(3):307-323.

Maryland School Performance Program
1991   *School System and Schools Reports.* Baltimore, Md.: Maryland State Department of Education and Baltimore City Public Schools.

Massachusetts Advocacy Center and Center for Early Adolescence
1988   Before It's Too Late: Dropout Prevention in the Middle Grades. Massachusetts Advocacy Center, Boston, Mass., and the Center for Early Adolescence, Carrboro, N.C.

Mayer, S.
1991   The Effect of School and Neighborhood Social Mix on Adolescents' Transition to Adulthood. Commissioned paper for Panel on High-Risk Youth, Commission on Behavioral and Social Sciences and Education, National Research Council, Washington, D.C.

McPartland, J.M., J.R. Coldiron, and J.H. Braddock
1987   *School Structures and Classroom Practices in Elementary, Middle, and Secondary Schools.* Baltimore, Md.: Center for Research on Elementary and Middle Schools, Johns Hopkins University.

Mortenson, T., and Z. Wu
1990   *High School Graduation and College Participation of Young Adults by Family Income Backgrounds 1970 to 1989.* Iowa City, Iowa: The American College Testing Program.

Mullis, I.V.S., and L.B. Jenkins
1990   *The Reading Report Card, 1971-88: Trends from the Nation's Report Card.* Princeton, N.J.: Educational Testing Service.

National Center for Education Statistics
1990   *Dropout Rates in the United States, 1989.* Washington, D.C.: U.S. Department of Education.
1991   *Conditions of Education.* Washington, D.C.: U.S. Department of Education.

Oakes, J.
1982   The reproduction of inequity: the content of secondary school tracking. *Urban Review* 14:107-120.
1985   *Keeping Track: How Schools Structure Inequality.* New Haven, Conn.: Yale University Press.
1990   *Multiplying Inequalities: The Effects of Race, Social Class, and Tracking on Opportunities to Learn Math and Science.* Santa Monica, Calif.: The RAND Corporation.

Odden, A.
1991   School finance in the 1990s. *Phi Delta Kappan* 73(6):455-461.

Pine, G.J., and A.G. Hilliard, III
1990   Rx for racism: imperatives for America's schools. *Phi Delta Kappan* 71(8):593-600.

Plunkett, V.R.L.
1991   The states' role in improving compensatory education: analysis of current trends and suggestions for the future. *Educational Evaluation and Policy Analysis* 13(4):339-344.

Ramey, C.T., and F.A. Campbell
1987   The Carolina Abcedarian project: an educational experiment concerning human malleability. Pp. 127-139 in J.J. Gallagher and C.T. Ramey, eds., *The Malleability of Children*. Baltimore, Md.: Brookes Publishing Co.

Reynolds, A.J.
1992   Grade retention and school adjustment: an explanatory analysis. *Educational Evaluation and Policy Analysis* 14(2):101-121.

Rist, R.C.
1970   Student social class and teacher expectations: the self-fulfilling prophecy in ghetto education. *Harvard Educational Review* 40:411-451.

Roderick, M.
1991   The Path to Dropping Out: Middle School and Early High School Experiences. Working paper #H-900-13. John F. Kennedy School of Government, Harvard University.

Rohwer, W.D., Jr.
1971   Prime time for education: early childhood or adolescence? *Harvard Educational Review* 41(3):316-341.

Rosenbaum, J.E.
1980   Social implications of educational grouping. In D.C. Berliner, ed., *Review of Research in Education*, Vol. 8. Washington, D.C.: American Educational Research Association.

Simons, J.M., B. Finley, and A. Yang
1991   *The Adolescent and Young Adult Fact Books*. Washington, D.C.: Children's Defense Fund.

Slavin, R.E.
1987a   An alternative to meta-analytic and traditional reviews: a best-evidence synthesis. *Review of Educational Research* 15(9):5-11.
1987b   Ability grouping and student achievement in elementary schools: a best-evidence synthesis. *Review of Educational Research* 57:293-336.
1990   Achievement Effects of Ability Grouping in Secondary Schools: A Best-Evidence Synthesis. National Center on Effective Secondary Schools, University of Wisconsin, Madison.
1991   Chapter 1: vision for the next quarter century. *Phi Delta Kappan* 72(8):586-592.

Smith, M.L., and L.A. Shepard
1987   What doesn't work: explaining policies of retention in the early grades. *Phi Delta Kappan* 69(2):129-134.

Smith, M.S., and J. O'Day
1991   Educational equality: 1966 and now. In D.A. Vestegen and J.G. Ward, eds., *Spheres of Justice in Education—The 1990 American Education Finance Association Yearbook*. New York: Harper Business.

Stringfield, S.
1991   Introduction to the special issue on Chapter 1 policy and evaluation. *Educational Evaluation and Policy Analysis* 13(4):325-327.

Swap, S.McA.
1990   *Parent Involvement and Success for All Children: What We Know Now*. Boston: Institute for Responsive Education.

Trimble, K.D., and R.L. Sinclair
1987   On the wrong track: ability grouping and the threat to equity. *Equity and Excellence* 23:15-21.

Turnbull, B.J., S. Zeldin, and T. Cain
  1990   State Administration of the Amended Chapter 1 Program. U.S. Department of Education, Washington, D.C.
U.S. Department of Education
  1992   *Dropout Rates in the United States, 1991*. Washington, D.C.: Office of Educational Research and Improvement, U.S. Department of Education.
U.S. General Accounting Office
  1987   *School Dropouts: Survey of Local Programs*. Washington, D.C.: U.S. General Accounting Office.
Wehlage, G.G., and R.A. Rutter
  1986   Dropping out: how much do schools contribute to the problem. *Teachers College Record* 87(3):374-392.
Wehlage, G.G., R.A. Rutter, G.A. Smith, N. Lesko, and R.R. Fernandez
  1989   *Reducing the Risk: Schools as Communities of Support*. New York: Falmer Press.
Wheelock, A.
  1992   *Crossing the Tracks*. New York: The Free Press.
Zeldin, S., M.C. Rubenstein, J. Bogart, et al.
  1991   Chapter 1 Beyond the Elementary Grades: A Report on Project Design and Instruction. Policy Studies Associates, Inc., Washington, D.C.
Zigler, E., and W. Berman
  1983   Discerning the future of early childhood intervention. *American Psychologist* 38:894-906.

7

From School to Work

About one-half of high school graduates in the United States do not go on to college, and of those who do, less than 25 percent obtain 4-year degrees. Yet the array of programs and services available to college-bound students completely overshadows those available to non-college-bound students. Students planning to attend college receive comprehensive academic offerings that are linked to college requirements; counseling is available to help them make decisions and to see the connection between academic achievement and college acceptance; once accepted into college, financial assistance is often available; and most institutions offer a variety of orientation services to help adolescents adjust to their new life.

For the larger number of adolescents who do not attend or finish college, however, assistance is far more limited. While in school, students are often tracked into low-quality classes that provide little stimulus and few academic benefits. In most schools, vocational education is the only specialized program offering for students who do not intend to go to college, and most schools have few services to help these adolescents obtain suitable employment. For example, the job placement function takes less of school counselors' time than any other major job duty (Chapman and Katz, 1981; Grant Foundation, 1988b).

After school, there is no institutional bridge or system to help noncollege youth make the transition from school to work—unlike most other industrialized countries. As discussed below, the

Job Training and Partnership Act (JTPA) constitutes the most organized "system" for school-to-work transitions. Unfortunately, JTPA is quite small relative to the need it addresses, and its contribution is severely limited in terms of financial resources, scope, and program approach. Indeed, from the end of compulsory education at age 16 through the age of 24, the federal government invests less than one-half as much—perhaps as little as one-seventh—in the education and training of each noncollege youth as it does for each college youth (U.S. General Accounting Office, 1990b; Grant Foundation, 1988b).

After a brief overview of the status of youth after high school, this chapter focuses on the two major government-supported programs for helping adolescents make the transition into the labor market: vocational education in the schools and the employment and training programs funded under JTPA and demonstrations programs supported by foundations. We do not consider other programs that might be included within the "transition system," such as community-based youth organizations, proprietary schools, community colleges, the military, or the juvenile justice system. For most adolescents not moving into college, the primary transitional opportunities lie in vocational education in the secondary school and in employment and training programs.[1]

THE DIFFICULT TRANSITION TO THE LABOR MARKET: LACK OF A SYSTEM

Providing an accurate picture of what happens to young people in the school-to-work transition is enormously difficult because the sorting-out process involves myriad decision paths, and there are no surveys to track those who drop out of school. The most comprehensive analysis of postsecondary experiences is a 1991 RAND study, *After High School, Then What?* (Haggstrom et al., 1991), which merged a number of survey data bases to construct a comprehensive picture of the high school graduating classes of 1980 and 1982. Overall, the high school graduation rate has consistently run at less than 75 percent of the 17-year-olds since the

---

[1] The Committee on Postsecondary Education and Training for the Workplace at the National Research Council is completing a comprehensive study of federal programs that provide training for individuals beyond high school age who seek jobs that do not require a 4-year college degree. Its report is expected to be published in fall 1993.

mid-1970s, although some dropouts subsequently obtain GED (general equivalency diploma) degrees, and many later pursue training in community colleges and vocational-technical schools. Initially, however, a large number flounder and are not employed in the legitimate economy: in 1982, the unemployment rates for recent high school dropouts were 28.1 percent for males and 21.5 percent for females (Haggstrom et al., 1991).

Table 7-1 shows the main activity of 1980 high school graduates in the October following their graduation: overall, 14.6 percent are not employed or in education or training programs. Among minority youth, however, a much higher percentage fail to make immediate connections, 28.8 percent for blacks. The sorting-out process continues over the next 5 years as some students drop out of college or training programs, others enter 2- or 4-year colleges, and still others leave the jobs they started immediately following graduation and seek training for specific fields of employment. As the RAND study noted (Haggstrom et al., 1991:52):

> . . . many if not most high school seniors have only vague notions as to where they are headed and how they will get there . . . lacking clear cut objectives and being subject to myriad factors that can deflect them from their pursuits, many will experience numerous diversions and setbacks before they find their niches in the adult world.

Left to themselves, then, many high school graduates flounder in the labor market, either jobless or obtaining jobs with low wages and little opportunity for advancement. These difficulties are illustrated by the labor market "inactivity rates" of young people—the percentage of the population that is not employed, serving in the military, or enrolled in school (employment-to-population ratios). High inactivity rates begin immediately after high school: a recent study showed that after graduation, 19.5 percent of blacks, 14.3 percent of Hispanics, and 9.2 percent of whites were not working or in school; 2 years later, 50 percent of blacks, 42 percent of Hispanics, and 32 percent of whites who had been inactive remained inactive (Fernandez, 1990).

And for those who do make it into the labor market, a compounding problem is that full-time employment seems harder to obtain. As shown in Table 7-2, 72 percent of all young adult males not enrolled in school were working full time in 1968; by 1988, only about 50 percent of all eligible male workers had full-time employment. Similar declines are witnessed for young women. For young blacks and Hispanics, both male and female, it is even harder to find full-time employment. And for young adults who have failed to graduate from high school, the opportunities for

TABLE 7-1 Main Activity of High School Graduates in October: Class of 1980

| | Main Activity in October Following Graduation (percent) | | | | | | |
| | Student | | | | | | |
Demographic Group	Number (in 1,000s)	4-Year College	2-Year College	Vocational/ Technical School	Military Service	Civilian Employment	Other
All	3,021	29.4	11.1	5.3	2.6	37.1	14.6
Male	1,485	28.3	11.0	5.0	4.5	39.4	11.8
Female	1,536	30.4	11.1	5.6	0.7	34.9	17.3
Race/Hispanic origin							
White	2,466	31.3	11.1	5.6	2.2	37.3	12.4
Black	341	24.0	8.1	3.8	4.6	30.7	28.8
Asian/Pacific Islander	45	37.3	19.2	2.3	3.1	22.9	15.2
Native American	15	13.2	13.9	5.8	3.8	42.2	21.1
Hispanic	154	17.8	12.2	4.9	3.0	43.2	18.7

SOURCE: Adapted from Haggstrom et al. (1991:87).

TABLE **7-2** Employment-to-Population
Ratios of High School Graduates (aged 16-
24) Not Enrolled in College, 1968-1986

Year	Males	Females
1968	72.1	57.0
1974	69.6	47.6
1986	48.9	41.9
1988	52.4	33.8
Black	37.6	20.3
Hispanic	47.5	26.6
White	56.9	38.9

NOTE: Employment is full time.

SOURCE: Calculated from data presented in Grant
Foundation (1988a); Sum and Fogg (1991).

full-time work are extremely limited (Holzer, 1991; see also Chapter
2). Adolescents from low-income families face the most difficulties. They are the least likely to attend college, and they also fare
substantially worse on all measures of employment success than
do their peers from more affluent families. For those under 20,
being raised in a low-income family is the strongest predictor of
labor market inactivity (Sum and Fogg, 1991).

The United States differs from most other industrialized countries in its reliance on market forces to effect the transition of
young people from school to work. This does not mean that the
United States does not have a range of programs. For example,
vocational education courses are provided in most secondary schools.
Nonprofit training organizations under JTPA and Aid to Families
with Dependent Children (AFDC) offer a range of employment
and training programs for students who are performing poorly in
school and for dropouts who have not obtained steady employment. Employment and training services are also offered to out-
of-school youth through the Carl Perkins Vocational Education
Act, the National Community Service Act, and the McKinney Act
for homeless families. Some nonprofit community-based programs
also provide employment and training. With age, other opportunities become available: many young people, usually older than

24, receive employment-related training through technical institutions, community colleges, and proprietary schools.

However, it is difficult to consider this range of programs a "system," and the various programs are not well tailored to the needs of adolescents and young adults. Youth provisions in the Perkins Act (vocational education) and JTPA (as proposed in current legislative amendments) generally reflect "add-ons" to policies for adults, rather than efforts to target young people for specialized service, as is the case in most European countries (Hahn, 1992). There are few structural links among the various programs; in fact, there are strong policy disincentives to such program collaborations (Lerman and Pouncy, 1990; Grubb et al., 1990). And also, in contrast to other industrialized countries, the school-to-work transition system that does exist in the United States currently acts almost exclusively on the supply side of the labor market equation. This has not always been the case: for example, as recently as 1979 an estimated 40 percent of all jobs held by black teenagers were generated by employment and training programs (Betsey et al., 1985).

In the absence of federal policy guidance, there have been a number of state and local efforts to create school-to-work transition systems with an integrated array of services for young people. School and work linkages have been established through cooperative education, apprenticeship, and other work-based learning programs (see Chapter 10). However, only an estimated 3 to 8 percent of all high school students are enrolled in such programs (Grant Foundation, 1988a; U.S. General Accounting Office, 1991). There are also a small number of multisite research and demonstration programs—typically funded by foundations—that seek to involve both public and private agencies to provide options for low-achieving students and dropouts to move into the labor market.

VOCATIONAL EDUCATION

Traditionally, helping adolescents make the transition into the labor market has not been an explicit part of the mission of public schools in the United States (Grant Foundation, 1988b; Bishop, 1989). As a result, vocational education remains isolated from both academic instruction and the labor market, and vocational education is seen as having little value among school administrators and teachers, many of whom argue that vocational education has become a dumping ground. The extent of the stigma is disputed, but there is little disagreement that vocational education and its administrators, teachers, and students have become isolated from the mainstream of secondary education, and that recent reforms have done little to reduce this isolation (Wirt, 1991; Gray, 1991; Rosenstock, 1991). And while private employers have increasingly established ties with schools, formal school-to-work transition programs continue to be the exception (Hamilton, 1990).

An estimated 97 percent of all students take at least one vocational class (often typing) during their high school careers (Wirt, 1991). This level of participation is declining, however, and in many comprehensive high schools, vocational offerings have dwindled to typing and other business-oriented classes, home economics, agriculture (in rural schools), and an assortment of courses in industrial arts or technology (Gray, 1991; Strickland et al., 1989). Increasingly, comprehensive high schools are unable to offer a coherent or progressive sequence of courses in many occupational areas. At least one-half of the students who take vocational courses do so unsystematically, whether by choice or lack of opportunity, and consequently fail to acquire vocationally useful training (Grubb et al., 1991; Hamilton, 1990). In contrast, a small number of specialized schools—such as vocational high schools (usually in metropolitan areas) and area vocational centers (usually in rural areas)—provide excellent vocational training and a more varied curriculum (Weisberg, 1983).

Within this context, inequalities in program quality exist between poor and affluent schools. Although federal law targets funds to economically depressed areas, such efforts appear insufficient and have shown mixed success. Analyses indicate that programs in schools with high concentrations of low-income and low-achieving students are of significantly poorer quality than programs in other schools (Hayward and Wirt, 1989; Anderson, 1982; Oakes, 1986a,b). Specifically, poor schools (those that ranked in the bottom quartile of average family income and academic ability of the students) were 40 percent less likely than schools in the top quartile to be able to send students to a vocational high school or area vocational center; poor schools offered vocational education in one-third fewer program areas; and poor schools offered less than half the number of advanced courses in a sequence of two or more occupationally specific courses.

There has been extensive debate as to whether vocational education serves a class-sorting function. There are some data indicating that students who take more vocational education classes are those who have been perceived historically as being destined for nonprofessional work, particularly women and students from minority families and families of blue-collar workers (those with semi-skilled or unskilled jobs); others point out, however, that high-achieving students also take vocational education courses (Powell et al., 1985; Wirt, 1991; Oakes, 1986a; Crowley et al., 1983). It is clear, however, that the sorting occurs *within* vocational education programs. Specifically, low-achieving students and students from blue-collar families, as well as women and minorities, are more likely to be placed in vocational programs that are deemed to be of low quality or to have little potential for future employment, and less likely to be placed in those programs that are deemed to be directly applicable to students' successful transition to the labor market. For example, high-achieving males are five times more likely than low-achieving males to earn credits in technical and communication courses, an important finding given the current emphasis on training for high-technology fields. Indeed, the consistent finding that young women are most likely to benefit from vocational training is due in part to their overrepresentation in business and office-oriented training (Bishop, 1989; Wirt, 1991; Hoachlander et al., 1992; Hayward and Wirt, 1989).

Effects on Occupational Success

If vocational education had benefits comparable to the regular curriculum, concerns over sorting might be lessened. Unfortunately, vocational education has at best mixed effects on occupational success. There is abundant evidence that the vocational education system has been only marginally successful in helping its students make the transition from schooling to work. For example, when vocational education graduates are placed in jobs for which they have related training, their earnings are significantly higher than would otherwise be expected on the basis of compensation for the investment costs (e.g., tuition, foregone wages) of the specialized training. Unfortunately, however, in too many vocational education programs, there is only a tenuous connection between training and placement (Bishop, 1989), and after these programs, there is no increase in earnings to offset the cost of training, and few participants find employment appropriate to their training. Finally, vocational students seldom accrue long-term benefits in comparison with other students, in terms of income, employment, or job status (Meyer, 1981; Campbell and Basinger, 1985; Wirt et al., 1989; Hamilton, 1990; Grubb and Lazerson, 1975; Gray, 1991).

There are many reasons for this pattern of findings. First, self-selection contributes to this lack of effectiveness. Many students—perhaps one-half of those enrolled in vocational programs—have no intention of entering the vocation for which they are ostensibly being trained. Others enter vocational classes because they find them more congenial than academic classes or because they believe that the knowledge and skills being taught are more applicable to the "real world" than those taught in their other courses (Claus, 1986). In brief, vocational education provides a comfortable place, and an alternative, for students who do not do well in academic classes; but it is career preparation only for a small minority of them (Berryman, 1982; Hamilton, 1990).

Another reason for the lack of payoff is that vocational education is often a haphazard array of courses that are not conceptually or programmatically linked. Yet research suggests that a well-planned vocational program can have positive benefits for participants: students who take a coherent series of courses in a single specialty demonstrated somewhat higher rates of employment and earnings than graduates of the general track, and students who were able to find jobs specifically related to their training had higher labor force participation, lower unemployment, and higher earnings than comparable graduates of the general track (Campbell et al., 1981).

Finally, employers often do not want to risk hiring recent graduates in a loose job market, especially given the reputation of vocational education courses (Reisner and Balasubramaniam, 1989). If placing students in related employment is the goal of vocational education, then cooperative education (a model in which students earn academic credit for working with employers) is the most effective means (U.S. General Accounting Office, 1990b). The reason for its success appears to be that employers are more likely to make an employment commitment if they can "try out" students in a training capacity (Hamilton, 1990).

Effects on School Achievement and Attainment

The notion that vocational education may serve as a mechanism for imparting basic and higher-order academic skills has received little research attention. The most sophisticated study, using longitudinal data from the High School and Beyond project, examined the achievement scores of males during 3 years of high school (Ekstrom et al., 1986). Controlling for individual differences, it found that students in academic courses gained 0.13 of a standard deviation over 3 years, but that those in vocational courses gained 0.03 standard deviation. This small but statistically significant difference indicates that vocational courses, in general, have little effect on academic achievement.

In contrast, vocational programs that are specifically designed to enhance achievement may have greater potential. One study, for example, found that vocational students who continue to take demanding academic courses, and whose vocational courses also include substantive academic content, gain in basic skills at a rate comparable to that of academic students (Kang and Bishop, 1988). Similarly, data from the National Assessment of Vocational Education reveal that students who took "mathematics-related" vocational education courses (e.g., electronics, drafting, accounting, agricultural science) showed achievement gains comparable to those of students in traditional mathematics courses, while vocational students in "non-mathematics-related" classes showed no gains (Meyer, 1989). And even this finding is narrow: the effects on student learning were only for work-bound students and not for college-bound students, suggesting that the content of the courses is pitched at a low level or that other factors are at work (Wirt, 1991). Furthermore, "mathematics-related" courses account for less than 20 percent of the vocational curriculum.

Vocational education does appear to reduce dropout rates, although vocational students are still more likely to leave school before graduation than are college preparatory or general track students. This finding seems to result from the "dumping ground" phenomenon: potential dropouts often transfer into vocational education as a last resort, and many students who stay in school do so because of their vocational courses (Grant Foundation, 1988b). Yet vocational education does little to motivate students to progress to higher education. Students who concentrate on vocational courses have lower educational aspirations than general students, but, even after controlling for initial differences, they are less likely to enroll in postsecondary education, and when they do, they are more likely to enroll in technical schools than in 4-year colleges (Mertens, 1983).

The "tech prep" approach represents a promising new development in bridging high school vocational training and community college education. As defined by Hoerner (1991:2):

> [Tech prep is an] articulated educational program of two years of high school and two years of post-secondary preparation which includes a common core of math, science, communications, and technologies designed to lead to an associate degree or certification in a specific career field.

The distinctive features of tech prep include not only a well-defined or articulated educational program, but a stress on the importance of applied academics (Hull and Parnell, 1991). Math, science, communications, and social studies are stressed as the foundation for study of more technical courses, and competency-based curriculums provide students with skills that support working during school if needed. An important element of tech prep programs is a carefully constructed interface between high schools and community colleges.

Although they show promising early results, innovations such as tech prep have not yet been widely implemented or evaluated. For the currently implemented vocational education programs that have been evaluated, the data clearly indicate little impact on students' occupation or academic success.

EMPLOYMENT AND TRAINING PROGRAMS

There have been four fundamental shifts in employment policy for youth over the past 20 years. In 1973, the Comprehensive Employment and Training Act (CETA) emphasized the creation of subsidized jobs in the public sector. The assumption was that if youth had supervised employment for a sufficient period of time, they would then be able to gain a foothold in the labor market. By 1977, disillusioned with the administration of CETA and its effectiveness, Congress amended CETA with the Youth Employment Demonstration Program Act (YEDPA). YEDPA had two primary, but occasionally, conflicting objectives: (1) to build service delivery infrastructure to meet the needs of large numbers of youth (the peak of the baby boom swell for teenagers was fast approaching in the early 1980s); and (2) to support a knowledge development process of research and demonstration projects to learn what works for youth. A wide range of initiatives retained the fundamental CETA principles—specifically, that work experience was the most effective "second-chance" opportunity—but also recognized that such work needed to be supplemented or preceded by occupational skills training or labor-market-preparation courses.

In 1983, before evaluations of YEDPA were completed, a new Job Training Partnership Act (JTPA) placed special emphasis on placing people into private-sector jobs, containing costs, and assuring program accountability. Programmatically, there was also a significant shift away from serving the most disadvantaged youth: by 1985, less than 30 percent of participants were high school dropouts. The programs became shorter, with a strong emphasis on job search and job placement services; previous emphasis on job experience was all but eliminated, and the emphasis on skills training was reduced.

Programs offered to youth by local service delivery areas and their Private Industry Councils with funding from and under the auspices of JTPA are the successors to the YEDPA-and CETA-supported programs of the 1970s. Out-of-school youths make up about 23 percent of the national JTPA population, and in-school youths account for the remaining 22 percent. JTPA programs are offered across the country, but funding is sufficient to serve only a small percentage of eligible disadvantaged youth. Although local delivery agents do not have to offer special programming for youth, they are subject to different performance standards than those governing programs for adults. In addition to placement, programs for youth are also rewarded if participants achieve certain competencies in the world of work, or a particular academic goal, such as obtaining a GED. In contrast to the three field demonstration projects described below, the average program offered under JTPA is more likely to be short in duration, to serve a less disadvantaged population, and to be less comprehensive in the range of support and education and training services offered.

Currently there are three programs within JTPA. Subsidized summer employment and training, the largest program, serves about 700,000 adolescents each year. The basic JTPA program (Title IIA) annually serves approximately 324,000 youths aged 14 to 17, or about 5 percent of the eligible low-income youth population. These varied programs emphasize job placement and work readiness skills. They last, on average, about 12 weeks, and 63 percent of the students in them are enrolled in school. The third program is the Job Corps, primarily a residential program, which serves about 70,000 adolescents each year; approximately 85 percent of participants are school dropouts. These programs provide intensive, long-term job training and remedial education, as well as health care, counseling, and job placement assistance.

Just as vocational education remains largely independent of academic instruction, so employment and training programs, under JTPA, are largely independent of the workplace. Employer subsidies and participant stipends for work experience programs have largely been eliminated, for example, and the average length of training was shortened from 26 weeks under CETA to approximately 12 weeks under JTPA. And because program performance is measured by short-term placement rates, program services appear to be predominantly geared to a limited set of occupations that can be easily filled by enrollees, such as food services, building services, and the like (U.S. General Accounting Office, 1990b). As a further consequence, JTPA has moved away from serving the youth at greatest risk of failure in the job market—dropouts and unemployed young adults who have been unable to find a niche in the labor market. More than three-quarters of youth served by JTPA are still in school or are high school graduates (Public/Private Ventures, 1987a; U.S. General Accounting Office, 1990a).

The most recent shift is still going on. A number of large demonstration programs have aimed at serving specific populations of highly disadvantaged youth. These initiatives, supported largely by private foundations, are under the rubric of "second-chance" programs. The strongest commonalities across the programs is their emphasis on imparting basic academic and problem-solving skills to participants and the belief that social support services are also necessary before disadvantaged youth can sustain meaningful employment.

Despite all these changes, however, the employment and training component of the transitional "system" remains quite small. Current allocations for youth programs are about $700 million; in 1989, JTPA served about 1.1 million adolescents. Even during the late 1970s, federal spending for all employment and training programs reached only $2 billion annually (U.S. General Accounting Office, 1990a).

Program Effectiveness

There have been two waves of research on the net effects of employment and training programs, the first during the 1977-1981 YEDPA era and the second on JTPA and the "second-chance" or post-YEDPA demonstrations. One of the strongest conclusions to be drawn from the first wave, unfortunately, is that the research had serious methodological flaws. Of the many evaluations conducted during the YEDPA years, for example, the National Research Council found only 14 with sufficient validity to draw conclusions on program outcomes (Betsey et al., 1985). In addition, the outcome variables examined were limited, with an almost exclusive focus on employment or earnings, with little assessment of other psychosocial, problem-solving, or academic benefits. Few of the evaluations assessed implementation or treatment integrity. To a large extent, the post-YEDPA demonstrations have addressed these limitations.

Despite recent improvements in methodology, the major conclusion from evaluations is that researchers have been unable to document consistent net effects among participants in employment and training programs. This conclusion holds for the YEDPA studies and the demonstration projects. Overall, across all evaluations, employment and training programs are more likely to produce neutral or positive net effects for women than for men. In contrast, young men are sometimes found to have diminished employment benefits as measured during short follow-up periods of less than 2 years (Betsey et al., 1985; Hahn, 1992; Cave and Doolittle, 1991). However, a recent evaluation showed modest gains for men under certain circumstances (Cave et al., 1993b). Many plausible explanations have been offered for the poor performance of employment and training programs, including the following:

• There are relatively few high-paying jobs for program graduates to move into, especially for students who have performed poorly in school.

• Most employment and training programs have been of short duration or of limited quality; hence, there may be little reason to expect positive effects.

• Program operators have had to respond to many shifts in regulations, accountability, and targeting procedures over the past two decades, which has made it difficult to establish and maintain high-quality programs.

• For disadvantaged minority males, especially, JTPA participation may not be a sufficient "credential" to encourage employers already hesitant to hire such young people.

• Many programs have high dropout rates, and both participants and controls enter the labor force before the program is completed.

• In the evaluations, the design of randomized field experiments included in the "treatment" group not only those who actually received the program intervention, but also those who were assigned to participate but never did. Conversely, those in the "control" group often received services from other sources, such as schools, tutoring programs, or a community-based organizations.

Studies of YEDPA Programs

The National Research Council concluded that the lack of reliable findings on the YEDPA programs precluded generalizable conclusions (Betsey et al., 1985). In two of the four major program areas reviewed—labor market preparation and job training assistance—very little could be concluded at all. Labor market preparation programs had positive effects for out-of-school youth for up to 8 months, but there were no reliable data on long-term effects. No conclusions could be drawn for in-school youth. Job training assistance programs for in-school and out-of-school youth were effective in increasing employment for up to 1 year, but such effects steadily dissipated over time and did not exist at all 2 years later.

Results were somewhat stronger for two of the most visible and innovative YEDPA demonstrations: the temporary (subsidized) jobs programs and the Job Corps. The most adequate data on temporary jobs programs come from the Supported Work Project (SWP) and the Youth Incentive Entitlement Project (YIEP). These large demonstrations—YIEP alone served approximately 76,000 youth—were designed to test the premise that work experience was the best second chance. SWP offered temporary, transitional 12- to 18-month employment opportunities to low-income school dropouts with little prior work experience, while YIEP served both in- and out-of-school disadvantaged youth. In addition to providing subsidized part-time employment during the school year, YIEP required that participants stay in school or return to school in order to stay in the program. Reliable findings included the following:

- SWP was successful in providing temporary, subsidized jobs to out-of-school youth. However, there was no evidence of long-term gains in permanent employment or earnings or in reduction of crime, alcohol, or drug use between the experimental and control groups (Manpower Demonstration Research Corporation, 1980).
- YIEP's saturation employment offer in participating cities was successful in increasing the employment and earnings of youth—indeed, employment rates doubled for some groups of youth, and the effects were of sufficient magnitude to eliminate racial differences in employment levels. YIEP also had modest success in attracting dropouts back to school and in retaining low-income students in high school. However, the program did not increase the likelihood of high school graduation. Because the postprogram follow-up period was short and because a comparison site design was used and differences between the comparison cities grew over time, long-term employment benefits could not be adequately assessed (Gueron, 1984; Betsey et al., 1985; deLone, 1991).
- High proportions of participating adolescents remained in their jobs throughout the demonstration. This led one analyst to see

"convincing evidence that the employment deficit is not of the youths' making. The shortage is jobs, not motivation" (Gueron, 1984).

Job Corps was the most comprehensive program offered during the YEDPA years. Job Corps began in the mid-1960s and was continued under YEDPA. Rather than focusing on work experience, Job Corps emphasized basic skills training, supportive services, occupational training, and job placement services for highly disadvantaged youth. Two models were implemented: (1) a residential program for out-of-school youth, reflecting the belief that youth needed a sustained period of time removed from high-risk settings; and (2) a nonresidential program offering similar services to in-school youth.

Of all the YEDPA programs, Job Corps showed the most powerful positive effects for one group (Betsey et al., 1985). For those in the residential program, increased earnings and improved social behavior were found in a 4-year follow-up (Mallar et al., 1982). Overall, those who maintained consistent participation in the year-long program showed the most favorable employment outcomes. In contrast, in-school youth (those in the nonresidential program) did not appear to benefit, although for some research questions the data were not reliable (Betsey et al., 1985). These residential-nonresidential differences were generally replicated in a closer examination of different Job Corps models, although the analysis also pointed out that this element represents only one of many factors that ultimately determine the effectiveness of Job Corps Programs (Public/Private Ventures, 1987b).

A review by Public/Private Ventures (1987a) concluded that findings from YEDPA offer a somewhat unreliable mixture of assertions and of positive and negative findings. Nevertheless, a number of lessons can be learned by integrating the findings of the impact studies with the insights gained across many YEDPA evaluations, including some that did not meet the methodological standards of the National Research Council study (Hahn and Lerman, 1984):

• Young women are more likely than young men to benefit from employment and training programs, yet services too often direct women to a limited range of occupations.

• Comprehensive residential programs appear to have the strongest effects among programs for which reliable data exist.

• Single-purpose "categorical" programs (e.g., those that offer only subsidized employment or job training) are less effective than programs that offer a range of services. The only exceptions are skills training and directed job search programs, which may also have short-term effects when implemented as categorical programs.

• In almost all programs, short-term projects have only short-term effects, and short-term effects erode over time. Young people who spend more time in programs or employment settings are more likely to have sustained gains.

In short, the data suggest that different combinations of work experience, skills training, academic remediation, and job placement are most likely to produce positive outcomes. Unfortunately, available data do little to identify the most favorable combination of program services, or the services that may work for in-school youth compared with out-of-school youth.

JTPA

The 18-month results from a Department of Labor commissioned evaluation of JTPA youth and adult programs was recently completed (Bloom et al., 1993). This study used a random assignment design in which youths who were eligible for JTPA were randomly assigned either to a program group to participate or to a control group that did not participate. Young people aged 16-21 were classified into three service strategy subgroups: classroom training, on-the-job training and job search assistance, and other services. This classification was made before random assignment occurred. The program assignees and controls were then followed over time, information was collected on their employment and earnings and other relevant variables. Since the only difference between the two groups is that one participated in the program and one did not, differences in employment and earnings can be reliably attributed to the program's effect. Findings for out-of-school youth (in-school programs were not evaluated) are discouraging 18 months following the point of random assignment. The program was judged to have little or no effect on young women (a statistically insignificant earnings loss of $–182, or –2.9 percent), and a large, statistically significant negative effect on the earnings of male youths. Almost all of the earnings loss for male youths is concentrated among youths who reported having been arrested at some point before assignment into the program.

Interestingly, JTPA did have a statistically significant effect on attainment of a GED or a high school diploma—about 12 percentage points among young women, and nearly 10 percentage points among young men. Thus, JTPA did increase the percentage of youths who obtained a credential, but these gains in educational attainment did not translate into increased employment and earnings within the first 18 months of follow-up. This lack of effect may have been because JTPA assignees incurred similar opportunity costs in foregone earnings as the JOBSTART enrollees experienced (see below) while JOBSTART enrollees had immediate earnings. If this is the case, one might expect the JTPA enrollees to catch up to their control counterparts in later follow-up periods. Unfortunately, the quarter-by-quarter trend over the first 18 months does not suggest such a pattern of large initial losses followed by smaller and smaller losses as time proceeds. Instead, the losses remain fairly constant across the quarters.

Within the overall pattern, however, results for women are somewhat more encouraging, implying that they have a greater likelihood of faring well in future quarters. This consistent difference for female youths in JTPA and in the JOBSTART demonstration indicates substantial differences in program effectiveness for women over men. This difference can be explained in part by the generally lower employment and earnings among female youths who were in the control group relative to male controls. In short, women are less likely to be in the labor market, so programs can make a difference simply by increasing their participation in the labor market. Men are more likely to work than women, but their employment is less stable and at low-paying jobs. For programs to succeed they must be able to get participants better jobs and more stable jobs than they could have gotten on their own, a task employment and training programs have had a difficult job accomplishing, especially for youth.

Post-YEDPA Field Demonstrations

Another source of information comes from a series of post-YEDPA demonstrations, initiated by foundations with modest government support. These demonstrations were targeted to specific high-risk populations, such as adolescent mothers, school dropouts who come from poor families, and unmarried males. In contrast to most JTPA-supported programs, the foundation-supported efforts also emphasize long-term interventions of at least 6 months. Furthermore, all of them seek to provide a range of academic and support services to participants. Work experience is used purely as a complement to other services and, in general, skills training is reserved for older participants. Most importantly, the studies used reliable random assignment research designs that follow both program group and control group members longitudinally. Because the research was designed to assess long-term outcomes, except in a few cases, findings are not yet available.

We discuss three programs—the Summer Training and Education Program (STEP), Career Beginnings, and JOBSTART—for which evaluation data are available. These demonstrations confirm a basic YEDPA conclusion: most interventions do not have powerful effects on participants' employment and social behavior, especially among young men. Indeed, one of the greatest challenges is to develop more effective strategies for ensuring that young men stay in programs for their duration.

Both STEP and Career Beginnings offer a range of services to high school students, aiming first, to keep students in school, and second, to prepare them for a successful transition into the labor market or postsecondary schooling. STEP is designed for 14- and 15-year-olds who are both poor and experiencing severe academic difficulty. Its goals are to reduce dropout rates, summer learning decay, and teenage pregnancy among these youth by offering a program of academic remediation, work experience, and life-skills instruction. Services are offered during two consecutive summers, with limited support during the intervening school year. In 1991, there were 100 STEP sites.

Overall, in-program results to date have been moderately encouraging, while postprogram effects have been very discouraging (see Public/Private Ventures, 1987c). Evaluations of nearly 5,000 STEP participants found that they outperformed control group students in reading, math, and "fertility-related attitudes and knowledge" at the end of the first summer of programming, but the academic gains were not sustained during the intervening school year, and learning gains were less impressive during the second summer of participation. But the in-program gains did not translate into lasting postprogram effects. STEP had no significant longer term effect when program-eligible youths who were enrolled in STEP were compared with randomly assigned control group youths.

Career Beginnings is a multisite program to serve high school juniors from low-income families with average grades. The 2-year intervention pairs students with adult mentors, who provide emotional support and advice and help the youth prepare for college or career. Students receive other services from college staff, such as career planning, tutoring, financial aid, family planning skills, and exposure to higher education environments. An evaluation using an experimental research design found positive but modest success in raising educational aspirations and increasing college entry rates relative to control groups (Cave and Quint, 1990). Whether these modest increases in college entry rates will translate into increases in college graduation is unknown.

From an implementation perspective, STEP (100 sites) and Career Beginnings (17 sites) illustrate that programs can be successfully replicated on a large scale. At the same time, the time and energy needed to replicate a program, even a successful one, cannot be discounted. Both evaluations found unevenness of program implementation from site to site. In the Career Beginnings evaluation, sites rated "well implemented" produced better outcomes that those rated "poorly implemented," suggesting that careful implementation is a critical aspect of overall program effectiveness (Hahn, 1992).

JOBSTART provided services to 17- to 21-year-old, low-income adolescents with a history of school failure. Operated in 13 sites, JOBSTART was modeled after Job Corps and provided a range of occupational and academic instruction in nonresidential settings, in addition to job placement assistance and training-related support services, such as transportation and job training. Because JOBSTART involved investments of time and effort in education and training, it also entailed opportunity costs in foregone employment and earnings. While program group members were participating in JOBSTART's education and training initiatives, their control group counterparts were more likely to obtain jobs. Thus, in the first year, earnings by those in the control group exceeded the earnings of those in the program group by about $500 (which was statistically significant). By the second year, the advantage had declined to around $120. Beginning in the third year and continuing through the end of the fourth follow-up year, JOBSTART enrollees were outearning those not enrolled by slightly more than $420 a year (which was not statistically significant, but the earnings trend over time follows a consistent and expected pattern). The opportunity costs for men were substantially higher than those for women, amounting to more than $800 in the first year for men and nearly $400 in the second; for women the first year loss in earnings was around $250, and in the second year JOBSTART women were generally outearning controls. In addition, the earnings of women in the program group began to catch up and move ahead of those of controls. Men, however, continued to lag behind until the third year. Even by the end of the fourth year, while the trend was in the right direction, when cumulative earnings over the 4-year period were compared for both program and control groups, men were modest net losers, while women were generally gainers.

Three additional findings are of interest. First, the subgroup of sample members who dropped out of school for school-related reasons (such as academic failure) had statistically significant earnings gains for follow-up years three and four of about $660 per year. Second, males with a prior arrest record appeared to gain substantially as a result of participation in JOBSTART by about $1,100 in earnings in the third year (which was not significant) and by nearly $1,900 in the fourth year (which was statistically significant). Finally, one program site produced significant cumulative earnings gains for the entire 4-year period of around $6,700 per enrollee. These subgroups and site-specific findings add support to the overall conclusion that JOBSTART is helping high school dropouts improve their position. Moreover, although the overall results are not as positive as originally hoped, they indicate that JOBSTART services may work better for some groups than others and when delivered in a particular format and environment. These findings also suggest the importance of limiting the foregone earnings period, possibly by making the training as intensive and short as possible (Cave et al., 1993a).

CONCLUSIONS

The current transition system for non-college-bound youths does little to help adolescents and young adults enter the job market. It is fragmented, is small relative to need, and does little for those at the highest risk of failure. Furthermore, the foundations of the system—vocational education and employment and training—have only marginal positive effects on those who receive service. Clearly, these systems need fundamental reform.

First and foremost, programs need to be reexamined in the light of what is known about labor market needs and about the programs' effects in preparing young people for the modern workforce. Resources should be directed to the types of education and training models that have shown results. Funding for higher education is regarded as a vital national economic investment, while support for labor market transitions, particularly for youths most at risk of failing to make the school-to-work transition, is viewed as a social, rather than an economic, responsibility. This reflects a consistent and continuing belief that employment and training are private matters, best left to individuals and the marketplace. As a result, vocational education and employment and training policies have not been directed to the demand side of the private sector of the labor market. Rather, supply-side policies aimed at changing the clients have dominated youth development policy.

Vocational education and employment and training have moved away from their immediate constituencies: vocational education maintains a high degree of isolation from academic schooling and the academic curriculum; employment and training programs have moved away from serving high-risk youth—those out of the labor market. There is also little attention to systematic early intervention. Vocational education programs do not offer a sequenced series of courses throughout high school, and only a minority of local JTPA jurisdictions serve 14- and 15-year-olds (U.S. General Accounting Office, 1990a).

Both vocational education and employment and training programs currently focus overwhelmingly on "employability." This one-dimensional emphasis tends to slight human development factors in favor of employment-related ones. Only recently has there been renewed recognition that young people in second-chance programs need to build a range of competencies before achieving a consistent degree of occupational success. Job training is not sufficient, especially for the many youths who enter the labor market with a range of needs; but only a very small proportion of JTPA funds are directed towards remedial education or support services (Public/Private Ventures, 1987a). The in-program effects for STEP and YIEP on educational gains and employment increases, respectively, and the moderately positive results from Career Beginnings and JOBSTART suggest some potential merit of more comprehensive programs than are usually offered in either vocational education or JTPA. Findings on differences in performance by site and for potential target groups also suggest the need to undertake additional field demonstrations to refine understanding of both what works best for whom and how to improve program efficacy and thus the magnitude of the program effects.

REFERENCES

Anderson, J.D.
    1982   The historical development of Black vocational education. In H. Kantor and D.B. Tyack, eds., *Work, Youth and Schooling*. Stanford, Calif.: Stanford University Press.
Berryman, S.E.
    1982   The equity and effectiveness of secondary vocational education. In H.F. Silberman and K.S. Rehage, eds., *Education and Work*. 81st Yearbook of the National Society of Education. Chicago: University of Chicago Press.

Betsey, C.L., R.G. Hollister, Jr., and M.R. Papageorgiou, eds.
1985   *Youth Employment and Training Programs: The YEDPA Years.* Committee on Youth Employment Programs, Commission on Behavioral and Social Sciences and Education, National Research Council. Washington, D.C.: National Academy Press.

Bishop, J.
1989   Occupational training in high school: when does it pay off? *Economics of Education Review* 8:1-25.

Bloom, H.S., L.L. Orr, G. Cave, S.H. Bell, and F. Doolittle
1993   *The National JTPA Study: Title II-A Impacts on Earnings and Employment at 18 Months.* Bethesda, Md.: Abt Associates, Inc.

Campbell, P., and K. Basinger
1985   *Economic and Noneconomic Effects of Alternative Transitions Through School to Work.* Columbus: National Center for Research in Vocational Education, Ohio State University.

Campbell, P.B., M.N. Orth, and P. Seitz
1981   Patterns of Participation in Secondary Vocational Education: A Report Based on Transcript and Interview Data of the 1979 and 1980 National Longitudinal Survey New Youth Cohort. National Center for Research in Vocational Education, Ohio State University, Columbus.

Cave, G., and F. Doolittle
1991   *Assessing JOBSTART: Interim Impacts of a Program for School Dropouts.* New York: Manpower Demonstration Research Corporation.

Cave, G., and J. Quint
1990   *Career Beginnings Impact Evaluation: Findings from a Program for Disadvantaged High School Students.* Executive Summary. New York: Manpower Demonstration Research Corporation.

Cave, G., F. Doolittle, and H. Bos
1993a   *Evaluating JOBSTART: Four Years Later.* New York: Manpower Demonstration Research Corporation.

Cave, G., H. Bos, F. Doolittle, and C. Toussaint
1993b   *JOBSTART: Final Report on a Program for School Dropouts.* New York: Manpower Demonstration Research Corporation, forthcoming.

Chapman, W., and M. Katz
1981   *Survey of Career Information Systems in Secondary Schools.* Princeton, N.J.: Educational Testing Service.

Claus, J.F.
1986   Opportunity or Inequality in Vocational Education? An Ethnographic Investigation. Dissertation, Cornell University, Ithaca, N.Y.

Crowley, J.E., T.K. Pollard, and R.W. Rumberger
1983   Education and training. In M.E. Borus, ed., *Tomorrow's Workers.* Lexington, Mass.: D.C. Heath.

deLone, R.H.
1991   School-To-Work Transition: Failings, Dilemmas, and Policy Options. Issue paper no. 5, Public/Private Ventures and Center for Human Resources, Brandeis University, Philadelphia, Pa.

Ekstrom, R.B., M.E. Goertz, J.M. Pollack, and D.A. Rock
1986   Who drops out of high school and why? Findings from a national study. *Teachers College Record* 87:356-373.

Fernandez, R.M.
1990   Structural Factors in Hispanic Youth Employment. Report to the Inter-

University Program for Latino Research and the Social Science Research Council Grants Program for Public Policy Research on Contemporary Hispanic Studies, Northwestern University, Evanston, Ill.

Grant Foundation (The William T.)
1988a   *The Forgotten Half: Non-College Youth in America.* Washington, D.C.: The William T. Grant Foundation, Commission on Work, Family and Citizenship.
1988b   *The Forgotten Half: Pathways to Success for America's Youth and Young Families.* Washington, D.C.: The William T. Grant Foundation, Commission on Work, Family and Citizenship.

Gray, K.
1991   Vocational education in high school: a modern Phoenix? *Phi Delta Kappan* 72(6):437-445.

Grubb, W.N., and M. Lazerson
1975   Rally 'round the workplace: continuities and fallacies in career education. *Harvard Educational Review* 45(4):451-474.

Grubb, W.N., C. Brown, P. Kaufman, and J. Lederer
1990   *Order Amidst Complexity: The Status of Coordination Among Vocational Education, Job Training Partnership Act, and Welfare-To-Work Programs.* Report to U.S. Congress. Berkeley, Calif.: National Center for Research in Vocational Education.

Grubb, W.N., G. Davis, J. Lum, J. Plihal, and C. Morgaine
1991   *The Cunning Hand, The Cultured Mind: Models for Integrating Vocational and Academic Education.* Berkeley, Calif.: The National Center for Research in Vocational Education.

Gueron, J.M.
1984   Lessons from a Job Guarantee: The Youth Incentive Entitlement Pilot Projects. Manpower Demonstration Research Corporation, New York.

Haggstrom, G.W., T.J. Blaschke, and R.J. Shavelson
1991   *After High School, Then What? A Look at the Postsecondary Sorting Out Process for American Youth.* Santa Monica, Calif.: The RAND Corporation.

Hahn, A.
1992   Job Training Policy for Core Youth: Where the Field Has Been, Where It Needs To Go. Paper prepared for Panel on High-Risk Youth, Commission on Behavioral and Social Sciences and Education, National Research Council, Washington, D.C.

Hahn, A., and R. Lerman
1984   *What Works in Youth Employment Policy?* Washington, D.C.: National Planning Association.

Hamilton, S.F.
1990   *Apprenticeship for Adulthood: Preparing Youth for the Future.* New York: The Free Press.

Hayward, B.J., and J.G. Wirt
1989   *Handicapped and Disadvantaged Students: Access to Quality Vocational Education, Final Report,* Vol. 5. Washington, D.C.: National Assessment of Vocational Education, U.S. Department of Education.

Hoachlander, E.G., P. Kaufman, K. Levesque, and J. Houser
1992   *Vocational Education in the United States: 1969-1990.* Washington, D.C.: National Center for Education Statistics, U.S. Department of Education.

Hoerner, J.
1991   *Tech Prep and Educational Reform.* National Center for Research in Vocational Education. Berkeley, Calif.: University of California.
Holzer, H.J.
1991   Youth and the Labor Market in the 1990s. Issue paper no. 10, Public/ Private Ventures and Brandeis University, Philadelphia, Pa.
Hull, D., and D. Parnell
1991   *Tech Prep Associate Degree.* Waco, Texas: Center for Occupational Research and Development.
Kang, S., and J. Bishop
1988   Vocational and Academic Education in High School: Complements or Substitutes. Working paper 88-10, New York State School of Industrial and Labor Relations, Center for Advanced Human Resource Studies, Cornell University, Ithaca, N.Y.
Lerman, R., and H. Pouncy
1990   The compelling case for youth apprenticeships. *The Public Interest* 101:62-77.
Mallar, C., S. Kerachsky, C. Thornton, M. Donihue, C. Jones, D. Long, E. Noggoh, and J. Schore
1982   Evaluation of the Economic Impact of the Job Corps Program. Second follow-up report, U.S. Department of Labor, Washington, D.C.
Manpower Demonstration Research Corporation
1980   *Summary and Findings of the National Supported Work Demonstration.* Cambridge, Mass.: Ballinger Publishing Company.
Mertens, D.M.
1983   The vocational education graduate in the labor market. *Phi Delta Kappan* 34:360-361.
Meyer, R.
1981   An economic analysis of high school education. In *The Federal Role in Vocational Education: Sponsored Research.* Washington, D.C.: National Commission for Employment Policy.
Meyer, R.H.
1989   Beyond Academic Reform: The Contribution of Applied Academics to Mathematical Skills. Unpublished paper, Institute for Research and Poverty, Madison, Wis.
Oakes, J.
1986a   *Keeping Track: How Schools Structure Inequality.* New Haven, Conn.: Yale University Press.
1986b   Beyond tinkering: restructuring vocational education. In G. Copa, J. Plihal, and M. Johnson, eds., *Re-Visioning Vocational Education in the Secondary School.* St. Paul: University of Minnesota.
Powell, A.G., E. Farrar, and D.K. Cohen
1985   *The Shopping Mall High School.* Boston: Houghton Mifflin.
Public/Private Ventures
1987a   *Youth and the Workplace.* Philadelphia: Public/Private Ventures.
1987b   Youth Conservation and Service Corps: Findings from a National Assessment. Public/Private Ventures, Philadelphia, Pa.
1987c   Summer Training and Education Program (STEP): Report on the 1986 Experience. Public/Private Ventures, Philadelphia, Pa.
Reisner, E.R., and M. Balasubramaniam
1989   *School-to-Work Transition Services for Disadvantaged Youth Enrolled in Vocational Education.* Prepared for the National Assessment of Vo-

cational Education, U.S. Department of Education. Washington, D.C.: Policy Studies Associates, Inc.

Rosenstock, L.
1991   The walls come down: the overdue reunification of vocational and academic education. *Phi Delta Kappan* 72(6):434-436.

Strickland, D., E. Donald, and N. Frantz
1989   *Vocational Enrollment Patterns Study: Preliminary Report.* Blacksburg, Va.: National Center for Research in Vocational Education, Virginia Tech Office.

Sum, A., and W.N. Fogg
1991   The adolescent poor and the transition to early adulthood. In P. Edelman and J. Ladner, eds., *Adolescence and Poverty: Challenge for the 1990s.* Washington, D.C.: Center for National Policy Press.

U.S. General Accounting Office
1990a   *Job Training Partnership Act: Youth Participant Characteristics, Services, and Outcomes.* GAO Report No. HRD-90-46BR. Washington, D.C.: U.S. General Accounting Office.

1990b   *Training Strategies: Preparing Noncollege Youth for Employment in the U.S. and Foreign Countries.* GAO Report No. HRD-90-88. Washington, D.C.: U.S. General Accounting Office.

1991   *Job Training Partnership Act: Racial and Gender Disparities in Services.* GAO Report No. HRD-91-148. Washington, D.C.: U.S. General Accounting Office.

Weisberg, A.
1983   What research has to say about vocational education and the high schools. *Phi Delta Kappan* 64:355-359.

Wirt, J.G.
1991   A new federal law on vocational education: will reform follow? *Phi Delta Kappan* 72(6):424-433.

Wirt, J.G., L.D. Muraskin, D.A. Goodwin, and R.H. Meyer
1989   *Summary of Findings and Recommendations: Final Report*, Vol. 1. Washington, D.C.: National Assessment of Vocational Education, U.S. Department of Education.

8

Juvenile and Criminal Justice

America's juvenile and criminal justice systems assume major roles in the lives of increasing numbers of adolescents, especially the adolescent children of racial and ethnic minorities and the inner-city poor. Involvement with the justice system often compounds other institutional difficulties, including failure in school and in finding work. As a result, it frequently foreshadows adverse occupational, marital, and health-related outcomes as an adult, as well as continuing contact with the police and courts.

The juvenile justice system that emerged early in this century included training and reform schools and other forms of institutionalization, but it also made frequent use of suspended sentences and probationary dispositions for the rehabilitation of delinquents in the community. Now, however, the juvenile justice system has many of the adversarial and punitive characteristics of the adult criminal justice system (Krisberg et al., 1986). The Supreme Court's 1967 Gault decision, for example, extended the Fifth Amendment's protection against self-incrimination and the Sixth Amendment's right to counsel to delinquency proceedings. At the same time, many states shifted their delinquency statutes toward deterrence and away from treatment and rehabilitation and also provided for waiving juvenile cases to adult courts and for more punitive treatment by juvenile court judges. The division between juvenile and criminal courts became more permeable, and the two systems became more alike.

Another important reform in juvenile justice in almost all jurisdictions involves handling "status offenses" differently from "juvenile crime." Status offenses are actions that are offenses solely because of the age of the offender: running away from home, truancy, curfew violation, being a "person in need of supervision," being "incorrigible," etc. The Juvenile Justice and Delinquency Act of 1974 required that states receiving federal delinquency prevention monies begin to divert and "deinstitutionalize" their status offenders. Overall, increasing numbers of young people pass directly or indirectly from the juvenile to the criminal justice system, and the latter system also is populated disproportionately by older teenagers and young adults.

CRIME, MINORITIES, AND CONCENTRATED POVERTY

An increasing number of adolescents engage in, and are arrested for, violent crimes. In 1991, 130,000 arrests of youths ages 10 to 17 were made for rape, robbery, homicide, or aggravated assault—an increase of 48 percent since 1986 (Annie E. Casey Foundation, 1993). Minorities, especially blacks, are very disproportionately both the victims and the perpetrators of crime in the United States. The U.S. Department of Justice's annual National Crime Survey, a nationwide residential survey of the general public about their experiences as victims of crime, shows that blacks experience rates of rape, aggravated assault, and armed robbery that are approximately 25 percent higher than those for whites, rates of motor vehicle theft that are about 70 percent higher, and rates of robbery victimization that are more than 150 percent higher. For much of the past half century, rates of black homicide deaths have ranged from six to seven times those for whites (Hawkins, 1986; Rose and McClain, 1990).

The experience of crime is felt disproportionately by the young and the poor, less well-off socioeconomic segments of black communities. For example, children under 16 are victims of robbery at a rate of over 1,000 per 100,000 population, which is three times the rate for persons 65 or older (Gottfredson and Hindelang, 1981). For many youths, victimization is a consequence of the risk of living in a highly criminal environment; for others, it is a consequence of direct participation in the criminal activities that prevail in this environment (Fagan et al., 1987). Victimization can sometimes lead to offending: some crime in minority neighborhoods may be a product of retaliation and revenge-seeking acts that are a frequent part of gang and peer group associations (Black,

1983; Stafford, 1984). In this context, the line between victimization and offending can be unclear; the act itself is partly a reflection and partly a cause of the youth's "diffuse aggression" (Blau and Blau, 1982).

Even living in proximity to high-crime areas may increase the risk of victimization. Although poor blacks do suffer greatly, middle-class and near-poor blacks seem to suffer the greatest losses from crime victimization (Jaynes and Williams, 1989). Public opinion surveys indicate that many middle-class blacks believe that the police and courts fail to protect them from the growing problems of crime, and at the same time mistreat them in their encounters with justice officials. These perceptions have been reinforced by the Rodney King beating and similar encounters, but middle-class blacks have long complained of such harassment (see Russell, 1966). Research confirms that black Americans, especially those who have achieved positions of high status, share a pervasive perception of injustice at the hands of the law enforcement system (Hagan and Albonetti, 1982).

Blacks make up about 12 percent of the U.S. population and Hispanic Americans about 8 percent, but both groups are arrested for a higher proportion of serious crimes against persons. Blacks account for more than 40 percent of all homicides, forcible rapes, armed robberies, and aggravated assaults, and Hispanic Americans account for about 14 percent of these violent crimes against persons. For less serious property crimes, blacks account for a quarter to a third of all arsons, car thefts, burglaries, and larceny/thefts (Harris, 1991); Hispanic Americans account for about 11 percent of these property crimes. Like homicide, these crimes also peak in mid- to late adolescence. Young black males who experience education and employment problems are at exceptionally high risk of arrest, imprisonment, or criminal victimization (Freeman, 1991). Consider the following:

- Homicide is the leading cause of death among black youth.
- Overall, blacks account for one-third of all arrests and one-half of all incarcerations in the United States.
- About one-fifth of all 16- to 34-year-old black males are under justice system supervision.
- One-half of all black male school dropouts under age 25, and three-quarters of the dropouts who are between the ages of 25 and 34, are under justice system supervision.
- Three-quarters of all black prison inmates have less than 12 years of schooling.

These facts confirm that delinquency, crime, and contacts with the juvenile and criminal justice systems are massive risk factors in the lives of poorly educated and economically disadvantaged black youth. Self-report studies confirm that black adolescents are far more likely to be involved in serious youth crime, particularly *violent* offenses involving theft (Hindelang et al., 1981; see also Elliot and Ageton, 1980). Research among prison inmates, most of whose past criminal involvement dates from their youth, reveals parallel racial differences (Petersilia, 1985).

Scholarly efforts to explain these facts have focused on two possibilities. First, race-linked patterns of discrimination, segregation, and concentrated poverty may produce pervasive family and community disadvantages, as well as educational and employment difficulties, that in turn cause high levels of delinquent and criminal behavior among young minority males. Second is the possibility that, at the hands of the juvenile and criminal justice systems, young black males are victims of prejudice and discrimination in the form of more frequent arrest, prosecution, and punishment for delinquent and criminal behavior.

Both possibilities are plausible, and together they have produced an additional important problem: a legacy of suspicion and distrust of the justice system. Some of this suspicion and distrust derives from the historical experience of slavery, lynching, and the discriminatory use of the death penalty by white juries (Sellin, 1935; Wolfgang and Riedel, 1973). It also reflects patterns of law enforcement following Reconstruction, extending well into this century, in which the harsher punishment of blacks for crimes against whites legally perpetuated a caste system born in slavery (Sellin, 1976).

Overall arrest rates increased markedly throughout the 1960s, 1970s, and 1980s, and continue at high levels into the 1990s. One researcher has calculated that more than half of the increase in crime in 12 of the largest U.S. cities was linked to a rise in the proportion of blacks living in those cities (Chilton, 1986). Street crime and victimization are increasingly concentrated in urban "underclass" neighborhoods, in large part because of the concentration of poverty and joblessness in these predominantly poor and minority neighborhoods (see Chapter 4; Wilson, 1987). In a penetrating analysis of "American apartheid," Douglas Massey (1990) argues that racial segregation was the key factor responsible for the social transformation of many black communities in the 1970s. Using experimental simulations and regression models based on census tracts, Massey shows how a pernicious interaction between rising poverty rates and high levels of segregation created a population often identified as the "underclass," transforming low-income communities into places where welfare-dependent, female-headed families are the norm. When this occurs, patterns of formal and informal community control may be undermined, in turn producing high rates of crime and related problems.

Racial segregation and related forms of discrimination may also find expression in forms of "diffuse aggression" and "hostility." Blau and Blau (1982:119) tested this thesis in a landmark study of violent crime in 125 of America's largest metropolitan areas. They began with the premise that "pronounced ethnic inequity in resources implies that there are great riches within view but not within reach of many people destined to live in poverty." They hypothesize that the result is "resentment, frustration, hopelessness, and alienation," producing a "sense of injustice, discontent, and distrust." This and subsequent research (Messner, 1989) reveals that while inequality generally promotes criminal violence, racial inequities are especially productive of such violence.

Ethnographic studies are especially persuasive in describing the ways in which concentrated poverty affects crime rates in minority neighborhoods (Hagedorn, 1988; Anderson, 1991; Sullivan, 1989; Lehmann, 1991; Sanchez-Jankowski, 1992). Recent accounts emphasize the growth of the underground drug economy focused around gangs, which substitutes for and competes with the legitimate labor market in many minority low-income communities. Anderson writes (1991:244):

> For many young men the drug economy is an employment agency superimposed on the existing gang network. Young men who 'grew up' in the gang, but now are without clear opportunities, easily become involved; they fit themselves into its structure, manning its drug houses and selling drugs on the street corners.

These descriptions also depict the danger, anger, risks, and strains of poverty and crime in poor urban areas. For example, in *There Are No Children Here*, Kotlowitz (1991) follows the early teenage years of brothers Pharoah and Lafeyette Rivers, who live in a Chicago housing project where the prospects for escaping poverty and crime seem remote. The younger brother poignantly confides, "I worry about dying, dying at a young age, while you're little." Surveys indicate that parents in these neighborhoods share the same fears as their children (National Commission on Children, 1991).

At the aggregate level, it is difficult to fully disentangle the factors linking concentrated poverty and violence. Recent epidemiological studies indicate that, at higher socioeconomic levels, blacks and whites experience similarly low rates of homicide; only in census tracts with high concentrations of poor families do blacks have higher levels of homicide victimization. Indeed, data from the Centers for Disease Control indicate that personal and neighborhood income are the strongest predictors of violent crime (see Lowry et al., 1988; Centerwall, 1984; Munford et al., 1976; Spivak et al., 1988). One analysis of 21 macrolevel studies found a cluster of factors that have a clear and pervasive causal influence, including median income, percent of families below the poverty line, an index of income inequality, the percentage of black population, and the percentage of single-parent families. These factors could not be fully separated into more specific causes (Land et al., 1990). However, a later analysis argued convincingly that aggregate lagged rates of unemployment have specifiable effects on property crime (Land et al., 1991). Joblessness and other factors are also implicated in the causal mechanisms that link concentrated poverty and family disruption to crime among young minority citizens. A study of race-specific rates of robbery and homicide in over 150 U.S. cities suggests a link between the scarcity of employed black men, the prevalence of families headed by women, and increased rates of black murder and robbery, especially among juveniles (Sampson, 1987; see also Matsueda and Heimer, 1987).

LAW ENFORCEMENT AND NEIGHBORHOODS

The lack of confidence in the ability of the juvenile and criminal justice systems to respond effectively to crime in minority urban communities presents a major public policy problem. Although these systems may have the ability to protect citizens in white communities and redirect adolescents who are from advantaged backgrounds, it is widely believed that the systems are far less effective in ghetto communities and with the ghetto youth who disproportionately are swept into the criminal justice system. In this view, the justice system is a source of new risks for urban minority youth—a view that is reinforced by research on the policing, prosecution, and punishment of blacks in both middle- and low-income neighborhoods.

Police work has changed dramatically over the past century, and much of this change has aimed to make the police officers more professional and efficient in their handling of youth as well as adults. It is useful to keep in mind that the police are a relatively modern invention, going back little more than a century in most American cities. In the early part of this century, police officers in most American cities were relatively uneducated recruits from the local neighborhood who retained strong neighborhood ties, in part by patrolling the community on foot or by horse. Today the police are more often well-educated, highly trained outsiders who are encouraged to limit compromising aspects of local ties and who patrol the community from radio-dispatched cruisers that roam well beyond local neighborhood boundaries (although this approach is increasingly questioned). These changes have had a substantial impact on the policing of youth, in part because of the high degree of discretion given by law to the police for handling juveniles.

A classic study by James Q. Wilson (1968) of the policing of juveniles describes these polar styles of policing as reflecting "fraternal" and "professional" departments. Both kinds still exist, and new efforts are being made to reestablish "community policing," but the professional type of department in large part displaced its more fraternal predecessors and is now the predominant type. One of the consequences has been a change in patterns of enforcement: officers in a professional department arrest a larger share of the juvenile suspects they encounter. When Wilson studied the impact of this difference on minority youth suspects, he found that the professional department was more even-handed in its arrest practices, but at the cost of arresting more minority youth overall. There is also much evidence that the police find the attitudes and behaviors of ghetto youth hostile and threatening, which further increases police use of harassment, brutality, and arrest in ghetto settings. The results include increasing levels of negative contact between ghetto youth and the police, with negative consequences for police-community relations and for the affected youth.

There are many plausible reasons for police perceptions of hostility by minority youths. The danger of violence in policing leads the police to treat large parts of the public as "symbolic assailants" (Skolnick, 1966), and young minority males are especially prone to this kind of stereotyped treatment. More than 20 years ago, a study in three of the largest U.S. cities reported that a majority of the police expressed "anti-Black" attitudes (Black and Reiss, 1967). And a common tactic in police-citizen encounters is to "take charge" and "freeze" situations through verbal and physical expressions of authority (see Reiss and Bordua, 1967). These factors tend to make police-suspect encounters emotionally charged and confrontational, especially in encounters with minority youth, thereby increasing the risks of brutality and indiscretion. There is no reason to believe that any of these factors has changed significantly in the high-crime inner cities of the 1990s.

A classic study of such encounters suggests that adolescents who do not display respect toward officers are most likely to be arrested (Piliavin and Briar, 1964). The demeanor of juveniles constitutes a basic set of cues that the police use in making arrest decisions in juvenile cases. This study found that, other than having a prior record, the juvenile's general demeanor, or "contriteness," was the most crucial determinant of decisions both on the street (i.e., whether to take the juvenile in) and in the station (i.e., whether to release or detain).

A number of studies have gone on to demonstrate that the demeanor of minority youth accounts for at least part of their higher risk of arrest (Ferdinand and Luchterhand, 1970; Black, 1970). One of the most useful of these studies suggests that policing is characterized by a normative expectation that requires that the police receive more deference than they give, so that (for example) a policeman or policewoman will expect to be addressed as "officer," while citizens in general and youths in particular are addressed by given names (Sykes and Clark, 1975). The "asymmetrical status norm" exists in part because the police represent the authority of the law and probably also because officers are usually older and of higher occupational status than the suspects they encounter. When minority youth are involved, their refusal to express deference may be viewed by the officer as a refusal to acknowledge assumed social obligations of all citizens and the officer's symbolic authority. Such encounters often lead to more punitive treatment of minorities.

Status-linked expectations may also be a problem across genders. While it is sometimes thought that female delinquents benefit from "chivalrous coddling" by the police, recent studies suggest that "paternalistic punitiveness" may often be the more pressing problem (McEachern and Bauzer, 1967; Krohn et al., 1983). Research by Visher (1983:6) suggests:

> . . . when law enforcement officials (e.g., police, prosecutors, judges), most of whom are male, interact with female violators, the encounter is transformed into an exchange between a man and a woman. In this situation, appropriate gender behaviors and expectations may become more salient than strictly legal factors in the official sanctioning of female offenders. Indeed, if women fail to conform to traditional female roles, then the assumed bargain is broken and chivalrous treatment is not extended.

Abandonment of chivalry may have especially serious implications in contacts with young minority women. Female adolescents still appear to be incarcerated for less serious offenses than their male counterparts, and young black women specifically are at risk of being treated more severely than young white women (Chesney-Lind, 1987; Datesman and Scarpetti, 1977; Pawlak, 1977; Visher, 1983). "The latter may reflect the dual impact of racism and sexism," according to one study, "or it may be that Black female arrestees and defendants are less likely than their White counterparts to exhibit submissiveness and other traditionally defined 'feminine' demeanors" (Horowitz and Pottieger, 1991:76). This element of distrust and hostility characterizes the interactions of many minority accused (male as well as female) with justice system personnel.

None of this explanatory analysis denies the significance of "strictly legal" variables, such as seriousness of offense and prior record, in determining police decisions. Nonetheless, a study of 742 suspect encounters with police in 24 U.S. cities found that antagonistic suspects are much more likely to be taken into custody than suspects who display deference, that black suspects are more likely to be arrested than whites, and that part of this race effect can be explained by the more hostile or antagonistic demeanor of black suspects (Smith, 1986). Antagonism is a thread that runs through a range of contacts of minority citizens in general—and minority youth in particular—with the criminal justice system, ultimately adding to the risks faced by this group.

Anderson's (1991) recent ethnographic description of the precarious position of young black males on the streets of a northeastern U.S. low-income community raises a serious dilemma in contemporary policing of minority neighborhoods. He notes that (Anderson, 1991:195): "In trying to do their job, the police appear to engage in an informal policy of monitoring young Black men as a means of controlling crime, and often they go beyond the bounds of duty." As a result (Anderson, 1991:195-196):

> Many youths . . . have reason to fear . . . mistaken identity or harassment, since they might be jailed, if only for a short time . . . . When law-abiding Blacks are ensnared by the criminal justice system, the scenario may proceed as follows. A young man is arbitrarily stopped by the police and questioned. If he cannot effectively negotiate with the officer(s), he may be accused of a crime and arrested. To resolve this situation he needs financial resources, money for an attorney, which often happens, he is left to a public defender who may be more interested in going along with the court system than in fighting for a poor Black person. Without legal support, he may well wind up "doing time" even if he is innocent of

the charges brought against him. The next time he is stopped for questioning he will have a record, which will make detention all the more likely.

Against this background, Anderson reasons that it is not surprising that many black youth develop an "attitude" toward the police. This picture contrasts sharply with Sullivan's (1989:196) finding in the white neighborhood he studied:

> [Youths] had resources for dealing with the criminal justice system that were not available to the youths in the other neighborhoods; when they did get caught, they sought to manipulate the system—and were often successful in doing so—by means of money and personal connections.

Finally, the geographical distribution of police work underlines the links between racial discrimination and the concentration of poverty and crime in poor minority neighborhoods. It has been argued that densely populated settings increase anonymity and freedom from surveillance and control (Thrasher, 1927; Newman, 1972). However, others argue that the press of people in high-density areas imposes on residents a unique kind of community organization characterized by a high level of mutual surveillance (see Jacobs, 1961; Plant, 1957). This surveillance restricts residents' privacy and makes activities, both legal and illegal, more frequently "public" (Stinchcombe, 1963). A result is that the same act detected, reported, and recorded as illegal in a densely populated minority community may go undetected, unreported, and unrecorded in more spaciously populated middle- and upper-class settings. This is one way in which some social and geographical areas are more "offensible" than others.

The term "offensible space" refers to areas in which the police perceive a disproportionate incidence of deviant behavior and so take some initiative in processing offenders (Hagan et al., 1978). In some cases, citizens have provided intelligence about patterned juvenile behavior, such as recurrent vandalism or rowdiness on their block, leading police to increase surveillance in an attempt to "clean up" the area (Black, 1970). In other cases, however, the police themselves designate certain neighborhoods, based on a set of internalized expectations derived from past experience. Unfortunately, the result can be a process of "ecological contamination" by which all residents of designated neighborhoods are viewed as potential suspects or threats (Smith, 1986). In other words, offensible space or ecological contamination involves areas where prior police conceptions encourage an aggressive and stereotyped pattern of police work.

A study designed to assess the impact of police conceptions of offensible space was undertaken in a Canadian community called Westport (Hagan et al., 1978). Using a mixture of quantitative and qualitative techniques, the study showed that a neighborhood's delinquency rates can be better explained by police preconceptions or by citizen complaints than by aggregated self-reported measures of delinquent behavior. That is, the contamination effect associated with offensible space results in the overpolicing of youth and adults from stigmatized areas.

Contextual analysis of data from the Seattle Youth Study also reveals a strong inverse effect of neighborhood socioeconomic status (SES) on police processing of juveniles, independent of self-reported delinquent behavior. The author concludes (Sampson, 1986:884): " . . . the influence of SES on police contacts is contextual in nature, and stems from an ecological bias with regard to police control, as opposed to a single individual-level bias against the poor" (see also Smith, 1986). Nevertheless, this kind of community-based discrimination is felt by individuals: it lowers the threshold (or raises the risk) that poor and minorities will enter the juvenile and criminal justice systems, and it is a part of the experience that builds resentment and distrust among these populations.

THE JUSTICE SYSTEMS

Processing

Once caught up in the juvenile or criminal justice system, the risks for minority youth increase. Even prolonged contact with the system during pretrial phases can be detrimental, so much so that one researcher argues that "the process is the punishment" (Feeley, 1979). It is hardly surprising that minority juvenile defendants can be uncooperative during the process of prosecution. The pervasive concern at the prosecution stage is with charge and plea bargaining, which has been defined as "the exchange of official concessions for the act of self-conviction" (Alschuler, 1979:213). This bargaining can be explicit or implicit, but it is usually assumed that a high percentage of guilty pleas in a court is a sure sign of plea bargaining (Haumann, 1975). Extensive plea bargaining is apparently a relatively modern development, taking center stage in the courts at about the middle of this century (compare Moley, 1928; Friedman, 1979). Prosecutors are known to regularly "overcharge" to strengthen their bargaining positions (Alschuler, 1968).

A key issue involves what kinds of charges and cases will get "bargained down" or dismissed instead of fully prosecuted. One determinant is the prosecutor's experience with offenders and cases that have been pursued successfully to conviction and sentencing in the past, a process that involves a stereotyping of strong and weak cases in terms of case-specific characteristics (see Cicourel, 1968; Sudnow, 1965; Myers and Hagan, 1979). These characteristics can include not only the seriousness of the offense and the amount and quality of evidence, but also the credibility of the victim(s) and offender(s) as witnesses. Nonwhite victims tend to be considered less credible witnesses, while white victims, especially of nonwhite defendants, are considered highly credible (Newman, 1966; Miller et al., 1978).

Although there is variation in results, two predominant patterns seem to emerge in analyses of the treatment of minorities, who are disproportionately young and male, at the prosecutorial stage: (1) prosecutors initially dismiss more cases involving nonwhite than white defendants; and (2) prosecutors offer the remaining nonwhite defendants fewer plea bargains than white defendants. These patterns are not as contradictory as they might seem. One possible explanation is that police tend to arrest minority suspects with insufficient evidence or probable cause; this speculation is supported by a finding that warrants are used more extensively in arrests of whites than of nonwhites. Prosecutors may simply use dismissals to eliminate the weakest cases against minority defendants (Petersilia, 1983).

When the cases are not dismissed, minority defendants are less likely to accept a plea bargain and therefore more likely to go to trial (Petersilia, 1983; LaFree, 1980; Mather, 1979; Uhlman, 1979; Welch et al., 1985; Zatz and Lizotte, 1985). This suggests that whites are getting better "deals" in the plea bargaining process, and there are several studies that support this view (Welch et al., 1985; Zatz, 1985). But other studies speculate that this results from the suspicion, distrust, and hostility that minority suspects have for the prosecutorial process. Thus, the hostility at earlier stages affects this stage: the justice system bears the costs of fully prosecuting a greater proportion of cases involving minority defendants, and the defendants are caught up in a system that consumes their time and resources and puts them at risk for imprisonment.

Punishment

The shift from an earlier emphasis on rehabilitation and treatment to the current emphasis on punishment has had important consequences for the sentencing and punishment of young offenders. The change has brought renewed attention to theories of crime that emphasize the consequences of punishment, with a view toward the protection of society. The reemergence of deterrence theory and strategies of "selective incapacitation" are part of this shift of theoretical attention (Blumstein et al., 1986). Associated with this shift in emphasis is an increased use of institutionalization and incarceration, especially for high-risk minority youth.

Although precise data are lacking on the use of institutional placements in juvenile facilities, much is known about the increased use of imprisonment, which inevitably involves large numbers of older minority adolescents and young adults. For example, state prisons hold 92 percent of our nation's inmates; in little more than a decade, commitments to prisons increased nationally nearly 2-1/2 times, from 96,073 in 1974 to 232,969 in 1986. During this entire period, the rate of incarceration for black Americans was more than six times the rate for whites (Chilton and Galvin, 1985). Between 1978 and 1982 alone, the number of black males in the U.S. prison population increased by 23 percent (Bureau of Justice Statistics, 1985). Black women constitute the majority of female prisoners.

There also has been growth in the use of institutional placements for juvenile offenders, although this growth has been less pronounced than that for adult imprisonment. In 1975, juveniles between 10 and 18 were confined in juvenile facilities at a rate of 241 per 100,000; by 1987 the figure was 353 per 100,000. Over the 1975-1989 period, the number of children in custody in public facilities increased by 19 percent, from less than 47,000 in 1975 to more than 56,100 in 1989.

Several explanations have been offered for the increase in imprisonment between 1974 and 1986 (Langan, 1991). Increasing levels of reported crime and overall arrests account for 9 percent of the increase. More specific increases in arrests and imprisonment for drug crimes account for another 8 percent. Changes in the proportion of young people in the U.S. population account for 20 percent of the increase. However, the largest factor by far, accounting for more than half of the change, is simply a renewed preference for institutional sentences. This tougher response to crime apparently involves not only judges, but also prosecutors, probation officers, and parole boards. For example, in 1974, parole boards returned 6 percent of their cases to prison; in 1986, they returned 14 percent; courts and parole boards together returned nearly a quarter of this population to prison in 1986.

Because crime is concentrated so heavily among youth and minorities, the increased use of imprisonment falls heavily on young minority males. Early studies of race and sentencing conducted in the 1940s and 1950s often concluded that racial discrimination occurred. A number of efforts have been made over the past several decades to reform sentencing practices in ways that would make discrimination less common. These include rules and guidelines for plea bargaining, mandatory minimum sentences, statutorily determined sentences, presumptive or prescriptive sentencing guidelines, and the establishment of sentencing councils. A number of recent contextual analyses indicate that ethnic- and race-based sentencing is still apparent for some types of offenders, at some decision points, and in some times and places (Zatz, 1987; Myers and Talarico, 1987; Peterson and Hagan, 1984; Hagan and Bumiller, 1983). However, few criminologists would argue that the current gap between black and white levels of imprisonment is mainly due to discrimination in sentencing or in any of the other decision-making processes in the criminal justice system. The higher rate of crime among blacks explains much of the differential (Jaynes and Williams, 1989).

Yet the reforms in sentencing practice have also often made imprisonment more likely for young minority males, in much the same way that the professionalization of police work has increased their risk of arrest. That is, more young minority males were imprisoned through an even-handedness that includes increased severity for whites as well as nonwhites. The even-handedness has also extended to women, with the result that judges have sentenced women to prison in record numbers in recent years (Chesney-Lind, 1987). The number of girls and women arrested increased by 203 percent between 1974 and 1984, and the number of women in prison jumped 258 percent (compared with a male increase of 199 percent). Again, even if white and minority women are treated equally, the biggest effect will be felt by young minority women because they encounter the system in disproportionate numbers.

Consequences

Enthusiasm for aggressive policing, prosecution, and punishment of a large number of youthful and highly active offenders is based on the policy of selective incapacitation, a strategy that usually focuses on "career criminals," mainly, repeat offenders. However, a large body of research on selective incapacitation suggests that it would not reduce crime significantly without very substantial increases in prison populations because the capacity to predict criminal careers is limited, there is relatively little specialization by type of crime, most criminal careers are brief, and new offenders quickly replace those who desist (Blumstein et al., 1986). This assessment is supported by the increasing level of violent crime that has occurred during a time of record use of imprisonment.

It is similarly unclear that institutionalization and related repressive measures have deterrent effects on young people. Attempts to assess effects of delinquency prevention programs have produced distinctively mixed results (compare Martinson, 1974; Whitehead and Lab, 1989). However, the most systematic of these reviews found that deterrence-based programs, including "shock incarceration" and the "scared straight" program that received much publicity a few years ago, produce more, not less, recidivism when they are systematically assessed in control group designs (Lipsey, 1991).

It is uncertain exactly how these negative effects occur. For many years the concern was that institutionalization resulted in "prisonization," a process by which new detainees take on the attitudes and values of older inmates. However, there now is more evidence that by the time they encounter the justice system, ghetto youth have already assumed self-concepts, attitudes, and values that make further impact, beyond perpetuation, unlikely (see Ageton and Elliott, 1974; Harris, 1976). This should not be surprising, given the hostile attitudes toward the justice system in the community. It might also help explain the weak effects of delinquency prevention and other programs for minority youth.

Meanwhile, prison experiences may actually solidify the networks of association that make continued involvement in crime likely. For example, racial associations and conflicts are imported to prisons from home communities, perpetuating gang and sexual violence (Lockwood, 1980). These continuing associations may also help inmates maintain connections with illegal markets that persist in prison (see Jacobs, 1977; Moore et al., 1978; Moore, 1991). Underground markets are alternatives to conventional employment, and for many ghetto youth illegal markets offer culturally accepted lines of economic opportunity (Sullivan, 1989), sometimes replacing or competing with legitimate labor markets (Freeman, 1991). Sullivan (1989) notes that youth crime provides otherwise unavailable funds for a short period but further separates inner-city youths from the labor market and stigmatizes them in their later careers.

There is mounting evidence of more general detrimental consequences of the processing and punishment of youthful offenders, especially in terms of adult economic outcomes, for those who are otherwise disadvantaged. Working-class males with conviction records are uniquely disadvantaged in finding employment, and even for adolescents who are arrested but do not go to jail, the experience of arrest and conviction can have long-term, even intergenerational repercussions in terms of occupational as well as criminal careers (Schwartz and Skolnick, 1964; Hagan and Palloni, 1990; Hagan, 1991). A criminal arrest record has negative effects on employment as much as 8 years later, in part because employers are reluctant to employ ex-offenders (Freeman, 1991; Grogger, 1991).

Incarceration, or even prolonged processing through the criminal justice system, can also date job skills and contact networks for employment. The attitudes and interests that signal employability to prospective employers may be undermined and otherwise discouraged, while attitudes of distrust and hostility are perpetuated. Factory jobs in the manufacturing sector once allowed for a toughness of demeanor among young minority males, but such attitudes are disabling in the new service economy jobs (Anderson, 1991). Juvenile and criminal justice system contact seems to perpetuate those attitudes.

A number of studies have established that former delinquents also experience disproportionate problems in securing and holding jobs (Robins, 1966; Sampson and Laub, 1990; Glueck and Glueck, 1950). A recent 13-year study also found that youth from working-class families who identify with a subculture of delinquency are distinctly disadvantaged in terms of occupational outcomes when compared with middle- and upper-class youth who also were involved in that subculture (Hagan, 1991). This study provides evidence that contact with the justice system is one way in which the low social and cultural capital of ghetto youths is further diminished.

The research reviewed by the panel suggests that the U.S. justice system is overburdened, and that its emphasis on punishment is expensive, unproductive of the desired gains in reducing levels of crime, and probably productive of increased hostility toward itself in ghetto communities. Studies suggest that Americans favor increasing the use of alternatives to incarceration, except for violent offenders (Doble, 1987). The diversion of status offenders from the juvenile justice system is an encouraging step along these lines, but simply ignoring these troubled youth is not a promising policy alternative. The most effective treatment programs are applied outside of public facilities, custodial institutions, and the juvenile justice system (Lipsey, 1991). They also tend to involve nonpunitive behavior and skill-orientation, multimodal treatments that offer alternatives to the more socially and fiscally costly mechanisms of justice system involvement.

CONCLUSIONS

The high levels of crime among black American youth are causally associated with the concentration of poverty in urban neighborhoods. Patterns of ethnic, especially racial, segregation have created the conditions in which economic downturns and concentrated poverty have torn the social fabric of black American communities. Social disruption has aggravated stereotypes of ghetto settings and has led to overpolicing and other kinds of discriminatory treatment that generate diffuse feelings of injustice, hostility, and aggression (Blau and Blau, 1982). Hostility is itself disorganizing and disruptive in ways that make crime and violence common.

The growing concentration of poverty in inner-city neighborhoods (see Chapter 4) has coincided with the entry into the crime-prone years of adolescence and early adulthood of the large postwar birth cohorts and—more recently—their children. The aging of these cohorts might have been expected to produce some relief in the following years, but after some positive signs in the early 1980s, rates of criminal violence have moved upward again. The decline of the rehabilitative ideal, a new emphasis on deterrence and selective incapacitation, and escalating rates of imprisonment have not altered these trends. Ghetto youth, especially minority males, have continued to experience high levels of crime as well as punishment.

The large-scale use of arrest and imprisonment has both fiscal and other implications. Race-linked inequalities further aggravate problems in an array of institutional settings in which blacks and whites meet. Because community-level policing practices display discriminatory patterns, and because the justice system is nevertheless expected to embody high standards of fairness, justice system interactions have become particularly difficult forums for black-white relations. A result is that many ghetto youth grow up in environments that, in addition to other difficulties, are characterized by hostility toward the justice system.

REFERENCES

Ageton, S., and D. Elliott
    1974   The effects of legal processing on self-concept. *Social Problems* 22:87-100.
Alschuler, A.
    1968   The prosecutor's role in plea bargaining. *University of Chicago Law Review* 36:50-112.
    1979   Plea bargaining and its history. *Law & Society Review* 13:211-245.
Anderson, E.
    1991   *Streetwise: Race, Class and Change in an Urban Community.* Chicago: University of Chicago Press.
Annie E. Casey Foundation
    1993   *Kids Count Data Book.* Washngton, D.C.: Center for the Study of Social Policy.
Black, D.
    1970   Police control of juveniles. *American Sociological Review* 35:63-77.
    1983   Crime as social control. *American Sociological Review* 48:34-45.
Black, D., and A.J. Reiss
    1967   Patterns of behavior in police-citizen transactions. In *Studies in Crime and Law Enforcement in Major Metropolitan Areas, Field Surveys III,* Vol. 2. President's Commission on Law Enforcement in Major Metropolitan Areas. Washington, D.C.: U.S. Government Printing Office.
Blau, J., and P. Blau
    1982   The cost of inequality: metropolitan structure and violent crime. *American Sociological Review* 47:114-128.
Blumstein, A., J. Cohen, J.A. Roth, and C.A. Visher, eds.
    1986   *Criminal Careers and Career Criminals,* Vol. 1. Washington, D.C.: National Academy Press.
Bureau of Justice Statistics
    1985   *The Prevalence of Imprisonment.* U.S. Department of Justice Special Report. Washington, D.C.: U.S. Government Printing Office.
Centerwall, B.
    1984   Race, socioeconomic status and domestic homicide, Atlanta, 1971-72. *American Journal of Public Health* 74:813-815.
Chesney-Lind, M.
    1987   Female offenders: paternalism reexamined. In L. Crites and W. Hepperle, eds., *Women, the Courts and Equality.* Beverly Hills, Calif.: Sage Publications.
Chilton, R.
    1986   Age, sex, race and arrest trends for twelve of the nation's largest central

cities. In J. Byrne and R. Sampson, eds., *The Social Ecology of Crime: Theory, Research and Public Policy.* New York: Springer-Verlag.

Chilton, R., and J. Galvin
1985   Race, crime and criminal justice. *Crime and Delinquency* 31:3-14.

Cicourel, A.
1968   *The Social Organization of Juvenile Justice.* New York: Wiley.

Datesman, S., and F. Scarpetti
1977   Unequal protection for males and females in the juvenile court. In T.N. Ferdinand, ed., *Juvenile Delinquency: Little Brother Grows Up.* Beverly Hills, Calif.: Sage Publications.

Doble, J.
1987   *Crime and Punishment: The Public's View.* New York: Public Agenda Foundation.

Elliot, D. and S. Ageton
1980   Reconciling race and class differences in self-report and official estimates of delinquency. *American Sociological Review* 45:95-110.

Fagan, J., F. Piper, and Y. Cheng
1987   Contributions of victimization to delinquency in inner cities. *Journal of Criminal Law and Criminology* 78:586-613.

Feeley, M.
1979   *The Process Is the Punishment.* New York: Russell Sage Foundation.

Ferdinand, T., and E. Luchterhand
1970   Inner-city youth, the police, the juvenile court and justice. *Social Problems* 17:510-527.

Freeman, R.
1991   Crime and the Economic Status of Disadvantaged Young Men. Paper presented to the Conference on Urban Labor Markets and Labor Mobility, Warrenton, Va.

Friedman, L.
1979   Plea bargaining in historical perspective. *Law & Society Review* 13(2):247-259.

Glueck, S., and E. Glueck
1950   *Unraveling Juvenile Delinquency.* Cambridge, Mass.: Harvard University.

Gottfredson, M., and M. Hindelang
1981   Sociological aspects of criminal victimization. *Annual Review of Sociology* 7:107-128.

Grogger, J.
1991   The Effect of Arrest on the Employment Outcomes of Young Men. Unpublished manuscript, University of California, Santa Barbara.

Hagan, J.
1991   Destiny and drift: subcultural preferences, status attainments, and the risks and rewards of youth. *American Sociological Review* 56:567-582.

Hagan, J., and C. Albonetti
1982   Race, class and the perception of criminal injustice in America. *American Journal of Sociology* 88:329-355.

Hagan, J., and K. Bumiller
1983   Making sense of sentencing: a review and critique of sentencing research. In A. Blumstein, J. Cohen, S.E. Martin, and M.H. Toury, eds., *Research on Sentencing: The Search for Reform*, Vol. II. Washington, D.C.: National Academy Press.

Hagan, J., and A. Palloni
1990   The social reproduction of a criminal class in working class London, circa 1950-80. *American Journal of Sociology* 96:265-299.

Hagan, J., A.R. Gillis, and J. Chan
1978   Explaining official delinquency: a spatial study of class, conflict and control. *Sociological Quarterly* 19:386-398.

Hagedorn, J.
1988   *People and Folks: Gangs, Crime and the Underclass in a Rustbelt City.* Chicago: Lake View Press.

Harris, A.
1976   Race, commitment to deviance and spoiled identity. *American Sociological Review* 41:432-442.
1991   Race, class and crime. In J. Sheley, ed., *Criminology.* Belmont, Calif.: Wadsworth.

Hawkins, D.
1986   *Homicide Among Black Americans.* Lanham, Md.: University Press of America.

Haumann, M.
1975   A note on plea bargaining and case pressure. *Law & Society Review* 9:515-528.

Hindelang, M., T. Hirschi, and J. Weis
1981   *Measuring Delinquency.* Beverly Hills, Calif.: Sage Publications.

Horowitz, R., and A.E. Pottieger
1991   Gender bias in juvenile justice handling of seriously crime-involved youth. *Journal of Research in Crime and Delinquency* 28(1):75-100.

Jacobs, J.
1961   *The Death and Life of Great American Cities.* New York: Random House.
1977   *Statesville: The Penitentiary in Mass Society.* Chicago: University of Chicago Press.

Jaynes, G.D., and R.M. Williams, Jr., eds.
1989   *A Common Destiny: Blacks and American Society.* Committee on the Status of Black Americans, Commission on Behavioral and Social Sciences and Education, National Research Council. Washington, D.C.: National Academy Press.

Kotlowitz, A.
1991   *There Are No Children Here.* New York: Doubleday.

Krisberg, B., I.M. Schwartz, P. Litsky, and J. Austin
1986   The watershed of juvenile justice reform. *Crime and Delinquency* 32:5-38.

Krohn, M., J. Curry, and S. Nelson-Kilger
1983   Is chivalry dead? An analysis of changes in police dispositions of males and females. *Criminology* 21:417-437.

LaFree, G.
1980   The effect of sexual stratification by race on official reactions to rape. *American Sociological Review* 45:842-854.

Land, K., P. McCall, and L. Cohen
1990   Structural co-variates of homicide rates: are there any invariances across time and space? *American Journal of Sociology* 95:922-963.

Land, K., D. Cantor, and S. Russell
1991   Unemployment and Crime Rate Fluctuations in the Post-World War II

United States: Statistical Time Series Properties and Alternative Models. Paper presented to the American Society of Criminology Meetings, San Francisco.

Langan, P.
1991   America's soaring prison population. *Science* 251:1568-1573.

Lehmann, N.
1991   *The Promised Land: The Great Black Migration and How It Changed America.* New York: Alfred Knopf.

Lipsey, M.W.
1991   Juvenile delinquency treatment: a meta-analytic inquiry into the variability of effects. In *Meta-Analysis for Explanation: A Casebook.* New York: Russell Sage Foundation.

Lockwood, D.
1980   *Prison Sexual Violence.* New York: Elsevier.

Lowry, P., S. Hassig, R. Gunn, and J. Mathison
1988   Homicide victims in New Orleans: recent trends. *American Journal of Epidemiology* 128:1130-1136.

Martinson, R.
1974   What works? Questions and answers about prison reform. *The Public Interest* 35:22-54.

Massey, D.
1990   American apartheid: segregation and the making of the under-class. *American Journal of Sociology* 96:329-357.

Mather, L.
1979   *Plea Bargaining or Trial? The Process of Criminal Case Disposition.* Lexington, Mass.: Lexington Books.

Matsueda, R., and K. Heimer
1987   Race, family structure and delinquency: a test of differential association and social control theories. *American Sociological Review* 52:826-840.

McEachern, A.W., and R. Bauzer
1967   Factors related to disposition in juvenile police contacts. In M. Klein, ed., *Juvenile Gangs in Context: Research, Theory and Action.* Englewood Cliffs, N.J.: Prentice-Hall.

Messner, S.F.
1989   Economic discrimination and societal homicide rates: further evidence on the cost of inequality. *American Sociological Review* 54(4):597-611.

Miller, H.S., W.F. McDonald, and J.A. Cramer
1978   *Plea Bargaining in the United States.* Washington, D.C.: National Institute of Law Enforcement and Criminal Justice, Law Enforcement Assistance Administration.

Moley, R.
1928   The vanishing jury. *Southern California Law Review* 2:97.

Moore, J., with R. Garcia, C. Garcia, L. Cerda, and F. Valencia
1978   *Homeboys: Gangs, Drugs and Prison in the Barrios of Los Angeles.* Philadelphia: Temple University Press.

Moore, J.W.
1991   *Going Down to the Barrio: Homeboys and Homegirls in Change.* Philadelphia: Temple University Press.

Munford, R.S., R. Kazev, R. Feldman, and R. Stivers
1976   Homicide trends in Atlanta. *Criminology* 14:213-221.

Myers, M., and J. Hagan
1979   Private and public trouble: prosecutors and the allocation of court resources. *Social Problems* 26:439-451.

Myers, M., and S. Talarico
1987   *The Social Contexts of Criminal Sentencing.* New York: Springer-Verlag.

National Commission on Children
1991   *Beyond Rhetoric: A New American Agenda for Children and Families.* Washington, D.C.: National Commission on Children.

Newman, D.
1966   *Conviction: The Determination of Guilt or Innocence Without Trial.* Boston: American Bar Association.

Newman, O.
1972   *Defensible Space.* New York: Macmillan.

Pawlak, E.
1977   Differential selection of juveniles for detention. *Journal of Research in Crime and Delinquency* 14:152-165.

Petersilia, J.
1983   *Racial Disparities in the Criminal Justice System.* Santa Monica, Calif.: The RAND Corporation.
1985   Racial disparities in the criminal justice system: a summary. *Crime & Delinquency* 31:15-34.

Peterson, R., and J. Hagan
1984   Changing conceptions of race: the sentencing of drug offenders in an American city, 1963-76. *American Sociological Review* 49:56-71.

Piliavin, I., and S. Briar
1964   Police encounters with juveniles. *American Journal of Sociology* 70:206-214.

Plant, J.S.
1957   The personality of an urban area. In P. Halt and A. Reiss, eds., *Cities and Society.* New York: The Free Press.

Reiss, A., and D. Bordua
1967   Organization and environment: a perspective on the municipal police. In D. Bordua, ed., *The Police: Six Sociological Essays.* New York: Wiley.

Robins, L.
1966   *Deviant Children Grown Up.* Baltimore, Md.: Williams and Wilkins.

Rose, H., and P. McClain
1990   *Race, Place and Risk: Black Homicide in Urban America.* Albany, N.Y.: SUNY Press.

Russell, W.F.
1966   *Go Up to Glory.* New York: Coward-McCann.

Sampson, R.
1986   Effects of socioeconomic context on official reaction to juvenile delinquency. *American Sociological Review* 51:876-885.
1987   Urban black violence: the effect of male joblessness and family disruption. *American Journal of Sociology* 93:348-382.

Sampson, R., and J. Laub
1990   Stability and change in crime and deviance over the life course: the salience of adult social bonds. *American Sociological Review* 55:609-627.

Sanchez-Jankowski, M.
1992   *Islands in the Stream.* Los Angeles: University of California Press.

Schwartz, R., and J. Skolnick
1964   Two studies of legal stigma. In H. Becker, ed., *The Other Side: Perspectives on Deviance.* New York: The Free Press.
Sellin, T.
1935   Race prejudice in the administration of justice. *American Journal of Sociology* 41:312-317.
1976   *Slavery and the Penal System.* New York: Elsevier.
Skolnick, J.
1966   *Justice Without Trial.* New York: Wiley.
Smith, D.
1986   The neighborhood context of police behavior. In A.J. Reiss and M. Tonry, eds., *Communities and Cities.* Chicago: University of Chicago Press.
Spivak, H., D. Prothrow-Stith, and A.J. Hausman
1988   Dying is no accident: adolescents, violence and intentional injury. *Pediatric Clinics of North America* 35(6):1339-1347.
Stafford, M.
1984   Gang delinquency. In R. Meier, ed., *Major Forms of Crime.* Beverly Hills, Calif.: Sage Publications.
Stinchcombe, A.
1963   Institutions of privacy in the determination of police administration practice. *American Journal of Sociology* 69:150-160.
Sudnow, D.
1965   Normal crimes: sociological features of the penal code in a public defender office. *Social Problems* (Winter):255-276.
Sullivan, M.
1989   *Getting Paid: Youth Crime and Work in the Inner City.* Ithaca, N.Y.: Cornell University Press.
Sykes, G., and J. Clark
1975   A theory of deference exchange in police civilian encounters. *American Journal of Sociology* 81:584-600.
Thrasher, F.
1927   *The Gang.* Chicago: University of Chicago Press.
Uhlman, T.
1979   *Racial Justice: Black Judges and Defendants in an Urban Trial Court.* Lexington, Mass.: Lexington Books.
Visher, C.
1983   Gender, police arrest decisions, and notions of chivalry. *Criminology* 21:5-28.
Welch, S., J. Gruhl, and C. Spohn
1985   Convicting and sentencing differences among black, Hispanics, and white males in six localities. *Justice Quarterly* 2:67-80.
Whitehead, J.T., and S.P. Lab
1989   A meta-analysis of juvenile correctional treatment. *Journal of Research in Crime and Delinquency* 26(3):276-295.
Wilson, J.Q.
1968   *Varieties of Police Behavior.* Cambridge, Mass.: Harvard University Press.
Wilson, W.J.
1987   *The Truly Disadvantaged: The Inner City, the Underclass, and Public Policy.* Chicago: University of Chicago Press.

Wolfgang, M., and M. Riedel
  1973   Race, judicial discretion, and the death penalty. *The Annals of the American Academy of Political and Social Science* 407:119.

Zatz, M.
  1985   Pleas, priors and prison: racial/ethnic differences in sentencing. *Social Science Research* 14:169-193.
  1987   The changing forms of racial/ethnic biases in sentencing. *Journal of Research in Crime and Delinquency* 24:69-92.

Zatz, M., and A. Lizotte
  1985   The timing of court processing: toward linking theory and method. *Criminology* 23:313-335.

9

Adolescents in the
Child Wefare System

The child welfare system in general, and foster care in particular, is supposed to provide a "safety net" for children and adolescents who face developmental risks because of dysfunctional families, high-risk neighborhoods, mental health, or behavioral problems. But there is clear evidence that this net has failed, that the child welfare system is doing an inadequate job of preparing the adolescents in its care to make the transition to productive, independent adulthood. For many adolescents who enter its care, the child welfare system has become a high-risk setting. Demographic trends (e.g., the "baby bust") and the efforts at deinstitutionalization in the 1970s and at community-based service alternatives in the early 1980s temporarily reduced the number of adolescents in the child welfare system, but by the mid-1980s the trend was reversed. It is not clear whether factors outside the service system (e.g., increased poverty and broken families) overwhelmed efforts to develop community service alternatives; it is clear that troubled and troublesome adolescents pose problems that, to date, have not been solved.

EVOLUTION OF THE SYSTEM

Early Reforms

At the beginning of this century, child welfare policy stressed the rights of individual children and enhanced the state's role in acting as parent to the child. This often meant separation from biological families and institutionalization in orphanages or similar settings (Katz, 1986). Reforms in the 1910s and 1920s brought with them the idea that children should not be separated from their families simply because of poverty (Meckel, 1985). The Social Security Act of 1935 expanded on existing "mother's pensions" at the state level to create a national Aid to Dependent Children program, which linked the act's provisions on economic maintenance, child protection, and foster care to form the structure on which subsequent reforms have been based.

As increasing numbers of children came to be reared in substitute care, concern arose that federal funds were being spent to separate children and parents, rather than in preserving families (Maas and Engler, 1959). Permanency planning—the provision of a stable family living arrangement with nurturing parents or caretakers and the opportunity to establish lifetime relationships—evolved out of this concern about "drift" in foster care (Maluccio and Fein, 1983).

Subsequent "reforms" were a mixed blessing. For example, the Civil Rights Movement of the 1960s provided a model for those who wanted to ensure that children, women, and people with disabilities also had full rights under the U.S. Constitution. The focus on individual liberties brought uneven results for children, however: handicapped children benefited by full entitlement to public education, and the prosecution of children for "state offenses" (activities that are not crimes if committed by adults) greatly declined. However, children who depended on government child welfare agencies were sometimes assured of their rights at the expense of the services they needed. When truancy or curfew violations were no longer delinquent activities, for instance, young people had to escalate their behavior before they could benefit from any community response.

In the 1960s, to "protect" clients from government intrusion—and to save money—many states eliminated one of the main roles of public social workers, that of helping clients acquire services and support. After nearly four decades, the casework relationship between a client and a social worker came to an end: social workers were responsible only for conducting financial assistance investigations; families were told to seek out social services on their own if they needed them.

This void in social services to families has been gradually filled by the child welfare system. For example, the Adoption Assistance and Child Welfare Act of 1980 (P.L. 96-272) responded to the long-standing concern that many children were staying in foster care for unnecessarily long periods and that no one was responsible for managing their exit from the system. To remedy these perceived problems, the law was designed to prevent foster care placement where possible, to facilitate quicker reunion with parents or placement in long-term foster care, and to subsidize hard-to-place children. Adolescents were covered by this legislation, but they were affected differently than younger children because many were in different circumstances than younger children. Since adolescents have less chance of either reunification or adoption than younger children, long-term placement in foster care, while not a preferred outcome, was included as a satisfactory outcome for adolescents. At the present time, the tide of change is running against these adolescents due to fiscal constraints and the growing caseloads of younger children. Many states, citing budget problems, have lowered from 21 to 18 the age at which adolescents are no longer eligible for services.

Recent Trends

Community-Based Services

Since the mid-1970s, the federal government and the states have sought noncorrectional alternatives for youths who engage in antisocial, but not serious criminal activities. These troubled and troublesome youths were typically classified as "minors in need of supervision," but they are neither treated as offenders nor incarcerated. A number of community-based alternatives have arisen to cope with this gentler system of social control. One of them, Community Based Youth Services (CBYS), uses local boards or agencies across a state to generate distinctive service packages for status offenders and other troubled youth. The goal is to reduce adolescents' contact with, and penetration into, the juvenile justice and child welfare systems by keeping them at home with community services. One evaluation of a CBYS system (Spergel and Hartnett, 1990) found that the services did not systematically reduce subsequent contacts with either the juvenile justice or child welfare systems, but the extent to which these results reflect national experiences with CBYS is not known. Community-based services appear to "widen the nets" of these systems by identifying young people whose needs exceed community resources and who ultimately need the protection or control of a correctional or child welfare setting. The only variable that seemed to reduce the likelihood of negative outcomes was the level of training of community service providers: staff members with graduate degrees were more likely than other staff to divert youth from these systems, which suggests that the complexity of problems required a more sophisticated understanding of troubled youth and a better sense of strategic interventions (Spergel and Hartnett, 1990).

Foster Care

The foster care population has experienced tremendous growth since the mid-1980s. There were an estimated 300,000 children in foster care during the mid-1980s, but the population is currently estimated to be over 500,000. Ten years ago, adolescents constituted a large portion of the child welfare population, but since then the number of adolescents in all types of foster care has remained relatively constant while the number of children in the youngest age groups has skyrocketed. As a result, the 13- to 18-year-old age group dropped from 45 percent of the total in 1982 to 34 percent of the total in 1988 (Tatara, 1992). (The lack of reliable and up-to-date national data may conceal further declines in the share, if not the absolute number, of adolescents in the foster care population.) In Illinois, for example, the rate for 15- to 19-year-olds being placed in foster care dropped from 13.2 per 10,000 in 1980 to 10 per 10,000 in 1990, while the placement rate for newborns to 4-year-olds increased from 26.3 per 10,000 to 49.7 per 10,000. Most of the overall decrease was due to fewer white adolescents being placed in foster care; the placement rates for minority youths remained constant or increased slightly (Goerge and Osuch, 1992). Substantial increases in the number of infants being placed in foster care, and resulting declines in the percentage of adolescents in the system, have also occurred in California, Michigan, and New York (Goerge and Wulczyn, 1990).

Several studies examined the duration of child welfare placement and reentry into the system for statewide populations of foster children of all children. The first showed that children who exited care and returned to their parents had stayed in care for an average of 1 year, those who were adopted had stayed in care for 1.2 years, and those who exited in other ways had stayed for 6 years (Maas and Engler, 1959). The second found that, once a child had been in foster care for over 90 days, there was a high probability that the child would remain in care for more than 3 years (Fanshel and Shinn, 1976). A more recent study of foster children in New York and Illinois showed that, for children discharged in 1986, the median duration of care for adolescents between 12 and 17 years old was between 10 and 14 months, the longest duration for any group except for children who were placed as infants (Goerge and Wulczyn, 1990). For young children, placements with relatives greatly increased the duration of foster care, but they also increased the stability of foster care (i.e., prevented multiple placements). However, this was not the case for adolescents. This difference suggests that even relatives find it difficult to care for adolescents separated from their parents (Goerge, 1990).

Unfortunately, research also shows that between 20 and 30 percent of children discharged from foster care will eventually reenter foster care (Rzepnicki, 1987). A study of foster children in New York showed that those who were placed between the ages of 10 and 12 had the highest risk of reentry, and that those who spent less time in care (less than 90 days) were also more likely to reenter care (Wulczyn, 1991). Another 1985 study in Illinois showed that 10- to 14-year-olds were most likely to reenter foster care (Wulczyn et al., 1986).

THE CHILD WELFARE SYSTEM FOR ADOLESCENTS

Structure and Problems

Child welfare services are a public-private partnership that includes many players:

- the federal government, which provides some funding and policy direction;
- state and local governments, which spend most of the funds and are responsible for administration, case management, and, in many cases, provision of services;
- private charitable organizations, which provide services;
- individuals, sometimes relatives, for the provision of foster care; and
- the families and children themselves, who sometimes play an integral part in service planning and provision.

Although state and local agencies are often blamed when the system fails, its success depends on all of these players and, beyond them, on the whole of society.

Many professionals have observed that there are actually two child welfare systems—one for young children and another for adolescents. And while the system for young children is viewed as deeply flawed, the system for adolescents faces even more complex and formidable problems. One example is the problem of recruiting and retaining foster parents. It is increasingly difficult to find foster parents for young children because of the tremendous increase in the number of infants entering the system and, at the same time, a decrease in the number of potential full-time foster parents. It is even more difficult to find foster parents for adolescents, for whom family life is often a source of conflict and whose behaviors may be both destructive and difficult to control. Hence, more restrictive living arrangements like group homes and residential treatment centers are often necessary for adolescents.

Other problems arise from the need to help adolescents with the developmental transition from childhood to adulthood. This increases the types of services that are required and poses complicated problems of institutional authority and responsibility. The task of preparing adolescents for adulthood is difficult to institutionalize, especially when adolescents are struggling with the wishes and fears that independence implies. In addition, the child welfare system must cope with many medical, social, and psychological problems that were present but not adequately addressed at earlier stages of adolescents' development. Finally, there are issues that relate to the reasons that adolescents come into the foster care system.

Places of Service

Adolescents reside or receive services in a range of kinds of homes and institutions, and there is variation in how states, cities, and counties take responsibility for certain populations and places. Thus, adolescents who are at risk of unsatisfactory development may receive services at home, in foster care, in institutional or residential homes, in custody of the justice systems, or on the street.

At Home

A large number of adolescents come into contact with the child welfare system while still living in the homes of their parents. These youths often come into the system because they are abused or neglected or because they are part of a sibling group in which the younger children have been abused or neglected. Services may be provided to the parents, but it is unusual for children to be the recipients of services. Parents receive homemaker services, day care, and parent-training classes to help them learn "alternative forms of discipline" or other caretaking skills. Occasionally, parents and children are referred to counseling, particularly when a child has been sexually abused. But the system rarely provides services directly to the adolescent. It is believed that the youth's problems will be resolved when a parent changes his or her behavior or when some of the stresses in a parent's life are relieved.

Foster Care

The most widespread and intensive service provided by the child welfare system is foster care. Children in foster care may be placed in foster family homes, with relatives (who may or may not be paid), in foster homes for children with special needs, in group homes, in institutions, and in independent living situations (that are supervised to varying degrees). Stable foster care or foster care with relatives may be acceptable as a long-term arrangement in some cases, but foster care is usually intended as a temporary placement for children. The primary goal for a child in foster care is permanency, achieved through either reunification with parents, adoption, or independence.

Independent and Residential Homes

Older adolescents often enter independent living programs in order to prepare themselves for adulthood. Since many of these young people return to their former foster families or birth families at the age of majority, one need is to help them learn how to manage these ongoing relationships.

Special settings are being developed to enable pregnant adolescents and adolescent mothers to stay with their children and to learn basic parenting skills. In comparison with other pregnant teenagers and young parents, those who are in the child welfare system have fewer financial, social, and personal resources with which to approach the difficult task of learning how to be a parent. Youths with handicaps, including those with developmental disabilities, serious emotional disturbances, or medically complex conditions, are often placed in specialized child welfare settings, such as residential treatment centers, group homes, and specialized foster care.

In Custody

Delinquent or "problem" youths who were once in the child welfare system often shuttle between systems: detention or correctional centers operated by juvenile courts and correctional departments, on one side, and group homes, residential treatment facilities, and halfway houses operated by the child welfare or mental health system, on the other. Like homeless youths, delinquent youths have often been abused or neglected without coming to the attention of the child welfare system. Many of these youths are beyond the control of their parents or foster parents and beyond the control or interest of the child welfare system, which often acts to exclude them (see below). Local service providers usually are unable or unwilling to provide the variety and intensity of services that these youths need, and the community may not respond to troubled youths until incidents bring them before the courts. The corrections system then becomes the custodial parent.

On the Street

Homeless adolescent "street kids" are often either former clients of the child welfare system or victims of maltreatment that was not discovered. Some adolescents who are wards of the state are formally runaways, although they are in contact with child welfare workers. An estimated 10 to 33 percent of street kids have been in the child welfare system at some point, and about 10 percent are runaways from foster placements. People who work with street youths say that most of those who were never in foster care could have been reported to the child welfare system for acute or chronic abuse (particularly sexual abuse) and neglect. Although some homeless youths are served by youth shelters and transitional living programs, many become detached from the community institutions, such as the schools, recreation centers, and health care services that they formerly used. Many older youths—especially males—are excluded from shelters that serve women and younger children.

Exclusion of Adolescents

The proportion of 14- to 17-year-olds reported as abused or neglected in Illinois increased from 7.6 per 1,000 in 1981 to 10.4 per 1,000 in 1984 and then stabilized at around 14.0 per 1,000 between 1988 and 1990. For younger children, however, the incidence of abuse and neglect continued to climb throughout the 1980s: for newborns to 3-year-olds, the rates increased from 23.4 per 1,000 in 1981 to 54.4 per 1,000 in 1990 (Illinois Department of Children and Family Services, 1981-1990). This difference may reflect the increasing abuse and neglect of small children, but it may also reflect a conscious or unconscious bias against adolescents, or even an attempt to exclude adolescents from the child welfare system.

A recent study of child welfare decisions in Illinois found that agency investigators were significantly more likely to reject reports of physical abuse involving adolescents than those for younger children. Similarly, the age of the child was significantly correlated with the decision to substantiate physical abuse allegations; workers were less likely to substantiate physical abuse cases involving older children. This statistical finding was corroborated by interviews with investigators, who listed age as an important factor in making this decision (Smith et al., 1992:19): "When children are older, there is a presumption that the child has means of protection other than direct state intervention, therefore, there is a greater tolerance for some injury (as from spanking or punishment)." Some investigators noted that older children are partly at fault and "deserve" punishment (Smith et al., 1992). The bureaucratic rationale for including age as a criterion rests on two principles that are applied to each substantiation decision: (1) the need for parents to provide basic necessities (protection, supervision, food, shelter, clothing, education, and a sanitary environment) lessens with age and maturity; and (2) the risk to the child decreases as the child's own ability to protect himself, comprehend danger, or provide basic necessities increases (Illinois Department of Children and Family Services, 1991).

The effect of applying these principles is to limit adolescents' access to the child welfare system, which may in turn be a way for administrators and workers to cope with rising caseloads. In other states, ostensibly in response to fiscal constraints, the cutoff age for eligibility has been lowered from 21 to 18. However, these policies may also reflect a generally hostile attitude toward adolescents. They are often blamed for being victimized, the physical and psychological damage of the abuse they suffer is minimized, and they are held accountable for their own protection. In fact, adolescents who have been abused are less able to protect themselves from harm than adolescents who have not been abused and often precipitate interactions in which they will be victims or through which they will victimize others (Green, 1985).

Adolescent Outcomes

Available information indicates that adolescents who pass through the child welfare system are at high risk of educational failure, unemployment, emotional disturbance, and other negative outcomes. Although these adolescents were at risk before they entered the system—indeed, many entered the system precisely because they had already been abused or neglected or had become truants or runaways—findings nevertheless suggest that the child welfare system is unable to meet their needs or to prepare them adequately for independent, self-supporting adult life. There is evidence that the system excludes many adolescents in need, fails to protect them from known abuse, and abandons them to their fate.

A national survey (Shyne and Schroeder, 1978) of young adults, 2.5 to 4 years after their discharge from foster care at age 16 or older, showed a dismal picture when they were compared with either low-income youths or a cross-section of the general population. The survey also found that 54 percent of youths had returned to live with extended family members when discharged, which suggests that the child welfare system must continue working with biological families even if the child has spent a great deal of time in the system and even if family reunification while the adolescent is in the custody of the state is unlikely. The study also found that high school completion prior to discharge led to better outcomes, regardless of skills training, but that skills training while in foster care (including money management, credit, consumer education, and employment skills) also led to better outcomes (Shyne and Schroeder, 1978).

A study of some 1,200 youths 18.5 years old and older who were in substitute care in Cook County, Illinois, during July 1991 found that they had multiple service needs: they were at risk of being unemployed, undereducated, and unable to support themselves. A high percentage of the youths (42 percent) had been in the system for longer than 10 years. Nearly 17 percent of the sample (a considerably higher proportion than in the general population) were identified as having a developmental disability; 55 percent were no longer in a school program; and only 40 percent had completed high school. Of the females, 41 percent were mothers; 8 percent were pregnant at the time of the study; and teenage mothers were more likely to be out of school and unemployed than other adolescent females. Overall, about 50 percent of the youths had some job experience, but only 16.5 percent were working and attending school (Goerge and Osuch, 1992).

Many children placed in foster care are at high risk of being emotionally disturbed, in large part because they have been raised in pathological families in which they were abused or neglected

(Joint Commission on Mental Health of Children, 1969; Knitzer and Allen, 1978; Fanshel and Shinn, 1976). Victims of abuse and neglect are more likely to exhibit significant cognitive and social deficits; to have moderate or severely impaired neurological competency; to demonstrate highly aggressive and antisocial behavior; to have lowered self-esteem and prosocial behaviors; and also to be at higher risk for mental illness (Hoffman-Plotkin and Twentyman, 1984; Green et al., 1981; Egeland et al., 1983; Main and George, 1985; Patterson et al., 1989; Kaufman and Cicchetti, 1989; Tuma, 1989). Children are also at risk when the parents are substance abusers, mentally ill, or welfare dependent (Institute of Medicine, 1989; Kaufman and Cicchetti, 1989).

Of course, the separation of a child from his or her family is traumatic and may itself cause emotional disturbance (Bowlby, 1973); in addition, the child may receive poor-quality care (Bowlby, 1973; Wolkind and Rutter, 1985). Children in foster care are at increased risk of suffering from emotional disturbance, although these findings may be the result of increased attention paid to children who are removed from their homes (Institute of Medicine, 1989). Discontinuous relationships (multiple placements) may affect the psychological health of children and adolescents in a variety of ways (Wolkind and Rutter, 1985).

Despite this evidence that foster children are at high risk of being emotionally disturbed, the child welfare system has not developed a comprehensive mental health delivery system for foster children. A child usually receives either restrictive institutional care (if he or she has been disruptive in less restrictive placements) or no mental health services at all. Services other than placement are in short supply for foster children (Goerge and Kranz, 1988; Schuerman et al., 1990).

Similarly, adolescents in the child welfare and juvenile justice systems are often underachievers, but little systematic research has been done to document the reasons for their educational problems. One recent study showed that adolescent foster children were twice as likely than were younger children to be in special education classes, primarily because adolescent foster children are more likely than younger foster children to be diagnosed as handicapped or behavior disordered (Goerge et al., 1991).

ISSUES IN PROVIDING SERVICES TO ADOLESCENTS

The definition of adolescence also remains a problem for the field of child welfare. Without a consistent definition, it is difficult to provide answers to several standard questions: When should certain types of services begin? When is a child nearly an adult and therefore appropriate for independent living programs? When can an adolescent be released from the system? When is it necessary to transfer an adolescent to adult human services?

It has been noted that the physical changes of adolescence begin earlier with each passing decade. Also, young adolescents are increasingly likely to be held accountable for their actions by the criminal justice system (see Chapter 8). In contrast to these trends, many young adults must endure long periods of preparation for occupations that will support them and their families, and they therefore continue to require economic and emotional support from families well into their 20s. As a result, the child welfare system faces growing but conflicting demands to both expand and contract its pool of services and clients.

Stable Care and Independence

The need for a permanent family is one that most Americans embrace without question, and research shows that unstable alternative living arrangements compound the effects of a child's separation from his or her birth family. Public policies now attempt to ensure children a permanent alternative when their birth parents cannot care for them. However, adoption specialists have discovered that a sizable proportion of the children in foster care have other problems that limit their chances for adoption. Consequently, foster families and relatives have been urged to adopt children, some of whom have needs that might require ongoing investment in special services and supports.

Optimism concerning the adoptability of most children has been tempered as families have needed more services than they could afford, and in some instances returned children whose needs overwhelmed them. Similarly, many adolescents who were previously consigned to long-term-care institutions (those with mental retardation, physical handicaps, incorrigible behavior, and emotional disturbance) now live in communities that are served by public schools. Yet, in many instances, schools and community institutions have been unable to adapt to the changes in the populations they are expected to accommodate, forcing families and children to cope without much help. The permanency planning and deinstitutionalization movements in child welfare have also placed many children with multiple service needs in community schools, recreation centers, and special service settings where staff resources are insufficient to meet their needs.

Taking care of children until their families can provide for them, or until they can function as independent adults, is part of the mission of a child welfare system. Over the last several decades, however, child development research has complicated the debate about what it means to "take care" of a child. There is consensus that it implies more than shelter, food, clothing, and basic education, but there are competing views about what other needs must be met in childhood if children are to become independent adults. The answers depend in part on what constitutes independence in complex societies in which even the most privileged and well-cared-for children are seldom fully independent at the age of majority.

Definitions of "independence" or "needs" cannot be arrived at solely by scientific means. Embedded in both words are social and class concepts that raise questions about whether needs or independence is different for the child welfare population than for children in general. Most children who are served by the child welfare system come from low-income families in which unmet needs and inadequate preparation for independence are common. Should services aim only to ensure that their chances are no worse than those of children in the class and milieu from which they came? How many needs should be met and by whom? Should medical, psychological, and educational problems be pursued vigorously? When a change of foster home is necessary, should emphasis be placed on keeping children close to service providers who are addressing their educational or mental health needs? Should services continue until every possible benefit has been achieved? Does it make sense to provide services to older adolescents if the child's case may soon be closed? These are potentially costly choices, and therefore difficult ones, yet it is clear from the limited existing data that children who are touched by child welfare systems have many more unmet—and possibly chronic—needs than other poor children from stable families.

Programs that prepare older youth for independence face challenges that are often overwhelming in light of scarce resources. For example, many youths have come to independent living programs with histories of unmet health needs, impoverished life experiences, inadequate social and academic skills, and poor self-regulatory mechanisms that conspire to defeat the best-organized efforts to prepare them for independent living. If achieving independence takes so long for most contemporary youth who have economic and psychological support from their families, it is not surprising that 18- and 19-year-olds who have personal limitations and lack family supports often fail the test of fully independent functioning.

Short-Term Services and Long-Term Needs

The vast majority of services currently provided to adolescents in the child welfare system are intended to be short-term services. Some are used longer than intended and even become permanent features in the lives of the affected children and families (e.g., foster care placements). Others are as short term in practice as in intent. Family preservation services, for example, are designed to last between 3 and 6 months. Transitional and independent living programs, while sometimes designed to last up to 2 years, are still short relative to their goals (teaching life skills to older youth) and their timing (at the end of a foster care experience, after the chronic problems of some adolescents have gone unaddressed for years). Most of these services are designed primarily to protect children rather than to solve the problems of children and families.

Those problems often require longer, more intensive intervention. Children who enter the child welfare care system are most often the victims of severe abuse or neglect, which places them at risk of negative developmental outcomes. However, many victims of abuse or neglect are not placed in foster care and do not even receive an immediate response by a child welfare agency (Stagner, 1992). Furthermore, with the possible exception of sex abuse, victimized children rarely receive therapeutic services. A recent Illinois study of service provision to both intact families and families whose children had been placed outside their homes revealed that only 50 percent of the families in each group received services while they were in the child welfare system. For most of these families, the services were not delivered until the family had been in the system for more than 6 months (Schuerman et al., 1990). In many cases, the lack of response is due in part to an insufficiency of service resources in the face of increasing numbers of substantiated cases of abuse or neglect.

The sheer number of adolescents with problems will result in some failures. Criticism of the foster care system often highlights incidents of abuse or neglect that occur in foster care. Similarly, newspapers often carry spectacular stories about children who have been harmed or killed after being left with abusive parents by child protection workers. At the same time, however, critics also point to the trauma of separation for children removed from their parents. Most children in foster care, while they may wish to return to abusive or neglectful parents, see that they benefit from being out of the home and living with foster parents. In a study of 60 young adolescent foster children, more than half of them thought that their removal from their homes might be preventing further abuse and was an overall help to the family. Nearly half of them believed the problems in their families would have gotten worse or stayed the same had their placement not occurred. They described their lives in substitute care positively and commented on the increased safety and consistency of care in their foster homes (Johnson et al., 1990).

There is no evidence to support the claim that children in foster care would be better off at home. On the contrary, the limited evidence from methodologically sound studies on the effects of foster care suggests that many children show improvement while in foster care on several developmental measures, and that foster care compares favorably to leaving children at home (Fanshel and Shinn, 1976; Wald et al., 1988). Nevertheless, almost all child welfare professionals believe that it is preferable to leave children with their natural parents whenever possible, although they may disagree about when this is possible. Some argue that if the comparative effects of foster care versus staying at home are not clearly understood, children should remain at home on the basis of value preferences or cost savings. Unfortunately, early studies of intervention models intended to prevent out-of-home placements have been faulted for using weak research designs (Frankel, 1988; Rossi, 1990). Subsequent evaluations with more rigorous designs have failed to find significant effects over time from such strategies (Yuan, 1990; Feldman, 1990; Schuerman et al., 1992).

CONCLUSIONS

No one in the child welfare field holds any illusions that the system is currently able to provide adequate resources to promote adolescent development or that it has been able to do so for the past decade. The absolute number of adolescents in the system has not changed, but their share of the available resources has dropped, and the increasing numbers of younger children in the system have shifted the focus of public attention and reform away from adolescents. Achieving the goal of adequate development and preparation for adulthood in the child welfare system will require additional interest in and commitment to adolescents. It will also require additional funding, although this seems unlikely at a time when states' budgets are severely constrained.

REFERENCES

Bowlby, J.
1973 *Separation: Anxiety and Anger.* New York: Basic Books, Inc.

Egeland, B., M. Erickson, and L.A. Sroufe
1983 The developmental consequence of different patterns of maltreatment. *Child Abuse and Neglect* 7:459-469.

Fanshel, D., and E.B. Shinn
1976 *Children in Foster Care: A Longitudinal Investigation.* New York: Columbia University Press.

Feldman, L.
1990 Evaluating the Impact of Family Preservation Services in New Jersey. Bureau of Research, Evaluation, and Quality Assurance, New Jersey Division of Youth and Family Services, New Jersey.

Frankel, H.
1988 Family-centered, home-based services in child protection: a review of the research. *Social Service Review* 62:137-157.

Goerge, R.M.
1990 The reunification process in substitute care. *Social Service Review* 64(3):422-457.

Goerge, R., and R. Kranz
1988 Appendix A. Data Requirements for Planning Child and Adolescent Mental Health Services in Illinois. Chapin Hall Center for Children, University of Chicago.

Goerge, R.M., and R. Osuch
1992 Older Youths in Foster Care: Transition into Adulthood: A Report to the Illinois Department of Children and Family Services. Chapin Hall Center for Children, University of Chicago.

Goerge, R.M., and F. Wulczyn
1990 Public Policy and the Dynamics of Foster Care: A Multi-State Study of Placement Histories, New York, Illinois and Michigan. Chapin Hall Center for Children, University of Chicago.

Goerge, R.M., J. Van Voorhis, S. Grant, K. Casey, and M. Robinson
1991 Special Education Experiences of Foster Children: An Empirical Study. Chapin Hall Center for Children, University of Chicago.

Green, A.
1985 Children traumatized by physical abuse. Pp. 135-154 in S. Eth and R.S. Pynoos, eds., *Post-Traumatic Stress Disorder in Children.* Washington, D.C.: American Psychiatric Press, Inc.

Green, A., K. Voeller, R. Gaines, and J. Kubie
1981 Neurological impairment in maltreated children. *Child Abuse and Neglect* 5:129-134.

Hoffman-Plotkin, D., and C.T. Twentyman
1984 A multimodal assessment of behavioral and cognitive deficits in abused and neglected preschoolers. *Child Development* 55:794-802.

Illinois Department of Children and Family Services
1981- Child Abuse and Neglect Statistics. Illinois Department of Children
1990 and Family Services, Chicago, Ill.
1991 Policy Transmittal 91.2. Illinois Department of Children and Family Services, Chicago, Ill.

Institute of Medicine
1989   *Research on Children and Adolescents with Mental, Behavioral and Developmental Disorders.* Washington, D.C.: National Academy Press.
Johnson, P., C. Yoken, and R. Voss
1990   *Foster Care Placement: The Child's Perspective.* Chicago: Chapin Hall Center for Children, University of Chicago.
Joint Commission on Mental Health of Children
1969   *Crisis in Child Mental Health: Challenge for the 1970s.* New York: Harper & Row.
Katz, M.
1986   *In the Shadow of the Poorhouse: A Social History of Welfare in America.* New York: Basic Books.
Kaufman, J., and D. Cicchetti
1989   Effects of maltreatment on school-age children's socioemotional development: assessments in a day-camp setting. *Developmental Psychology* 25(4):516-524.
Knitzer, J., and M.L. Allen
1978   *Children Without Homes: An Examination of Public Responsibility to Children in Out-of-Home Care.* Washington, D.C.: Children's Defense Fund
Maas, H.S., and R.E.J. Engler
1959   *Children in Need of Parents.* New York: Columbia University Press.
Main, M., and C. George
1985   Responses of abused and disadvantaged toddlers to distress in agemates: a study in the day care setting. *Developmental Psychology* 21(3):407-412.
Maluccio, A., and E. Fein
1983   Permanency planning: a redefinition. *Child Welfare* 62:195-201.
Meckel, R.
1985   Protecting the innocents: age segregation and the early child welfare movement. *Social Service Review* 59:455-475.
Patterson, G.R., B.D. DeBarsyshe, and E. Ramsey
1989   A developmental perspective on antisocial behavior. *American Psychologist* 44(2):329-335.
Rossi, R.J.
1990   Demographic accounting for special education. *Social Indicators Research* 22(1):1-30.
Rzepnicki, T.L.
1987   Recidivism of foster children returned to their own homes: a review and new directions for research. *Social Service Review* 61:56-70.
Schuerman, J.R., P. Johnson, M.W. Stagner, and S. Smith
1990   Study of Non-Placement Service Provision in DCFS: A Report to the Illinois Department of Children and Family Services. Chapin Hall Center for Children, University of Chicago.
Schuerman, J.R., T.L. Rzepnicki, J.H. Littell, and S. Budde
1992   Implementation issues. *Children and Youth Services Review* 14(1/2):193-206.
Shyne, A., and A. Schroeder
1978   *National Study of Social Services to Children and Their Families— Overview.* Washington, D.C.: Children's Bureau, U.S. Department of Health and Human Services.

Smith, S.L., Q. Sullivan, and A. Cohen
    1992   Final Project Report of Handling of Abuse Reports from Mandated Reporters. A report to the Illinois Department of Children and Family Services, Chicago.
Spergel, I.A., and M.A. Hartnett
    1990   Evaluation of the Illinois Department of Children and Family Services (DCFS) Comprehensive Community Based Youth Services System (CCBYS). Chapin Hall Center for Children, University of Chicago.
Stagner, M.W.
    1992   *An Analysis of Client Transitions in a Child Welfare Caseload.* Chicago: University of Chicago.
Tatara, T.
    1992   Characteristics of Children in Substitute and Adoptive Care: A Statistical Summary of the VCIS National Child Welfare Data Base Based on FY 82 through FY 88 Data. American Public Welfare Association, Washington, D.C.
Tuma, J.M.
    1989   Mental health services for children: the state of the art. *American Psychologist* 44(2):188-199.
Wald, M.S., J.M. Carlsmith, P.H. Leiderman, and R.D. French
    1988   *Protecting Abused and Neglected Children.* Stanford, Calif.: Stanford University Press.
Wolkind, S., and M. Rutter
    1985   Separation, loss and family relationships. Pp. 34-57 in *Child and Adolescent Psychiatry: Modern Approaches.* Oxford: Blackwell Scientific Publications.
Wulczyn, F.
    1991   Caseload dynamics and foster care reentry. *Social Service Review* 65(1):133-156.
Wulczyn, F., R.M. Goerge, M.F. Testa, and M.A. Hartnett
    1986   Substitute care in Illinois. In M. Testa and E. Lawlor, eds., *State of the Child 1985.* Chicago: Chapin Hall Center for Children, University of Chicago.
Yuan, Y.T.
    1990   *Evaluation of AB 1562 In-Home Care Demonstration Projects*, Volumes I and II. Sacramento, Calif.: Walter MacDonald and Associates, Inc.

10

Good Practice: Community-Based Interventions and Services

As detailed throughout this report, many of the major institutions, or settings, in which adolescents are growing up are unable to provide the guidance and support young people need for positive development. Policies that might change high-risk settings into ones that promote adolescent development have been neglected, and existing policies often diminish the viability of families and neighborhoods. The urgent need for increased support of the major settings of adolescent life as well as very basic changes within these institutions has been argued throughout the report. The primary institutions that serve youth—health, schools, employment, training—are crucial and we must begin with helping them respond more effectively to contemporary adolescent needs. Effective responses will involve pushing the boundaries of these systems, encouraging collaboration between them and reducing the number of adolescents whose specialized problems cannot be met through primary institutions.

Even if categorical systems become more effective, however, some adolescents will continue to experience problems that transcend the response capacities of primary institutions. For these adolescents and their families, specialized service programs may fill the gaps or compensate for failures in major life settings (Schorr et al., 1991). This chapter reviews the experience of service programs that attempt to meet the needs of adolescents experiencing complex, often health- or life-compromising problems. Information for the chapter was developed through a special symposium held in New York City and attended by the directors of adolescent programs that are thought to be particularly successful in turning around the lives of young people who are caught in a web of failure. The panel also heard from a number of adolescents served by the programs. This chapter summarizes what was learned at the symposium as well as through our review of the growing literature on this subject.

There are numerous examples of locally designed and operated programs through which communities are beginning to address the risks that face many of America's adolescents. Many local efforts aim at supporting families and strengthening communities. The commonality among such efforts is that they seek to enable and empower parents and community residents to increase their capabilities to nurture young people. Communities have also implemented a range of innovative initiatives in response to the risks that often arise from service systems themselves. The innovative strategies, and the experiences of the local practitioners that created them, may provide models for national programs and policies in the years ahead. They certainly offer a rich lode of examples that should be drawn upon by primary systems as they evolve in response to current needs. All of the examples of "good practice" exhibit a number of common characteristics. First and foremost, their services for adolescents are comprehensive: the programs transcend categorical labels, organizations, and funding sources to bring together a coherent package of service to young people. Whether programs are offered in a single site or through interagency collaboration, the goal is to provide services that ensure that the emotional, recreational, academic, and vocational needs of adolescents are explicitly addressed. Comprehensiveness also means that these programs provide adolescents from high-risk settings with the developmental opportunities that are too often missing in their lives.

This chapter describes innovative programs in three broad categories: (1) strengthening families and communities; (2) improving institutional services; and (3) comprehensive service for adolescent development. We use the label "good practice" to identify those programs and interventions that have strong research and theoretical justification. Such judgments should also be supported by evaluation research, but few of the programs have been rigorously evaluated. In other cases, new evaluation methodologies must be developed that adequately assess the quality and outcomes of multipurpose programs or comprehensive service systems (see Chapter 11).

STRENGTHENING FAMILIES AND NEIGHBORHOODS

Assisting adolescents requires attention to the settings—families and neighborhoods—that they experience on a daily basis. In good practice initiatives, community residents—both adults and, increasingly, adolescents—are viewed as integral resources who can contribute substantially to the change process. That is, good practice programs focus on the conditions for change—engagement and empowerment—rather than the problems per se of families, neighborhoods, and young people. They provide participants with legitimate opportunities to contribute in ways that are directly relevant to their concerns and interests.

Supporting Parents

If parents are not supported, they have a diminished capacity to support their children (Bronfenbrenner, 1978). In response to the conditions described in Chapters 3 and 4, many communities have implemented family support programs directed toward low-income parents. Such parents not only suffer from economic hardship, but also face additional challenges arising from the lack of personal networks—friends, coworkers, and extended family members—that contributes directly to emotional distress and continued isolation from the labor market (Cochran, 1990). Family support programs vary tremendously, but one common feature is an attempt to "extend" families by helping parents form both functional and emotional attachments to other parents. Most programs also have educational components, aimed at enhancing parenting skills, and many have training components to help parents enter, or progress within, the labor market.

Traditionally, family support programs focused on parent education, as in the case of Head Start, with the goal of teaching parents effective caregiving skills. Over time, the goals broadened to include a range of activities and strategies, the development of personal networks, and peer supports for childrearing and employment. Evaluation research indicates the potential strengths of family support programs: when programs are well implemented, they are found to enhance the emotional well-being of parents, broaden their social networks, and facilitate child development (Cochran, 1990; Kagan et al., 1987; Weiss, 1987).

There are an estimated 2,000 family support programs across the country, most of which are implemented by nonprofit organizations (Zigler and Black, 1989). Unfortunately, only a small minority provide family support for parents with adolescent children, especially those in high school, and these programs tend to be taught in class-like settings and aimed at middle-class families. Some of the more innovative programs not only focus on imparting caregiving skills, but also help parents cope with stress in their lives—such as fear for children's well-being—and difficulties in funding appropriate services for their children. Such programs help parents develop personal networks through which parents can help solve problems of guidance, monitoring, and communication (Small, 1990).

The increasing number of parents unable to care for their children has overwhelmed the child welfare system (see Chapter 9). Absent economic supports and employment training (which are often unavailable), a number of "family preservation" or "homebuilder" programs seek to prevent the placement of children in foster care or other supervised settings. Typically, a trained case manager provides a family with intense short-term counseling and parent education, arranging for a broader spectrum of child welfare, health, and mental health services as needed. Evaluations of family preservation programs remain open to multiple interpretations, and their effectiveness is disputed. Some studies suggest that the program works better with families with young children, rather than families with adolescents (Rossi, 1991; Farrow, 1987).

Interagency collaboration is often necessary to provide comprehensive service to families and their children. In Ventura County, California, for example, a project seeks to strengthen families' ability to manage and to care for adolescents with behavioral and emotional disorders by linking schools and agencies that provide mental health services—welfare, juvenile justice, and health. Staff and funding are integrated across agencies to support the program, and case management ensures continuity of care. Evaluation indicates that the project decreased rates of out-of-home placement and facilitated earlier return of adolescents to their home and school when placement did occur: since 1985, out-of-county juvenile justice and social services placements have been reduced by 46 percent in Ventura County (U.S. Office of Technology Assessment, 1991).

Teenage mothers are often poor and lack the knowledge, skills, and social support needed to be good parents. Further, they commonly lack the education, training, and connections to employment that would enable them to obtain jobs and become self-sufficient. One result is the high proportion of welfare dependency among adolescent mothers discussed in Chapter 2. Exemplary programs directed toward teenage mothers are therefore unusually comprehensive—seeking to impart the parenting skills discussed above, but also to assist the mothers over the numerous hurdles standing between them and self-sufficiency, such as job training, child care, and transportation. Some family resource centers—for example, those operated by Friends of the Family (Commission on Chapter 1, 1992)—have had some success in providing essential services in a single site and offering referrals for services that cannot be provided. Two exemplary programs—Project Redirection and New Chance—have been successful in the complex task of arranging necessary services.

Project Redirection operated at 11 sites, delivering services to very low-income teenagers who were either pregnant or parents of young children. It linked participants with existing educational and support services in the community and also provided direct services, including parenting workshops, peer group support sessions, counseling, and mentoring. In a 5-year follow-up, Project Redirection participants had better outcomes than a comparison group on measures of weekly wages, welfare recipiency, and parenting skills. In addition, their children showed better cognitive skills and fewer behavioral problems. Nonetheless, disadvantage was still prevalent: fewer than one-half of the participants had completed high school, only one-third were working full time, and one-half were receiving Aid to Families with Dependent Children (AFDC) (Polit et al., 1985).

Building on the Project Redirection experience, New Chance offers similar services to highly disadvantaged young mothers. Rather than using a "brokered service" or "case management" model, New Chance provides the majority of services in a program setting, with an emphasis on direct services to children in a developmental day care setting. Although studies of project effects are not yet available, lessons have been learned regarding the implementation of family support programs. For example, while the parenting programs are relatively easy to put into place, the implementation of employment and training and family planning components is more difficult. Participant absenteeism remains a significant problem, requiring extensive outreach with highly skilled staff (Quint et al., 1991).

Mobilizing Neighborhoods

Other local initiatives aim not to strengthen specific families, but instead, to rebuild and strengthen neighborhoods. This approach is based on historical evidence indicating that sustained change occurs most readily when local residents invest themselves and their resources in the effort (Cochran, 1990; McKnight and Kretzman, 1992; Davies, 1991).

Successful neighborhood mobilization has occurred through at least four mechanisms: (1) community organizing and development, (2) collaboration in service delivery, (3) the implementation of community-based programs, and (4) the involvement of families in school governance and instruction. Fundamental to each strategy is the importance of building on existing resources and engaging the people—adult and adolescent residents—typically excluded from such efforts.

Community organizing and development initiatives run the gamut from simple networking and coalition building to resource leveraging. The common focus is an effort to realign the political, financial, and institutional forces in neighborhoods. In the most distressed neighborhoods, there is often a need for residents to coordinate traditional grassroots organizing with larger initiatives in the form of community development corporations (CDCs). CDCs, often organized and funded by public-private collaborations, provide service not currently supported by government. For example, a CDC might undertake a housing rehabilitation program that renovates existing housing stock, which it then rents to citizens. Another housing program might seek to turn the program into a community-based effort that requires potential homeowners to participate in the renovation program in many ways, from management to remodeling (Leavitt and Saegert, 1989; Rivlin, 1991).

CDCs often seek to enhance the beauty and safety of neighborhoods as a strategy for retaining residents and businesses. In one area of New York City, for example, the Grand Central Partnership supplements municipal services with a 50-person security force, a 40-person sanitation force, and an extensive program for homeless persons. Another partnership has renovated a major park in Manhattan, providing a place for adults and young people to relax and play in safety. Other CDC programs broaden the array of services available to parents through the provision of family support and education, child care, and after-school programs (Edelman and Radin, 1991; Leinberger, 1992).

Increasingly, programs for young people are also seen as an integral part of community organizing and development efforts. The rationale is two-sided: on one side, youth are viewed as a threat to the viability of housing and community cohesion; on the other side, young people are untapped resources for positive change and can often make irreplaceable contributions to their own neighborhoods. For these reasons, some CDCs operate day care, after-school tutoring programs, child-family activities, recreational programs, employment and training programs, and counseling (Sullivan and DeGiovanni, 1991).

The provision of services through collaboration between federal, state, and community-based entities is another method of neighborhood mobilization. Programs of the U.S. Office of Economic Opportunity were developed on this model. One barrier is that government agencies are hesitant to share authority with neighborhood residents, who are too often viewed only as prospective clients. Nonetheless, collaboration has long been the mechanism for delivering employment and training services, and in recent years similar programs have successfully delivered youth-oriented services traditionally provided by the police, justice system, social services, and health and mental health agencies (Spergel, 1976; Sauber, 1983; Eisenhower Foundation, 1990).

Collaborative or jointly organized services can offer tangible benefits not easily accomplished through more traditional modes. However, successful implementation demands concrete knowledge of the neighborhoods in which programs operate, including resource availability, past history and present conditions, income mix, and cultural norms and beliefs. Consequently, using neighborhood residents as professional staff and as members of governing bodies better ensures that the problems defined and the solutions offered are consistent with local conditions. Collaboration also appears to enhance the attachment of the involved adults to the neighborhood, and in some studies services have been provided more efficiently and with improved client outcomes (Camino, 1992; Cochran, 1990; Suttles, 1972).

It must be remembered, however, that the most beneficial effect of community initiatives is likely to be on the individuals involved in the effort. The tangible, but modest, achievements of CDCs benefit a small number of people and are easily overwhelmed by the major structural changes in neighborhoods as discussed in Chapter 4. We know far too little about the ecology of urban change—why certain neighborhoods implode into disorganization and disintegration while others do not.

As a response to the unsuccessful efforts of the juvenile justice system in decreasing crime and hostility, many community organizations have become directly involved in providing services to offenders. Often, community and justice system collaborations focus on juvenile restitution programs, in which young people are ordered by the court to pay restitution to their victims or to engage in community service to pay back the neighborhood. While these programs have benefits for young people and crime victims, their potential may be even greater as a vehicle for mobilizing neighborhoods.

In the Juvenile Justice Alliance in Oregon, government officials and community organizations have created a model for services to all young people. The restitution program, for instance, has led to coalitions between business and labor organizations, trained a large cadre of paid and volunteer staff, and developed ties to organizations not traditionally associated with juvenile justice or youth service, such as forestry, fish and game, and wildlife groups (Bazemore, 1988). Other interventions have focused on providing new opportunities for young people, mediating with schools and law enforcement agencies to change policies, and developing job and community service programs. On the whole, programs that emphasize advocacy and institutional mediation appear to be more effective than approaches based on mobilizing residents to provide traditional educational and social services (Fagan, 1987).

Community-based youth programs are often implemented to fill the void in adolescents' lives that results from extremely stressed families and to provide developmental experiences typically offered by schools, health programs, or employment training agencies. Such programs play a key role in development by giving young people a sense of membership, a chance to develop supportive relationships with a range of adults and peers, and an opportunity to develop functional and interpersonal skills necessary for healthy adolescent development (Pittman and Wright, 1991). Not surprisingly, community-based youth programs have been found to be an integral factor contributing to resiliency and positive self-identities among young people (Werner and Smith, 1982; Heath and McLaughlin, 1991).

Viewed as neighborhood institutions, these diverse organizations—ranging in size from volunteer-run organizations to multi-million-dollar entities—can collectively provide young people with a critical array of opportunities and services, as well as a place to form interpersonal relations with adults and peers. Because community-based services typically make little or no distinction between clients that are served, they are able to implement programs that remove stigmatizing distinctions like "undeserving" or "high risk." Often staffed by neighborhood residents and volunteers, these programs have sought to fill the gaps by providing services not extensively supported by government and not readily available elsewhere: group counseling, life-skills training, family counseling, substance abuse education, and supportive services for abused children (Sauber, 1983; Pittman and Cahill, 1992; Independent Sector, 1992; Littell and Wynn, 1989; Wynn et al., 1987). They can also serve as protective institutions that promote adolescent development and prevent entry into the child welfare and criminal justice systems (Bronfenbrenner, 1979; Garbarino, 1985; Pittman and Wright, 1991). Neighborhoods can also be directly strengthened through the contributions of young people. Community action youth programs demonstrate the value of using local residents in the effort to rebuild neighborhoods. In El Puente, for example, they have initiated a recycling program, formed an advocacy/action group ("The Toxic Avengers") to oppose the concentrations of toxic wastes in their neighborhood, established an AIDS education drama group, and conducted a measles immunization campaign. At YouthBuild, participants have organized a construction company that renovates city-owned buildings and are developing a local child care center. In other programs that employ youth service, youth are conducting community needs assessments, renovating housing, serving as tutors, and providing service to elders, to list only a few examples (Nathan and Kielsmeir, 1991; Quinn, 1992).

The school building is an integral part of all communities. Not only is it the setting in which the majority of young people spend each day, but ideally, it is also a place where parents, other neighborhood adults, and service providers can form personal relationships and collaborate in the change process. Hence, changing schools can help strengthen neighborhoods. Furthermore, the active involvement of parents can help to transform the culture of the school itself (Lightfoot, 1975; Davies, 1991). Family involvement in all phases of schooling—from governance to the instructional process—provides direct mechanisms of parent empowerment.

Several recent initiatives seek to engage parents and school staff in a collaborative efforts:

• The social development model creates organizational structures whereby stakeholders (students, parents, teachers) meet on a regular basis to make decisions regarding the climate of schools, with an emphasis on ensuring that the academic and social needs of all students are explicitly addressed in all school activities (Comer, 1988).

• In the accelerated schools model, school stakeholders collaborate in creating school structures and instruction consistent with "new" school norms, with an emphasis on reflection, trust, risk taking, and communication (Levin, 1987).

• The schools reaching out model emphasizes experimentation and "participatory inquiry" among stakeholders, aimed at identifying the major barriers to quality education in schools, and developing consensus and plans to address priority issues (Davies, 1991).

Moreover, family involvement has direct benefits for students. Program evaluations consistently find that such involvement enhances the academic achievement of students, particularly when parents take an active role as classroom tutors or engage in structured home-based instruction that is complementary to, and reinforces, classroom instruction (Epstein, 1991a; Swap, 1990; Eastman, 1988).

Regardless of the type of involvement, schools must confront the fact that low-income and minority parents are often isolated from and distrustful of schools. In part, this lack of involvement is because it is difficult for parents to arrange for child care for younger children or time off from work. But it also stems from the structure of schools: teachers are granted little time to work with parents and are given little training to learn how to engage parents. It is also due in part to explicit and implicit messages from the school that parents are not welcome (Lightfoot, 1975; Lareau, 1989; McLaughlin and Shields, 1987; Slaughter and Schneider, 1986; Boutte, 1992).

Yet for each of these barriers, many communities and school districts have implemented programs with demonstrated effectiveness. A fundamental ingredient for success is that schools must create opportunities for partnership—teachers need time for collaboration, and principals need to instill an organizational ethos that encourages the development of sustained relationships. For example, studies of Chapter 1 and Head Start have shown that teachers and parents will engage in governance activities if they are given genuine opportunities to participate in key decision-making forums. Studies of home-school partnership consistently demonstrate that parents will become involved if teachers expect participation and provide parents with sufficient interpersonal and technical support (Epstein, 1991b; Zeldin, 1990; Krasnow, 1991; Swap, 1990).

IMPROVING INSTITITIONAL SERVICES

In this section we highlight some good practice initiatives—in the areas of health, education, and employment training—that seek to replace current institutional practice with alternatives better suited to the developmental needs of adolescents.

New Settings for Health Services

The U.S. health system, built around and financially sustained by the treatment of pathology and physical disorders, provides strong incentives for service to be provided in traditional settings, such as hospitals and physician offices. But these settings are not well suited to the provision of comprehensive health services and are often inaccessible for low-income adolescents and their families. A number of communities have attempted to fill this gap by developing alternative school- and community-based centers—some are linked to and supported by hospitals, others are freestanding.

There are only about 400 school-linked health programs in the country, which serve less than 1 percent of all adolescents. School-linked health centers convey a number of benefits. They are readily accessible and provide a confidential setting in a familiar environment, and they integrate health and education to promote preventive interventions. Sports and health examinations and immunizations are often the most frequently offered services. School-linked health centers rarely provide contraception or refer pregnant teenagers for abortions; reviewers often note that the weakest components of school-based adolescent health centers are their family planning programs (Kirby and Waszak, 1989; Dryfoos, 1988; Levy and Shepardson, 1992).

Research indicates that the centers reach a large percentage of the student population in the schools where they are located and that they identify significant numbers of untreated or unrecognized health conditions. Some centers have demonstrated positive effects in delivering preventive services with measurable outcomes, such as reduction in pregnancy rates, delay in onset of sexual activity, increased contraceptive use, and improved school attendance (Dryfoos, 1990; Packard Foundation, 1992).

The heaviest demand on school-linked health services is for individual counseling to address adolescent depression, stress, and substance use. However, the lack of insurance coverage for these conditions means that most centers can only provide crisis intervention and short-term treatment. In response, some schools are forming collaborative programs with local family support and mental health services to provide counseling and early intervention services to students, both self-referrals and those identified by teachers. Because the centers value confidentiality and are easily accessible, they are able to provide preventive services to many young people who would otherwise not have them (Lorian et al., 1984; Orr, 1987; Millstein, 1988; G. Reynolds, 1991, personal communication; A. Shirley, 1992, personal communication).

Community-based multiservice centers (e.g., drop-in centers, life options centers, community clinics) provide access to both in-school and out-of-school young people. Community centers are accessible to dropouts and are not subject to school regulations, but they are not linked to a primary institutional base. They are able to consolidate and link services, however, and they often use an array of creative strategies to make services attractive, relevant, and developmentally appropriate for youth. At the highly regarded New York City programs, The Hub and The Door, for example, health services are supplemented with peer-based interventions and supports, mentoring, and classes in the arts, life skills, and job and career training.

The greatest strength of community-based centers is their emphasis on outreach. The most vulnerable teenagers are often isolated, living either on their own or in dysfunctional family settings. Such youths are unlikely to engage the health system, through either a school or community clinic; street-based outreach is the most effective means for reaching them. However, this strategy for adolescents from high-risk settings requires aggressive outreach by talented providers who know and are trusted in the community; see, for example, Joseph (1992) on outreach programs for adolescents at risk for HIV infection (also, K. Hein, 1991, personal communication). For example, midnight basketball leagues in New York appear to be effective settings for conducting outreach to populations at risk for health problems (M. Cahill, 1992, personal communication). Regardless of the setting in which service is provided, however, five strategies appear most effective in ensuring accessibility and outreach (H. Spivak, 1992, personal communication):

1. modifying hours of operation to include service after school and in the evening;
2. locating services in settings familiar to youth;

3. having a culturally diverse staff;

4. developing collaborative outreach and service provision efforts between health institutions and other settings, such as courts and police, public housing corporations, youth centers, recreation programs, and schools; and

5. consolidating services into comprehensive, multiservice environments.

New Academic Approaches

Perhaps the most important step in fostering adolescent development and achievement is the improvement of education. Beginning with *A Nation at Risk* (National Commission on Excellence in Education, 1983), there has been a stream of highly negative assessments of the education system. Schools have responded by broadening the range of programs that they offer. Indeed, the education system is becoming the dominant setting for preventive health services, as well as for substance abuse prevention, sex education, and violence prevention programs. The call for greater emphasis on basic skills has led to broader requirements for courses in math, reading, and science. Increasingly, schools are integrating "work-readiness" components into their curriculums. Many schools have also sought to improve accountability and performance from principals, teachers, students, and parents: for example, schools are beginning to implement policies of school-based management, parent choice, and common curriculums as mechanisms for accountability and vehicles for change.

Changes in policy are important only if they contribute to more effective school and classroom environments in which students are strongly motivated to work hard at challenging learning tasks. As yet, there has been relatively little national attention to issues of school organization and instruction, although these are clearly critical to schools' effectiveness. Research shows that fundamental instructional practices—ability grouping (tracking), grade retention, Chapter 1 programs, categorical dropout prevention programs—create many disadvantages for low-achieving students and have not been effective in improving academic achievement among such students.

Some school districts are implementing alternatives to these practices, many of which have empirical support, and others that are justified by research on student learning and motivation. The common denominator is an effort to provide quality programming for low- as well as high-achieving students. Specifically, explicit efforts are made to ensure low achievers are afforded the caring teachers, energetic instruction, and high expectations for success that have traditionally been principally offered to higher achieving students. In so doing, they create a positive setting for learning and growth.

In some schools, rigid forms of tracking have been replaced with a mix of heterogeneous and "accelerated" classes that provide extra assistance from the school's most accomplished teachers. One example is for ability grouping in only one or two subjects, with the rest of the student's program occurring in heterogeneous classes. Instead of attempting to fine-tune track assignments into the most homogeneous groupings, other schools use broadband groupings that separate only the students at the extremes of ability (Oakes and Lipton, 1992; Newmann and Thompson, 1987; Cohen, 1986).

Because being retained in grade is one of the most stressful experiences for students, with clear negative effects on subsequent achievement, some schools have implemented alternatives to traditional grade retention practices. Other models allow students to advance in grade level while concurrently taking "bridging classes" and receiving extra help to make up deficiencies (Goodlad and Anderson, 1987; Slavin, 1990; Braddock and McPartland, 1992).

Chapter 1 and dropout prevention programs are the traditional means for providing extra assistance to the most needy students. However, they are often de facto lower tracks for students who have been retained. There are alternative strategies that do not require tracking and that have been found to produce less grade retention and higher achievement. For example, some schools form interdisciplinary teacher teams that allow scheduled time with small groups of "remedial" students. Other schools use peer tutoring or direct tutoring by teachers during scheduled periods (MacIver and Epstein, 1991; Lloyd, 1978; Kelly et al., 1964; Madden et al., 1991; Hedin, 1987; Cohen et al., 1982).

Other models provide extra assistance through methods that allow students to remain in their regular classrooms. Some programs use instructional strategies that allow all students to learn common course contents; others use multiple textbooks and instructional methods to accommodate different learning styles (Epstein and Salinas, 1991; The Civic Achievement Award Program, n.d.; Levin, 1987). Less frequently, students are given options as to the type of extra assistance they receive, a strategy that appears to be successful in enhancing the student's motivation to engage in the learning process (Treisman, 1985; Ascher, 1991).

Finally, some schools are replacing traditional Chapter 1 "pull-out" programs and dropout prevention programs with initiatives that seek to avoid labeling and further isolating low-achieving students by instead implementing schoolwide programming for the benefit of all students. The most promising programs directly address student motivation by complementing traditional instructional strategies with more diverse pedagogies, including experiential and cooperative learning. Explicit efforts are made to ensure that instruction is directly relevant to students' interests and concerns (LeTendre, 1991; Massachussets Advocacy Center and Center for Early Adolescence, 1988).

A positive school climate—one in which students feel "membership" in their schools and in which they perceive that teachers care about them as individuals—is considered a prerequisite for student engagement in either academic or vocational learning. The large size of many high schools is seen as a strong institutional barrier to a positive school climate. In large schools, teachers are most likely to form close supervisory relations with only the most accomplished students, while others (most often minority students and low achievers) remain isolated from ongoing adult attention (McPartland, 1990, 1991; Bryk et al., 1990; Powell et al., 1985).

Available evidence indicates that low-achieving students are most likely to prosper in smaller schools. Accordingly, some districts have created alternative schools and schools-within-schools to make schools feel smaller. Alternative schools, which are usually much smaller and more student oriented than the typical comprehensive high school, have been found to be effective with many students who would otherwise have dropped out (Wehlage et al., 1989; Gold and Mann, 1984; Glatthorn, 1975; Garbarino, 1980). The Bronx Regional High School (New York) provides one of the most inspiring examples of success, educating a student body composed exclusively of students with serious behavior problems and a record of academic failure. The success of the program is built on respecting the students, challenging them to succeed, and providing the individual level of attention that they need. The success of Job Corps and of vocational academies is attributed, in part, to the fact that academic instruction is provided in smaller, independent learning centers (Mangum, 1987; Dayton et al., 1992).

Other schools have implemented alternatives to departmentalized staffing as a strategy for making a school smaller and more personal, an approach that may be especially effective for minority students. There is some evidence that achievement may be fostered by specialist teachers, but other research indicates that student motivation may be so tightly tied to relations with teachers that they actually have greater achievement and improved social behavior with fewer teachers (Bryk and Driscoll, 1988; Becker, 1987; Massachusetts Advocacy Center and Center for Early Adolescence, 1988; Gottfriedson and Daiger, 1979; Wehlage et al., 1989). Most schools seek to find a balance. Some schools use only two or three different teachers covering all subjects for each student, a strategy seen especially valuable in helping young people succeed in the difficult school transitions—from elementary school into middle school and from middle school into high school. The more common strategy is to implement programs of interdisciplinary team teaching. Teams of four teachers covering each of the major subjects share the same four classrooms of students, with regularly scheduled team time to address individual student needs and with each adult team member having special responsibilities for a homeroom subgroup, including providing students with extra help.

Vocational Education and Employment and Training Programs

As discussed in Chapter 7, the United States does not have well-articulated school-to-work transition programs for adolescents who do not enter college, enter technical training programs, or join the armed services—in other words, for a majority of the young people leaving high school each year. One consequence is that many adolescents move into the labor market without adequate training or experience. Many experts believe that more uniform and integrated school-to-work transition systems are needed (Hahn, 1991; Nothdurft, 1990; Hamilton, 1990). In the absence of national policy support and guidance, many schools and communities have begun to develop alternatives to existing vocational education and employment and training programs, and in doing so, have begun to create their own systems.

Most students in vocational programs and Job Training Partnership Act (JTPA) programs have few opportunities to test their skills on the job. Employers have limited opportunities to work with prospective employees. In response to this lack of connection, the most innovative local initiatives in vocational education are designed for employers to provide supervised work experience to young people. In some models, complementary academic instruction is provided by the school.

In cooperative education programs, there are agreements between a school and a cooperating employer. In general, both schools and employers offer close supervision to students and ensure that the student engages in relevant classroom instruction and meaningful work experiences. Cooperative education programs have been shown to enhance high school graduation rates and the postsecondary education enrollment. And, of all vocational programs, participants in cooperative education are most likely to gain permanent employment in an area for which they were trained (U.S. General Accounting Office, 1991; Hamilton, 1990).

Apprenticeship models are another strategy for integrating work experience with academic instruction. During the late 1970s, the U.S. Department of Labor funded eight school-to-apprenticeship programs, some of which continue to operate. These programs are similar to cooperative education: the primary difference is that students in the apprenticeship programs are primarily engaged in the building trades, with the expectation that they become registered apprentices at the completion of their schooling. Interpretations of evaluations range from positive to "spotty" (U.S. General Accounting Office, 1991; CSR, Inc., 1981; Siedenberg, 1989).

More recently, a small number of school-based apprenticeship programs have been implemented. Their fundamental characteristic is that progressive instruction is provided for a minimum of 3 years. In general, schools release students for about one-half day to engage in their apprenticeship; they also provide opportunities to students to relate their work experience to their academic classes, for example, by assigning special projects. These programs differ from traditional apprenticeship programs in that they are not concentrated in the building trades, and students are not necessarily expected to take full-time work at the completion of the apprenticeship. After graduation, students are given several options, including full-time work, contingent on good performance, and opportunities to enter postsecondary education while continuing the apprenticeship (Hamilton and Hamilton, 1992a; Hoyt, 1990, 1991; Lerman and Pouncy, 1990; Hamilton et al., 1991).

In lieu of providing young people with structured work experience, many schools have opted for modifying instructional approaches, with particular emphasis on improving vocational education. Some efforts aim to integrate academic and vocational instruction by incorporating academic concepts into vocational programs or by coordinating the academic and vocational curriculum so that students are provided with complementary instruction in both settings. Either way, many models are currently being implemented.

In recent years, curriculums have been designed that seek to foster work-oriented competencies in the context of academic course offerings (U.S. Department of Labor, 1992). The goal is to deemphasize essays, book reports, and research papers in favor of brochures, memorandum, advertising copy, and planning documents, while at the same time, providing a traditional liberal arts education that focuses on general competencies and an appreciation of learning through exposure to course content that is often independent of explicit occupational purposes (Grubb, 1992; Nothdurft, 1989). Alternatively, other schools are beginning to consider vocational education as an alternate route for academic instruction. In some programs, for example, students learn academic concepts through problem-solving activities: geometry can be taught as part of a curriculum on carpentry; physics and reading can be taught through curriculums on automotive repair or plumbing (Brandt, 1992).

A fundamental barrier to these initiatives is that they often require schoolwide changes not only in the vocational curriculum, but in the academic curriculum as well, and such reforms are often poorly implemented (Grubb et al., 1991; Rosenstock, 1991). There are few systematic evaluations, but some research indicates that the most successful programs concentrate resources in a single setting, such as a specialized high school or a regional vocational center, that allows educators to provide integrated and progressive learning experiences to young people—similar to the approach used in core academic courses (Goodlad, 1984; Wirt, 1991; Hamilton, 1990; Bishop, 1989). For example, secondary school "vocational academies" are one of the few models of vocational education that consistently has positive outcomes in terms of increasing graduation rates, enrollment in postsecondary education, and earnings. Organized as schools-within-schools, staffing for these academies often consists of three academic teachers and one vocational teacher who stay with cohorts of students for 2 or 3 years. They focus on a specific field (e.g., health, electronics, business), building field-specific vocational courses around a core of academic courses (Grubb, 1992; Hayward et al., 1988; Dayton et al., 1992).

Many of the themes reflected in good practice in vocational education have been adopted by recent initiatives in employment and training programs. There is an emerging consensus that academic instruction is necessary to supplement traditional occupational training and job placement services. And while basic education currently constitutes only a small component of JTPA programs, recent demonstrations reverse this emphasis: for example, in JOBSTART, each participant is required to take at least 200 hours of basic skills remediation. In the Summer Training and Education Program (STEP), participants hold half-time jobs, with the rest of the day spent in basic skills remediation (Public/Private Ventures, 1987a; Cave and Doolittle, 1991; see also Chapter 7). Experience in these innovative programs suggests that a range of services is necessary for positive results. For example, some evidence supports the combination of early work experience with job training, the inclusion of remedial education in the array of services, and the combination of self-directed job search strategies and job placement programs. The program with the strongest positive effects—Job Corps—provides basic skills training, work experience, occupational training, and job placement services (Bailis, 1991; Carnevale, 1991; Hahn, 1991; Grant Foundation, 1988; U.S. General Accounting Office, 1991; Public/Private Venture, 1987b). Because participants are at high risk for dropping out of school or not sustaining participation in employment and training programs, for example, outreach and case management are essential components. Employment programs that incorporate counseling, peer group supports, and mentoring components are increasing. The actual quality and mix of such services vary widely, however, and often they remain secondary or are offered only on a referral basis. To be effective, programs need to view them as essential components, of a level of importance comparable to the core employment services that are traditionally provided (Public/Private Ventures, 1987c). Although the need for comprehensiveness has been well understood since the 1960s, such programs have high front-end costs, and resources have rarely been available to support them. As a result, the overwhelming majority of programs have been narrowly focused.

Finally, the stigma attached to employment and training graduates has led other programs to take actions to inform potential employers about the skills and motivation of participants. Other approaches include "job portfolio" program components that provide graduates with a "credential" listing their special strengths, accomplishments, skills, and references; such programs have had promising effects (Charner, 1988; Stemmer et al., 1992). Career Beginnings provides participants with instruction in self-directed job search strategies; so does Jobs for America's Graduates, in which staff help participants secure their first jobs and then provide ongoing case management assistance to help them retain those jobs (Cave and Quint, 1990; Jobs for America's Graduates, 1989).

KEY ELEMENTS OF COMPREHENSIVE SERVICE

Researchers and practitioners agree that adolescents (as well as families) in high-risk settings require comprehensive services, but there is less agreement regarding the most useful conceptualization of comprehensive services. In general, however, "comprehensive" highlights the emerging consensus that rather than offering a single type of service or adopting a single categorical program goal (e.g., substance abuse prevention, school retention, family counseling), programs should offer a range of services and have multiple goals. (Indeed, almost all of the programs cited in this chapter are comprehensive.) This perspective reflects the well-documented finding that adolescents who engage in one type of problem behavior often concurrently engage in others. It suggests that, to the extent possible, all needed services should be offered in a single site or at least under a single administrative structure. Not all comprehensive programs, however, are implemented within single sites by single agencies. More recently, some programs are comprehensive by virtue of integrating program components provided by different service entities. Regardless of the structure, the goal of comprehensive service delivery systems is to transcend categorical labels, organizations, and funding sources to bring together an appropriate package of service that is easily accessible to young people and their families.

Current national policies are not supportive of comprehensive service: almost all federal and state funding is allocated by "problem" to designated agencies responsible for designated services (Dryfoos, 1990). In the absence of policy support, an increasing number of communities have taken the initiative, sometimes supported by public and private funds, to implement comprehensive programs. Schools are often the settings for comprehensive services because almost all children use them, at least initially. Other sites are also being used successfully, including housing projects and community centers. "Second-chance" employment demonstrations, school-linked health and mental clinics, family resource centers, street-based clinics, community-based youth development programs, and the Cities in Schools models are just a few illustrations of comprehensive programs. These initiatives have had documented success in increasing the accessibility and use of available services by adolescents from high-risk settings, but there is a paucity of evaluation research that identifies the outcomes of that use.

In this section, we highlight four cross-cutting program strategies that appear particularly important for adolescents from high-risk settings—independent of institutional setting: (1) sustained adult support, nurturance, and guidance; (2) opportunities to become involved in the community through structured community learning and service experiences; (3) opportunities to engage in structured experiences, including cooperative activities with peers, aimed at learning how to cope productively with the stress and pressures emanating from high-risk settings; and (4) demonstrations of respect and trust from adults, by having choice and "voice" within programs, and by learning about and experiencing different cultures and traditions.

Sustained Adult Support

Perhaps the most serious risk facing adolescents in high-risk settings is isolation from the nurturance, safety, and guidance that comes from sustained relationships with adults. Parents are the best source of support, but for many adolescents, parents are not positively involved in their lives. In some cases, parents are absent or abusive. In many more cases, parents strive to be good parents, but lack the capacity or opportunity to be so. In response, mentoring and case management are becoming an essential element of most programs; additional services are needed for adolescents in transition from the foster care system.

Mentors, in the traditional sense of the term, are adults, typically unrelated volunteers, who assume quasi-parental roles as advisers, teachers, friends, and role models for young people. Mentors are often expected to be confidants and advocates and, in some programs, to develop collaborative relations with parents and school staff. The empirical foundation for mentoring programs stems from the literature on resiliency, which indicates that a key factor in successful adolescent development is the presence of a sustained and nurturing relationship with adults (Garmezy, 1987; Rutter, 1987). Evaluation data are scarce, however, primarily because most research has examined the effects of mentoring within the context of other program services (see below).

Most recently, mentoring programs have been used as a vehicle for preventing teenage pregnancy and delinquency and as a means for addressing isolation in high-poverty neighborhoods. Young males from poor families are a particular focus, because they are less likely to maintain sustained participation in pregnancy prevention and employment programs. Other mentoring programs seek to reduce the isolation of young people from the labor market by matching older adolescents with community adults who hold positions of authority in business and government (Mincy and Weiner, 1990; Dryfoos, 1990; Children's Defense Fund, 1988; Mentoring International, 1989).

It is questionable if mentoring programs can replicate the parent-adolescent relationship, and few programs have that expectation. However, mentoring relationships with young people can be effective if they extend over time and if mentors themselves have clear goals, adequate training, and adequate support from the sponsoring organization. These requirements create a dilemma: as the number of young people who need mentors increases, the demands on mentors to be "full-service providers" makes it increasingly difficult to enlist volunteers. Because of this dilemma, perhaps the primary goal of "freestanding" mentoring programs should be to help young people build competencies. Other positive outcomes—such as trust and close affiliation—are likely to surface as a result of the skill-building process (Hamilton and Hamilton, 1992b; Roche, 1979).

Even under the best of circumstances, it is difficult for parents to connect their children with necessary educational and service programs. In other cases, parental involvement may not be appropriate or desired by adolescents who must arrange services on their own. In response, many programs have found it necessary to implement extensive case management services.

Most often, case managers (also known as counselors, advocates, or mentors) work directly with adolescents to arrange service delivery. In most community-based youth development programs, such as The Door and El Puente, young people are given a primary counselor or mentor immediately on entering the program. Some schools have found that the traditional school counselors fail to meet the needs of at-risk youth and so are institutionalizing alternative methods of providing youth with close personal relationships. At the South Brooklyn Alternative School, for example, every staff member is assigned as a "counselor-advocate" for specific students (Pittman and Cahill, 1992).

The use of case managers is well established in programs for teenage mothers, for whom there is a need for interagency coordination and flexibility. In the Teenage Pregnancy and Parenting Project (TAPP) model, for example, the counselors are not tied to any particular service delivery system, but help link clients with a broad array of programs, including school, social, nutritional, employment, obstetrical, public health services, and infant day care. The counselors, primarily social workers, also provide counseling and conduct follow-up to ensure that clients received services. In comparison with national and local norms, TAPP clients had fewer repeat pregnancies, stayed in school for a longer period after delivery, and had fewer low-birthweight babies. Clients who maintained consistent contact with their counselors generally had the most positive outcomes (Brindis et al., 1987). Another program, the Adolescent Pregnancy and Dropout Prevention Model, has reported an 88 percent school retention rate among teenage mothers served in the program. Success appears in part to be due to the case managers, who meet with teenage mothers on a regular basis to inform them about academic alternatives, help them identify job interests, and arrange for tutoring and home teaching (Earle, 1989).

Other programs rely on case management as an integral strategy to prevent entry into the justice and foster care systems. The Adolescent Diversion Project (ADP), for example, focuses on youth who have already committed delinquent acts but have not yet been formally adjudicated. The ADP is designed to develop empowerment skills in young people and their parents by building on the personal strengths existing within their families. The instrument for change is an extensively trained family worker (university student or community volunteer) who spends 3 hours per week with the assigned youth for 4-5 months. Evaluation results showed less recidivism among ADP participants than among other delinquent adolescents (Davidson and Redner, 1988).

The effectiveness of case management depends on case managers who can work across service domains. Whether directed at parents or at-risk youth, case management is a difficult and labor-intensive service. Because of the heavy demands on their time, case managers in all programs report that caseload size is a major barrier to performance. For those who work across agencies, confidentiality of information is often a problem. Finally, case managers must confront the lack of available services: adequate child care, housing, and employment opportunities remain limited, despite the best efforts of case managers (Brindis et al., 1987; Quint et al., 1991).

Adolescents in foster care face special barriers to making a successful transition into young adulthood. All have experienced the effects of severely troubled families, and many have spent their childhoods in many homes. They often need sustained emotional relationships with adults, as well as counseling or mental health services. The availability of an individual who provides continuous care and attention to the adolescent for an extended period of time is especially crucial as part of planning "discharge" from foster care.

Ideally, discharge planning, a process that engages the adolescent and all guardians as full participants, should begin well before age 18, both to ensure that adolescents develop necessary skills and to arrange necessary support services. In the most comprehensive models, child welfare agency staff serve as case managers who coordinate with government agencies and community-based youth programs to ensure the availability of counseling, recreational, and competency-building services, and often to arrange transitional housing as well (Merry, 1987; Spergel and Hartnett, 1990).

Community Learning and Service

One of the realities of daily life for adolescents from high-risk settings is impoverished neighborhoods—neighborhoods that lack recreational and employment opportunities, safety, and many role models of successful adults. Such adolescents often develop feelings of alienation and hopelessness; they do not develop feelings of caring or attachment to their neighborhoods. In response to this situation, many programs have begun to incorporate community learning and service into their array of services.

Empirical and evaluation research supports this approach. A broad body of literature indicates that community participation—in the form of community service, internships, and experiential learning—has measurable effects on young people in terms of preventing problems and in promoting competencies and achievements. For example, there is evidence that community learning and service programs enhance attachments to neighborhoods. That is, in well-designed programs, young people have been found to develop a greater interest in local issues and a perceived competence that they can bring about change (Hamilton and Zeldin, 1987; National Task Force on Citizenship Education, 1977; Calabrese and Shumer, 1986; Newmann, 1975).

Community learning and service can also be considered an alternative pedagogy to assist young people to develop a range of competencies. For example, planned community experiences have been found to promote gains in basic academic skills (Agnew, 1982; McKensey and White, 1982; Hamilton and Zeldin, 1987;

Rutter and Newmann, 1989). Other studies indicate that youth with structured community experiences and service show greater increases in problem-solving skills, personal and social responsibility, and earnings, and in accepting attitudes toward those different from themselves (Conrad and Hedin, 1982a,b; Hamilton, 1980; Hamilton and Fenzel, 1988; Bucknam and Brand, 1983).

Developing Emotional Strengths and Life Skills

Young people from high-risk settings often need special services to confront the emotional pain and feelings of hopelessness that can interfere with positive development. Some community programs are implementing interventions that facilitate collaborative peer group relations so that young people can learn from, and support, each other. Other programs are providing structured opportunities for young people to practice and develop the social, decision-making, and life skills necessary to succeed in high-risk settings.

An emerging body of research indicates that various forms of peer counseling and instruction, when conducted with adult guidance, can serve as supports for coping with the influences of high-risk settings. For example, the Teen Outreach program combines volunteer community service with after-school group counseling sessions to help young people confront the stress in their lives. A 3-year evaluation indicated that Teen Outreach participants had fewer pregnancies and were less likely to drop out of school or get suspended than a comparable group of students. Benefits were greatest for those at greatest risk and were related to the number of volunteer hours worked and attendance at the counseling meetings (Philliber et al., 1988). In the Teen Choice program, social workers staff three components: small groups, individual counseling and referral, and classroom dialogues. This approach has also had success in increasing contraceptive use among young people (Stern, 1988).

The power of peer counseling and group discussion have also been demonstrated in the use of high school curriculums on substance abuse and violence prevention. An analysis of drug prevention programs found that, of five approaches examined, peer programs were the most effective on all outcome measures, especially on indices of actual drug use (Tobler, 1986). In violence prevention programs, staff seek to create a process by which young people discuss and analyze violent behavior and identify and practice alternative behaviors to deal with their anger. Simulations and group feedback allow participants to respond to their peers regarding their behavior. Preliminary studies are encouraging, particularly with respect to young people with the highest number of risk factors (Spivak et al., 1989; Education Development Center, 1989).

Similarly, cooperative learning is being used to transform classrooms into settings in which students collaborate to achieve learning goals. Data generally support this approach, which is used extensively in elementary grades and often in middle grades. It is ironic that cooperative learning is not widely adopted in high schools, where student responsiveness to peer group pressures is even stronger than at younger ages (Johnson and Johnson, 1987; Slavin, 1990; Braddock and McPartland, 1992).

Most programs for at-risk youth focus on preventing problem behaviors; less attention has focused on building the emotional strengths of young people. This approach has led to prevention programs that try to scare young people, ask them to "just say no," or disseminate didactic information. But studies consistently find that these traditional strategies of problem prevention (of substance abuse, sexual activity, violence) have little or no positive impact, especially when they constitute the primary program intervention, and they may even stimulate further acting out (Dryfoos, 1991; Falco, 1988; Hayes, 1987).

The history of failure among prevention programs has led some service providers to develop alternative strategies. There is an emerging body of research indicating that programs that try to strengthen adolescents' coping, decision-making, and assertive skills lead to better outcomes. These programs—grouped under the label of "social and life-skills training"—help adolescents to identify and resist the social pressures that encourage problem behaviors. The most successful programs have taken a progressive approach, first teaching adolescents strategies to address general life dilemmas and then focusing on coping with the specific pressures to use drugs or engage in sexual activity. Most programs develop activities to promote responsible behavior as a step toward future abstinence. Other models shown to be effective are peer taught, use older adolescents or young adults as role models, include media analysis, and make counseling available for those with special needs (Tobler, 1986; Hansen et al., 1988; Stringham and Weitzman, 1988).

Social and life-skills training programs share many features of current "social competence promotion" or "mental health promotion" programs. In general, the programs that demonstrate positive outcomes seek to help adolescents develop an overall sense of well-being, flexibility in dealing with stress, and a repertoire of behavioral skills needed to solve both interpersonal problems and problems of daily living. Most of these programs are integrated into school curriculums, and involve between 8 and 20 sessions conducted by teachers with special training. The programs combine informational and experiential activities, complemented by group discussion and counseling. Early evaluations indicate that these programs are successful in improving adolescents' impulse control and self-identity, ability to understand the perspective of others, ability to solve problems, and school performance (Elias et al., 1986; Weissberg et al., 1988; Felner and Felner, 1989).

Demonstrating Trust and Respect for Adolescents

Explicit in good practice models is the recognition that young people, like all people, need to feel a sense of comfort and need to be offered a sense of autonomy in order to profit from program teachings and experiences. For this reason, many community programs seek to design programs that encompass principles of trust and respect for young people. Consistent demonstrations of caring and high expectations for young people are a prerequisite. Many programs are also providing young people with choice and "voice" regarding program operation, and, in response to the racial and ethnic diversity of adolescents, many practitioners incorporate cultural traditions and values into programs.

Choice and "Voice" for Adolescents

Personal attachments to institutions and engagement in program activities occur most readily when participation is voluntary or when individuals have options about how and when to participate (Newmann, 1981). Many school-linked health centers, for example, attribute their effectiveness to the fact that participation is voluntary, discussions are confidential, and young people are encouraged to bring friends along for support. Few youth development programs have enrollment requirements, so young people can immediately participate in activities. Adolescents are given choices about participation in the activities: a "drop in, test things out" approach is essential to effective programming. The almost universal use of small groups, flexible grouping practices, symbols of membership (uniforms, T-shirts), and clear structures (regular meetings, codes of conduct) reflects an organizational and programmatic recognition of the importance of group membership. Not surprisingly, adolescents in high-risk settings are most likely to identify community-based youth programs as their major source of institutional attachment (Pittman and Cahill, 1992; Heath and McLaughlin, 1991).

Youth development programs also use their institutional advantage to allow young people to participate in program decision making. In many programs, adolescents are given the responsibility of developing, implementing, and enforcing rules regarding drugs, violence, and conduct. Similarly, most community-based youth programs provide opportunities and expect adolescents to take responsibility for themselves and for others. For example, in The City, Inc., an alternative school and youth program, participants decide how to address problems when their peers break established rules (Pittman and Cahill, 1992). In the Youth Action Program (which provides job training and education for young people from poor neighborhoods), the youths participate in every level of program governance, from staffing and budget decisions to program and policy initiatives. Similarly, in a program sponsored by the Kalamazoo Youth United Way, participants conduct needs assessments, raise money for youth programming, and then decide how and where to expend the money (The Union Institute, 1991).

It is more difficult to promote institutional membership in schools, since attendance is mandatory. Nonetheless, evidence suggests that teachers can form personal relationships with students—a prerequisite for membership—if students spend sustained time with teachers on an individual basis or in small groups and if they engage together in such activities as recreation, counseling, and the study of more than one subject (Bidwell, 1970; Newmann, 1981). Choices can also be provided to students within the confines of schools. In some schools, adolescents choose whether to engage in cooperative or independent learning in certain classes, with the provision that they engage in both during a given week. Students in need of remedial instruction show improved outcomes when offered choices among a range of high-quality special assistance programs (Treisman, 1985; Ascher, 1991). In other schools, students vote on how to spend extracurricular funds or participate in working groups to decide the content of school assemblies. Schools can expect student assistance in tasks such as tutoring, media work, meal preparation, fundraising, and plant maintenance (Wynne, 1980).

Issues of Race, Ethnicity, and Culture

Racial and ethnic discrimination is a continuing reality in the United States: discriminatory practices, and responses to them, affect the development of young people from racial and ethnic minority populations. And although members of such populations share most of the values and orientations of the dominant social groups, important cultural differences also exist, which not only influence the nature of personal interactions with those in the dominant culture, but equally important, influence the ways in which parents and their adolescent children view the world, including social institutions (Gibbs and Huang, 1989; Batts, 1988). In response, many programs try to develop strategies for addressing the complex issues of discrimination, race, ethnicity, and culture. The most fundamental commonality of such programs is that they do not attempt to adopt a "color-blind" view of young people, which essentially denies that race and ethnicity are deeply rooted aspects of individual identity. On the contrary, good practice requires explicit attention to race, ethnicity, and culture, not as add-on program dimensions, but through strategies that are embedded within all aspects of the program (Camino, 1992; Comer, 1989; Pine and Hilliard, 1990).

Most practitioners see the recognition of racial and ethnic differences, as well as the promotion of open dialogue and expression regarding differences, as necessary prerequisites to instilling mutual respect among youth. For example, the SEED (Students Educating Each Other about Discrimination) project, which is being designed and targeted for implementation in Ann Arbor, Michigan, uses group discussion to train high school students to serve as role models and change agents who challenge racism (Polakow-Suransky and Ulaby, 1990). In other programs, understanding of multicultural differences emanates from shared experiences in purposeful activities. Pursuit of common goals among cross-ethnic peers has been documented as instrumental in reducing negative stereotypes and prejudices (Slavin, 1991). Such activities can also help to forge meaningful bonds between adults and young people. In one multicultural training program for youth workers in Montgomery County, Maryland, youth and adults were grouped cross-racially and cross-ethnically. Evaluations indicate that the experiences provided a good basis for building rapport (Washington School Anti-Racism/Anti-Oppression Training Group, 1991).

Multicultural competence, cooperation, and problem solving can also be promoted by curriculums that incorporate elements of various cultural and ethnic histories and traditions. For example, one program engaged Puerto Rican children and teenagers in New York City in telling and responding to stories about Puerto Rican heroes and heroines who negotiated tough situations in order to achieve success; an evaluation showed that participants enhanced their repertoire of positive coping skills (Costantino et al., 1988). Programs based on cultural pride stimulate the development of solid racial and ethnic identities, which serve as focal points from which to develop firm cross-ethnic relationships (Rosenthal, 1987; Wigginton, 1991). Some schools have incorporated multicultural referents throughout the curriculum, instead of relegating information on minorities to separate chapters, courses, or months.

Attention to race and ethnicity requires caring and sensitive staff. Although it is important to have minority staff in decision-making positions in all programs, membership in a racial or ethnic minority does not in and of itself guarantee cultural competence. Therefore, most programs that address issues of race and ethnicity ensure that all staff receive multicultural training. Training—if implemented over time, and not as a "one-time" initiative—has been found to have positive outcomes, such as increased knowledge about cultural differences and similarities, fewer stereotypic assumptions about minority adolescents and their families, improved cross-cultural interactions, and greater client satisfaction (Pederson, 1988; Lefley, 1989; Pine and Hilliard, 1990; Viadero, 1990; Ascher, 1991).

CONCLUSIONS

This chapter has highlighted "good practice" programs to help adolescents in high-risk settings—interventions that have strong research and theoretical justifications. However, such initiatives are not and should not be seen as substitutes for improving the basic institutions of adolescent life. The key to providing for adolescent needs is an approach based on the ideal of comprehensive services. In most instances this will mean pushing primary institutions to expand their horizons and build bridges, e.g., between schools and health care systems. Good practice programs have demonstrated the advantages of changing the institutional service settings that adolescents experience on a daily basis and redesigning programs to have multiple goals and a range of interventions. In pursuing these objectives, service providers must overcome formidable obstacles in the form of narrowly defined categorical program funding streams that place rigid and arbitrary restrictions on grantee programs.

Adolescents from high-risk settings need a comprehensive set of developmental opportunities and experiences that, too often, are not an integral part of their lives. That is, adolescents need opportunities to confront and address the difficult realities existing in their lives. They need opportunities to form sustained and positive relationships with adults and peers. They need opportunities to succeed and to be rewarded for success. They need opportunities to contribute, to feel in control, and to demonstrate competencies. In brief, young people need a comprehensive array of services that are empowering and that provide legitimate opportunities to develop and use their interpersonal, academic, and vocational skills. We recognize that there are limitations in relying on research, theory, and expert consensus without the additional insight gained from program evaluations. These issues are addressed in greater detail in Chapter 11. At the same time, studies clearly document the significant risks existing within current institutions and programs. Furthermore, there is sufficient accumulated knowledge to eliminate or reduce these risks by designing alternative models. At a minimum, implementation of best practice models would better ensure that institutional programs "do no harm" to adolescents. In a more optimistic light, it is likely that the programs highlighted in this chapter offer models that will aid the reform of primary settings as well as demonstrating effective interventions for adolescents whose experiences place them in extreme jeopardy.

REFERENCES

Agnew, J.
1982   Better education through application. *Synergist* 10(3):44-48.
Ascher, C.
1991   *School Programs for African American Male Students.* Trend and Issues paper no. 15. New York: Teachers College, Columbia University.
Bailis, L.N.
1991   Process Evaluation of the Career Beginnings Program: Final Report. Paper prepared for the Center for Corporate and Education Initiatives, Brandeis University, Waltham, Mass.
Batts, V.
1988   *Modern Racism: New Melodies for the Same Old Tunes.* Cambridge, Mass.: VISIONS, Inc.
Bazemore, G.
1988   Promoting accountability in juvenile justice: the role of youth development agencies. *Youth Policy* 19(2):40-42.

Becker, H.J.
1987   *Addressing the Needs of Different Groups of Early Adolescents: Effects of Varying School and Classroom Organizational Practices on Students from Different Social Backgrounds and Abilities.* Report No. 16. Center for Research on Elementary and Middle Schools. Baltimore, Md.: Johns Hopkins University.

Bidwell, C.
1970   Students and schools: some observations on client trust in client-serving institutions. In W.R. Rosengren and M. Lefton , eds. *Organizations and Clients.* Columbus, Ohio: Merrill.

Bishop, J.H.
1989   Incentives for learning: why American high school students compare so poorly to their counterparts overseas. *Investing in People: A Strategy to Address America's Workforce Crisis.* Background papers, Vol. 1, Commission of Workforce Quality and Labor Market Efficiency. Washington, D.C.: U.S. Department of Labor.

Boutte, G.S.
1992   Frustrations of an African-American parent: a personal and professional account. *Phi Delta Kappan* 73(10):786-788.

Braddock, J.H., and J. McPartland
1992   Education of At-Risk Youth: Recent Trends, Current Status, and Future Needs. Commissioned paper for the Panel on High-Risk Youth, Commission on Behavioral and Social Sciences and Education, National Research Council, Washington, D.C.

Brandt, R., ed.
1992   *Readings from Educational Leadership.* Alexandria, Va.: Association for Supervision and Curriculum Development.

Brindis, C., R. Barth, and A. Loomis
1987   Continuous counseling: case management with teenage parents. *Social Casework: The Journal of Contemporary Social Work* March:164-172.

Bronfenbrenner, U.
1978   Who needs parent education? *Teachers College Record* 79(4):767-787.
1979   *The Ecology of Human Development: Experiments by Nature and Design.* Cambridge, Mass.: Harvard University Press.

Bryk, A., and M.W. Driscoll
1988   The High School as Community: Contextual Influences and Consequences for Students and Teachers. National Center on Effective Secondary Schools, University of Wisconsin, Madison.

Bryk, A., V.E. Lee, and J.L. Smith
1990   High school organization and its effects on teachers and students: an interpretive summary of the research. Pp. 135-226 in W.H. Cline and J.F. Witte, eds., *Choice and Control in American Education*, Vol. 1. New York: Falmer Press.

Bucknam, R.B., and S.G. Brand
1983   EBCE really works: a meta-analysis on experience based career education. *Educational Leadership* 40(6):66-71.

CSR, Inc.
1981   *Report on Impacts Study of New Youth Initiatives in Apprenticeship.* Washington, D.C.: CSR, Inc.

Calabrese, R.L., and H. Shumer
1986   The effects of service activities on adolescent alienation. *Adolescence* 21:675-687.

Camino, L.
1992   Racial, Ethnic, and Cultural Differences in Youth Development Programs. Commissioned paper prepared for the Task Force on Youth Development and Community Programs, Carnegie Council on Adolescent Development, Washington, D.C.

Carnevale, A.P.
1991   *America and the New Economy.* Alexandria, Va.: The American Society for Training and Development. Washington, D.C.: U.S. Department of Labor.

Cave, G., and F. Doolittle
1991   *Assessing Jobstart: Interim Impacts of a Program for School Dropouts.* New York: Manpower Demonstration Research Corporation.

Cave, G., and J. Quint
1990   *Career Beginnings Impact Evaluation: Findings from a Program for Disadvantaged High School Students.* New York: Manpower Demonstration Research Corporation.

Charner, I.
1988   Employability credentials: a key to successful youth transition to work. *Journal of Career Development* 15:30-40.

Children's Defense Fund
1988   *What About the Boys? Teenage Pregnancy Prevention Strategies.* Washington, D.C.: Adolescent Pregnancy Prevention Clearinghouse.

Civic Achievement Award Program (The)
n.d.   Close Up Foundation. Unpublished manuscript, Arlington, Va.

Cochran, M.
1990   Personal networks in the ecology of human development. Pp. 3-34 in M. Cochran, M. Larner, D. Riley, L. Gunnarsson, and C.R. Henderson, Jr., eds., *Extending Families: The Social Networks of Parents and Their Children.* New York: Cambridge University Press.

Cohen, E.G.
1986   *Designing Groupwork: Strategies for the Heterogeneous Classroom.* New York: Teachers College Press.

Cohen, P.A., J.A. Kulik, and C.L. Kulik
1982   Educational outcomes of tutoring: a meta-analysis of findings. *American Educational Research Journal* 19:237-248.

Comer, J.P.
1988   Educating poor minority children. *Scientific American* 259(5):42-48.
1989   Racism and the education of young children. *Teachers College Record* 90(3):352-361.

Commission on Chapter 1
1992   *Making Schools Work for Children in Poverty.* Washington, D.C.: American Association for Higher Education.

Conrad, D., and D. Hedin, eds.
1982a   The impact of experiential education on adolescent development. *Youth Participation and Experiential Education.* New York: Haworth Press.
1982b   The impact of experiential education on adolescent development. *Child and Youth Services* 4:57-76.

Costantino, G., R. Malgady, and L. Rogler
  1988   Folk hero modeling therapy for Puerto Rican adolescents. *Journal of Adolescence* (special issue D) 11:155-175.

Davidson, W., and R. Redner
  1988   The prevention of juvenile delinquency: diversion from the juvenile justice system. In R. Price, E. Cowen, R. Lorion, and J. Ramos-McKay, eds., *14 Ounces of Prevention.* Washington, D.C.: American Psychological Association.

Davies, D.
  1991   Schools reaching out: family, school, and community partnerships for student success. *Phi Delta Kappan* 72(5):376-382.

Dayton, C., M. Raby, D. Stern, and A. Weisberg
  1992   The California partnership academies: remembering the "forgotten half." *Phi Delta Kappan* 73(7):539-545.

Dryfoos, J.
  1988   School-based health clinics: three years of experience. *Family Planning Perspectives* 20(4):193-200
  1990   *Adolescents at Risk: Prevalence and Prevention.* New York: Oxford University Press.
  1991   School-based social and health services for at-risk students. *Urban Education* 26(1):118-137.

Earle, J.
  1989   Adolescent Pregnancy and Dropout Prevention Project of NASBE. Unpublished report, National Association of State Boards of Education, Washington, D.C.

Eastman, G.
  1988   *Family Involvement in Education.* Madison, Wis.: Department of Public Instruction.

Edelman, P., and B. Radin
  1991   *Serving Children and Families Effectively: How the Past Can Help Chart the Future.* Washington, D.C.: Education and Human Services Consortium.

Education Development Center
  1989   Preventing Interpersonal Violence Among Teens: Field Test and Evaluation. Final report of Grant No. 87-IJ-CX-0009, National Institute of Justice, Washington, D.C.

Eisenhower Foundation (Milton S.)
  1990   *Youth Investment and Community Restructuring: Street Lessons on Drugs and Crime for the Nineties.* Washington, D.C.: Milton S. Eisenhower Foundation.

Elias, M.J., M. Gara, M. Ubriaco, et al.
  1986   Impact of a preventive social problem solving intervention on children's coping with middle-school stressors. *American Journal of Community Psychology* 14:259-275.

Epstein, J.L.
  1991a   Paths to partnership: what we can learn from federal, state, district, and school initiatives. *Phi Delta Kappan* 72(5):344-349.
  1991b   School and family partnerships. Pp. 1139-1151 in M. Alkin, ed., *Encyclopedia of Educational Research,* 6th ed. New York: Macmillan.

Epstein, J.L., and K.C. Salinas
  1991   *Promising Practices in Major Academic Subjects in the Middle Grades.* Reston, Va.: National Association of Secondary School Principals.

Fagan, J.
1987   Neighborhood education, mobilization and organization for juvenile crime prevention. *Annals of the American Academy of Political and Social Science* 493:54-70.
Falco, M.
1988   Preventing Abuse of Drugs, Alcohol and Tobacco by Adolescents. Working paper, Carnegie Council on Adolescent Development, New York.
Farrow, F.
1987   Preventing Out of Home Placement: Programs That Work. Testimony at hearing of Select Committee on Children, Youth and Families. U.S. House of Representatives, June 9, Washington, D.C.
Felner, R.D., and T.Y. Felner
1989   Primary prevention programs in the educational context: a transactional-ecological framework and analysis. In L.S. Bond and B.E. Compas, eds., *Primary Prevention and Promotion in the Schools.* Newbury Park, Calif.: Sage Publications.
Garbarino, J.
1980   Some thoughts on school size and its effects on adolescent development. *Journal of Youth & Adolescence* 9(1):12-31.
1985   *Adolescent Development: An Ecological Perspective.* Columbus, Ohio: Charles E. Merrill.
Garmezy, N.
1987   Stress, competence, and development: continuities in the study of schizophrenic adults, children vulnerable to psychopathology, and the search for stress-resistant children. *American Journal of Orthopsychiatry* 57:154-174.
Gibbs, J.T., and L.N. Huang
1989   *Children of Color: Psychological Interventions with Minority Youth.* San Francisco: Jossey-Bass.
Glatthorn, A.A.
1975   *Alternatives in Education: Schools and Programs.* New York: Dodd, Mead and Co.
Gold, M., and D. Mann
1984   *Expelled to a Friendlier Place: A Study of Effective Alternative Schools.* Ann Arbor: University of Michigan Press.
Goodlad, J.I.
1984   *A Place Called School,* New York: McGraw-Hill.
Goodlad, J.I., and R.H. Anderson
1987   *The Nongraded Elementary School,* revised ed. New York: Harcourt, Brace, and World.
Gottfriedson, G.D., and D. Daiger
1979   *Disruption in Six Hundred Schools.* Baltimore, Md.: Center for Social Organization of Schools, The Johns Hopkins University.
Grant Foundation (The William T.)
1988   *The Forgotten Half: Pathways to Success for America's Youth and Young Families.* Washington, D.C.: The William T. Grant Foundation, Commission on Work, Family and Citizenship.
Grubb, W.N.
1992   Giving high schools an occupational focus. *Educational Leadership* 49(6):36-41.
Grubb, W.N., G. Davis, J. Lum, et al.
1991   *The Cunning Hand, the Cultured Mind: Models for Integrating Voca-*

tional and Academic Instruction. Berkeley, Calif.: The National Center for Research in Vocational Education.

Hahn, A.
1991   Inside Youth Programs: A Paper on the Limitations of Research. Columbia University Teachers College, New York.

Hamilton, S.
1980   Experiential learning programs for youth. *American Journal of Education* 88:179-215.
1990   *Apprenticeship for Adulthood: Preparing Youth for the Future*. New York: The Free Press.

Hamilton, S.F., and L.M. Fenzel
1988   The impact of volunteer experience on adolescent social development: evidence of program effects. *Journal of Adolescent Research* 3:65-80.

Hamilton, S.F., and M.A. Hamilton
1992a   A progress report on apprenticeships. *Educational Leadership* 49(6):44-47.
1992b   Mentoring programs: promise and paradox. *Phi Delta Kappan* 73(7):546-550.

Hamilton, S., and R.S. Zeldin
1987   Learning civics in the community. *Curriculum Inquiry* 17(4):407-420.

Hamilton, S., M.A. Hamilton, and B.J. Wood
1991   Creating Apprenticeship Opportunities for Youth. A Progress Report from the Youth Apprenticeship Demonstration Project in Broome County, New York.

Hansen, W.B., C.A. Johnson, B.R. Flay, D. Phil, J.W. Graham, and J. Sobel
1988   Affective and social influences approaches to the prevention of multiple substance abuse among seventh graders: results from Project Smart. *Preventive Medicine* 17(2):135-154.

Hayes, C.D., ed.
1987   *Risking the Future: Adolescent Sexuality, Pregnancy, and Childbearing*, Vol. 1. Committee on Child Development Research and Public Policy, National Research Council. Washington, D.C.: National Academy Press.

Hayward, B.J., N. Adelman, and R.N. Apling
1988   *Exemplary Secondary Vocational Education: An Exploratory Study of Seven Programs*. Washington, D.C.: Policy Studies Associates.

Heath, S.B., and M.W. McLaughlin
1991   Community organizations as family. *Phi Delta Kappan* 72(8):623-627.

Hedin, D.
1987   Students as teachers: a tool for improving school climate and productivity. *Social Policy* 17:42-47.

Hoyt, K.B.
1990   A proposal for making transition from schooling to employment an important component of educational reform. *Future Choices* 2(2):73-83. Washington, D.C.: Youth Policy Institute.
1991   Education reform and relationships between the private sector and education: a call for integration. *Phi Delta Kappan* 72(6):450-453.

Independent Sector
1992   Highlights and Summary Data from Nonprofit Almanac, 1983-1993, Dimensions of the Independent Sector. Independent Sector, Washington, D.C.

Jobs for America's Graduates
1989   1989 Annual Report. Jobs for America's Graduates, Inc., Alexandria, Va.

Johnson, D., and R. Johnson
1987   *Learning Together and Alone*, 2nd ed. New York: Prentice-Hall.

Joseph, S.C.
1992   AIDS and adolescence: a challenge to both treatment and prevention. Pp. 96-103 in D.E. Rogers and E. Ginzberg, eds., *Adolescents at Risk: Medical and Social Perspectives*. San Francisco: Westview Press.

Kagan, S.L., D.R. Powell, B. Weissbourn, and E.F. Zigler
1987   *America's Family Support Programs: Perspectives and Prospects*. New Haven, Conn.: Yale University Press.

Kelly, F.J., D.J. Veldman, and C. McGuire
1964   Multiple discriminant prediction of delinquency and school dropouts. *Educational and Psychological Measurement* 24:535-544.

Kirby, D., and C. Waszak
1989   *An Assessment of Six School-Based Clinics: Services, Impact and Potential*. Washington, D.C.: Center for Population Options.

Krasnow, J.
1991   *Building Parent-Teacher Partnerships: Prospects from the Perspective of the Schools Reaching Out Project*. Boston: Institute for Responsive Education.

Lareau, A.
1989   Family-school relationships: a view from the classroom. *Educational Policy* 3(3)245-259.

Leavitt, J., and S. Saegert
1990   *From Abandonment to Hope: Community-Households in Harlem*. New York: Columbia University Press.

Lefley, H.P.
1989   Empirical support for credibility and giving in cross-cultural psychotherapy. *American Psychologist* 44:1163.

Leinberger, C.B.
1992   Where good jobs go: business flees to the urban fringe. *The Nation* 255(1):10-14.

Lerman, R.I., and H. Pouncy
1990   The compelling case for youth apprenticeships. *The Public Interest* 101:66.

LeTendre, M.J.
1991   Improving Chapter 1 programs: we can do better. *Phi Delta Kappan* 72(8):576-580.

Levin, H.M.
1987   Accelerated schools for disadvantaged students. *Educational Leadership* 44:19-21.

Levy, J.E., and W. Shephardson
1992   Look at current school-linked service efforts. *The Future of Children* 2(1):44-55.

Lightfoot, S.L.
1975   Families and schools: creative conflict or negative dissonance. *Journal of Research and Development in Education* 9:34-43.

Littell, J., and J. Wynn
1989   *The Availability and Use of Community Resources for Young Adoles-*

cents in an Inner-City and a Suburban Community. Chicago: Chapin Hall Center for Children, University of Chicago.

Lloyd, D.
1978   Prediction of school failure from third-grade data. *Educational and Psychological Measurement* 38:1193-1200.

Lorian, R.P., W.C. Work, and A.D. Hightower
1984   A school based multi-level preventive intervention: issues in program development and evaluation. *The Personnel and Guidance Journal* 62(4):479-484.

MacIver, D.J., and J.L. Epstein
1991   Responsive practices in the middle grades: teacher teams, advisory groups, remedial instruction, and school transition programs. *American Journal of Education* 99(4):587-622.

Madden, N.A., R.E. Slavin, N.L. Karweit, L. Dolan, and B.A. Wasik
1991   Success for all. *Phi Delta Kappan* 72(8):593-599.

Mangum, G.L.
1987   *Youth Transition from Adolescence to the World of Work.* Washington, D.C.: The William T. Grant Foundation, Commission on Work, Family and Citizenship.

Massachusetts Advocacy Center and Center for Early Adolescence
1988   Before It's Too Late: Dropout Prevention in the Middle Grades. Massachusetts Advocacy Center, Boston, Mass., and the Center for Early Adolescence, Carrboro, N.C.

McKensey, A.A., and R.T. White
1982   Fieldwork in geography and long-term memory structures. *American Educational Research Journal* 19:623-632.

McKnight, J.L., and J.P. Kretzman
1992   *Mapping Community Capacity.* Evanston, Ill.: Center for Urban Affairs, Northwestern University.

McLaughlin, M.W., and P.M. Shields
1987   Involving low-income parents in the schools: a role for policy? *Phi Delta Kappan* 69(2):156-160.

McPartland, J.M.
1990   Staffing decisions in the middle grades: balancing quality instruction and teacher/student relations. *Phi Delta Kappan* 71:465-469.
1991   How Departmentalized Staffing and Interdisciplinary Teaming Combine for Effects on Middle School Students. Paper presented at annual meeting of the American Education Research Association, Chicago.

Mentoring International
1989   *Journal of the International Camp for Mentoring* 3(3).

Merry, S.
1987   *Caring for Adolescents in Care: An Action Plan for Illinois.* Chicago: Chapin Hall Center for Children, University of Chicago.

Millstein, S.G.
1988   The Potential of School-Linked Centers to Promote Adolescent Health and Development. Working paper, Carnegie Council on Adolescent Development, New York.

Mincy, R.B., and S.J. Weiner
1990   A Mentor, Peer Group, Incentive Model for Helping Underclass Youth. Working paper, The Urban Institute, Washington, D.C.

Nathan, J., and J. Kielsmeir
1991   The sleeping giant of school reform. *Phi Delta Kappan* 72(10):738-742.

National Commission on Excellence in Education
1983   *A Nation at Risk: The Imperative for Educational Reform.* Washington, D.C.: U.S. Government Printing Office.
National Task Force on Citizenship Education
1977   *Education for Responsible Citizenship.* New York: McGraw-Hill.
Newmann, F.M.
1975   *Education for Citizen Action: Challenge for Secondary Curriculum.* Berkeley, Calif.: McCutchan.
1981   Reducing student alienation in high schools: implications of theory. *Harvard Educational Review* 51(4):546-561.
Newmann, F.M., and J.A. Thompson
1987   Effects of Cooperative Learning on Achievement in Secondary Schools: A Summary of Research. National Center on Effective Secondary Schools, Madison, Wis.
Nothdurft, W.
1989   *Schoolworks: Reinventing Public Schools to Create the Workforce of the Future.* Washington, D.C.: The Brookings Institution.
1990   Youth Apprenticeship, American Style: A Strategy for Expanding School and Career Opportunities. Report of a conference, Washington, D.C.
Oakes, J., and M. Lipton
1992   Detracking schools: early lessons from the field. *Phi Delta Kappan* 73(6):448-454.
Orr, M.T.
1987   *Keeping Students in School.* San Francisco: Jossey-Bass.
Packard Foundation (The David and Lucile)
1992   *The Future of Children: School Linked Services,* Vol. 2. Los Angeles: Center for the Future of Children.
Pederson, P.
1988   *The Anthropological Lens: Harsh Light, Soft Focus.* Cambridge: Cambridge University Press.
Philliber, S., J. Allen, N. Hoggson, and W. McNeil
1988   Teen Outreach: A Three Year Evaluation of a Program to Prevent Teen Pregnancy and School Dropout. Unpublished report, Association of Junior Leagues, Washington, D.C.
Pine, G., and A.G. Hilliard, III
1990   Rx for racism: imperatives for America's schools. *Phi Delta Kappan* 71(8):601-609.
Pittman, K., and M. Cahill
1992   *Youth and Caring: The Role of Youth Programs in the Development of Caring.* Academy for Educational Development. Indianapolis, Ind.: The Lilly Endowment.
Pittman, K., and M. Wright
1991   *A Rationale for Enhancing the Role of the Non-School Voluntary Sector in Youth Development.* Academy for Educational Development. New York: Carnegie Council on Adolescent Development.
Polakow-Suransky, S., and N. Ulaby
1990   Students take action to combat racism. *Phi Delta Kappan* 71(8):601-609.
Polit, D., J. Kahn, and D. Stevens
1985   *Final Impacts from Project Redirection: A Program for Pregnant and Parenting Teens.* New York: Manpower Demonstration Research Corporation.

Powell, A.G., E. Farrar, and D.K. Cohen
    1985   *The Shopping Mall High Schools: Winners and Losers in the Educational Marketplace.* Boston: Houghton Mifflin.
Public/Private Ventures
    1987a   Summer Training and Education Program (STEP): Report on the 1986 Experience. Public/Private Ventures, Philadelphia, Pa.
    1987b   Youth Conservation and Service Corps: Findings from a National Assessment. Public/Private Ventures, Philadelphia, Pa.
    1987c   *Youth and the Workplace.* Philadelphia: Public/Private Ventures.
Quinn, J.
    1992   Draft Report of the Carnegie Council on Adolescent Development Task Force on Youth Development and Community Programs. Unpublished paper, Carnegie Corporation, New York.
Quint, J.C., B.L. Fink, and S.L. Rowser
    1991   *New Chance: Implementing a Comprehensive Program for Disadvantaged Young Mothers and Their Children.* New York: Manpower Demonstration Research Corporation.
Rivlin, R.
    1991   *Reviving the American Dream.* Washington, D.C.: The Brookings Institution.
Roche, G.B.
    1979   Much ado about mentors. *Harvard Business Review* 57:17-28.
Rosenstock, L.
    1991   The walls come down: the overdue reunification of vocational and academic education. *Phi Delta Kappan* 72(6):434-436.
Rosenthal, D.A.
    1987   Ethnic identity development in adolescents. Pp. 156-179 in J.S. Phinney and M.J. Rotheram, eds., *Children's Ethnic Socialization: Pluralism and Development.* Newbury Park, Calif.: Sage Publications.
Rossi, P.H. (with assistance of Elizabeth Denny)
    1991   Evaluating Family Preservation Programs. A report to the Edna McConnell Clark Foundation, Social and Demographic Research Institute, University of Massachusetts, Amherst.
Rutter, M.
    1987   Psychosocial resilience and protective mechanisms. *American Journal of Orthopsychiatry* 57:316-331.
Rutter, R.A., and F.M. Newmann
    1989   The potential of community service to enhance civic responsibility. *Social Education* 53(6):371-374.
Sauber, S.R.
    1983   *The Human Service Delivery System.* New York: Columbia University Press.
Schorr, L.B., D. Both, and C. Copple, eds.
    1991   *Effective Services for Young Children: Report of a Workshop.* National Forum on the Future of Children and Families, National Research Council and Institute of Medicine. Washington, D.C.: National Academy Press.
Siedenberg, J.M.
    1989   Isolating co-op as a predictor of monetary rewards: an economist's view. *Journal of Cooperative Education* 25(3):8-15.
Slaughter, D.T., and B. Schneider
    1986   *Newcomers: Blacks in Private Schools.* Washington, D.C.: National Institute of Education.

Slavin, R.E.
1990   *Cooperative Learning: Theory, Research, and Practice.* Englewood Cliffs,
        N.J.: Prentice-Hall.
1991   Synthesis of research on cooperative learning. *Educational Leadership*
        48(5):71-82.
Small, S.A.
1990   *Preventive Programs that Support Families with Adolescents.* New
        York: Carnegie Corporation.
Spergel, I.
1976   Interactions between community structure, delinquency, and social policy
        in the inner city. In M. Klein, ed., *The Juvenile Justice System.* Beverly
        Hills, Calif.: Sage Publications.
Spergel, I.A., and M.A. Hartnett
1990   *Evaluation of the Illinois Department of Children and Family Services
        (DCFS) Comprehensive Community Based Youth Services System (CCBYS).*
        Chicago: Chapin Hall Center for Children, University of Chicago.
Spivak, H., A. Hausman, and D. Prothrow-Stith
1989   Public health and the primary prevention of adolescent violence. *Vio-
        lence and Victims* 4:203-212.
Stemmer, P., B. Brown, and C. Smith
1992   The employability skills portfolio. *Educational Leadership* 49(6):32-35.
Stern, M.
1988   Evaluation of school-based pregnancy prevention programs. *TEC News-
        letter* 19:5-8.
Stringham, P., and M. Weitzman
1988   Violence counseling in the routine health care of adolescents. *Journal
        of Adolescent Health Care* 9:389-393.
Sullivan, M., and F. DeGiovanni
1991   Community-Based Nonprofit Housing Management as a Strategy for
        Community-Building in Poor Neighborhoods. Paper presented at a meeting
        of the Association for Public Policy and Management.
Suttles, G.D.
1972   *The Social Construction of Communities.* Chicago: University of Chi-
        cago Press.
Swap, S.M.
1990   Comparing three philosophies of home-school collaboration. *Equity
        and Choice* 6(3):9-19.
Tobler, N.S.
1986   Meta-analysis of 143 adolescent drug prevention programs: quantita-
        tive outcome results of program participants compared to a control or
        comparison group. *Journal of Drug Issues* 15:10-14.
Treisman, P.U.
1985   A Study of Mathematics Performance of Black Students at the Univer-
        sity of California, Berkeley. Unpublished doctoral dissertation, Univer-
        sity of California, Berkeley.
Union Institute (The)
1991   *Disadvantaged Young Men in Urban Areas: A Summary of the First
        Year of the Forum on Public/Private Social Concern.* Washington, D.C.:
        The Union Institute Center for Public Policy.
U.S. Department of Labor
1992   *Learning a Living: A Blueprint for High Performance.* A SCANS report

for America 2000. The Secretary's Commission on Achieving Necessary Skills. Washington, D.C.: U.S. Government Printing Office.

U.S. General Accounting Office
  1991   *Transition from School to Work: Linking Education and Worksite Training.* GAO/HRD-91-105. Washington, D.C.: U.S. General Accounting Office.

U.S. Office of Technology Assessment
  1991   *Adolescent Health—Volume III: Cross-Cutting Issues in the Delivery of Health and Related Services.* OTA-H-467. Washington, D.C.: U.S. Government Printing Office.

Viadero, D.
  1990   Battle over multicultural education rises in intensity. *Education Week* 10(13):1, 11, 13.

Washington School Anti-Racism/Anti-Oppression Training Group
  1991   *Evaluations of Training for Montgomery County Youth Workers.* Washington, D.C.: Institute for Policy Studies, Washington School.

Wehlage, G.G., R.A. Rutter, G.A. Smith, N. Lesko, and R.R. Fernandez
  1989   *Reducing the Risk: Schools as Communities of Support.* New York: Falmer Press.

Weiss, H.B.
  1987   Family support and educational programs: working through ecological theories of human development. Pp. 3-36 in H.B. Weiss and F.N. Jacobs, eds., *Evaluating Family Programs.* Hawthorne, N.Y.: Aldine/de Gruyter.

Weissberg, R.P., M.S. Caplan, and L. Bennetto
  1988   *The Yale-New Haven Social Problem-Solving Program for Young Adolescents.* New Haven, Conn.: Yale University.

Werner, E.E., and R.S. Smith
  1982   *Vulnerable but Invincible: A Longitudinal Study of Resilient Children and Youth.* New York: McGraw Hill.

Wigginton, E.
  1991   Culture begins at home. *Educational Leadership* 49(4):60-64.

Wirt, J.G.
  1991   A new federal law on vocational education: will reform follow? *Phi Delta Kappan* 72(6):425-433.

Wynn, J., H. Richman, R.A. Rubenstein, and J. Littell
  1987   *Communities and Adolescents: An Exploration of Reciprocal Supports.* Washington, D.C.: William T. Grant Foundation, Commission on Work, Family and Citizenship.

Wynne, E.A.
  1980   *Looking at Schools: Good, Bad, and Indifferent.* Lexington, Mass.: Heath.

Zeldin, S.
  1990   The implementation of home-school-community partnerships: policy from the perspective of principals and teachers. *Equity and Choice* 6(3):56-63.

Zigler, E., and K. Black
  1989   America's family support movement: strengths and limitations. *American Journal of Orthopsychiatry* 59(1):6-19.

11

Conclusions and
Research Directions

This report describes the conditions and consequences of increasing numbers of America's youth who are growing up in circumstances that limit their development, compromise their health, impair their sense of self, and restrict their futures. The focus is on the major contexts or settings in which young people are growing up in contemporary American society and the deterioration that has occurred in them over the last two decades. Our decision to focus on settings reflects the panel's appreciation of the profound influence that context has on adolescent behavior and youth and our judgment that the power of settings on adolescent development has not been fully appreciated. The lack of attention to settings has resulted in concentration on individual adolescent behaviors and categorical programs, such as teenage pregnancy prevention, drug abuse prevention, smoking prevention, and dropout prevention. Because these problems are interrelated and have common predictors that are largely environmental, more comprehensive integrated approaches are needed to reduce the exposure of children and adolescents to high-risk settings. Reducing the risks generated by these settings is virtually a precondition for achieving widespread reductions in health- and life-compromising behavior by adolescents.

Describing the destructive effects of high-risk settings is far easier than recommending specific policies and programs to improve them. The demographic changes that are creating large numbers of poor, single-parent families are not well understood, and it is not at all clear what effect specific changes in public policies might have on those trends. We therefore limit most of this concluding chapter to describing the broad changes that we believe are essential if settings are to become less pernicious for a large share of American children and adolescents. If sound empirical evidence exists for policy recommendations, we are more specific. Because understanding of adolescent development in social context is very limited, the second part of this chapter describes a framework for research on adolescent health and development that should yield better information for program and policy development over the next decade. We strongly believe, however, that some of the problems we describe are far too acute and their effects far too destructive to delay action until more research is completed and other demands on national resources reduced. In particular, the diverse ways in which poverty harms children and adolescents, inflicts lasting damage, and limits their future potential points to the reduction of poverty as a key step toward improving the condition of many of the nation's youths.

Four conditions create and sustain high-risk settings. First, as noted, is the large and increasing number of families who are living in or near poverty and experiencing the emotional stress it brings. In 1991 the Census Bureau estimated that 35.7 million Americans were living in poverty (14.2 percent of the population), the largest percentage since the late 1960s. Families with young children make up the largest proportion of those living in poverty. The dramatic increases in single-parent, female-headed households both contributes to the growth in poor families and independently creates a high-risk setting for adolescent development. In fact, many of these families are headed by teenage mothers, creating a kind of double jeopardy. Parents in poor and near-poor families face significant challenges in rearing their children. Aside from their struggle to provide basic necessities, the stress of "making do" with very little money diminishes parents' ability to form personal networks and institutional attachments and to develop the caretaking skills critical to positive adolescent development. Such parents express the difficulties they face and the need for help in providing the guidance, support, and supervision that adolescents need.

Second is the concentration of poor families in some urban and rural neighborhoods and the increase in the numbers of intensely deprived neighborhoods. Such neighborhoods are characterized by racial stratification, homelessness or very degraded housing, inadequate schools, a lack of recreational and employment opportunities, and, in metropolitan areas, a high level of crime and violence. Constructing a family life that can guide children and adolescents into healthy, constructive behaviors is a challenge of heroic dimensions in these settings.

Third, the nation's major service institutions and systems—health, academic and vocational education, and employment and training—are not meeting the needs of many young people. Too often, they are high-risk settings, especially for those with emerging behavioral, emotional, or academic problems. Not all of these institutions have become worse over time, but they have been unable to respond to the increased needs of adolescents and the society. Similarly, the child protection and criminal and juvenile justice systems not only are unable to respond to the complex needs of adolescents who come under their care, but in many situations exacerbate the difficulties of young people.

Fourth, the strong influence of racial and ethnic discrimination on employment, housing, and the criminal justice system limits the options of minorities and, hence, their ability to rear their children. Limited opportunities and the many and painful indignities that racial and ethnic minorities endure in their daily lives place children and adolescents at risk for early academic and behavioral problems.

The interplay of these conditions creates very different developmental opportunities for adolescents according to the income and race of their parents, the communities in which they live, and whether they live with one or both parents. Children born into families of low socioeconomic status are likely to live in high-risk neighborhoods and attend poor schools, and they are likely to grow up in a single-parent household. They know that their opportunities are limited, and significant numbers become alienated, lose hope, and fail to acquire the competencies necessary for adulthood.

Unless progress is made in ameliorating the conditions that produce high-risk settings, large numbers of young people will fail the transition into roles as healthy, productive, contributing adults. The increasing size of the problem suggests that the response must be powerful and comprehensive. Attention to policies supporting families and neighborhoods and restructuring service institutions is necessary to impart the functional academic, vocational, social and psychological competencies needed by young people.

DIRECTIONS FOR CHANGE IN THE 1990s

This section discusses changes that could transform high-risk settings and create a more supportive environment for adolescents. We offer program models and intervention strategies that have shown success here or abroad and have strong theoretical, empirical, or evaluation support. However, it is true that little is understood about many of the causal relationships that might affect change in these settings; therefore, we describe the outcomes that we believe are necessary rather than recommend specific programs or policy directions for achieving them.

Supporting Families

A declining economy and changes in family structure and functioning over the past two decades have pushed large and increasing numbers of children and adolescents into poverty. At the same time, increasing numbers of young people are living in homes without a biological parent, and growing numbers are in foster care. Increases in maternal employment and the dramatic rise in numbers of single-parent families mean that adolescents are spending less time with their parents. These changes have increased the numbers of adolescents exposed to one or more high-risk settings.

A return to strong economic growth in the nation will improve employment opportunities for prime-age adults. The evidence suggests, however, that growth in the overall economy will not reach a large proportion of young families. The long expansion of the mid-1980s did not arrest the increase in the number of low-income families, nor did it contribute to a reduction in high-risk settings in neighborhoods or service institutions. Instead, structural economic and social changes overwhelmed the effects of expansion. Consequently, targeted interventions will be needed to enhance job skills, provide entry employment opportunities, and improve access to critical support services, such as child care. For those whose labor market connections are very weak or do not exist at all, more directed interventions may be needed. We consider improving the economic position of large numbers of families the first priority.

For many poor or low-income parents, jobs alone will not provide families with an adequate standard of living because of low wages. Income transfer programs will have to be extended and improved for families to have adequate incomes, safe housing, and access to essential services, such as health care. In addition, the major institutions or settings serving children and youth—schools, health and mental health, child protection, juvenile justice, employment training—will have to be revitalized if they are to fulfill their missions. At the same time, efforts must be made to deal with youths who need help beyond traditional categorical boundaries. Existing institutions must be not only comprehensive within their domains but also flexible at their boundaries. Finally, there is a need for community-based resource centers where sustained, integrated care and support can be given to youths who face special problems of isolation and harm.

Rebuilding and Strengthening Low-Income Neighborhoods

The continuing deterioration of many neighborhoods condemns growing numbers of parents and their children to live in high-risk settings. Increasing numbers of adolescents—disproportionately those who are poor and minorities—live in neighborhoods characterized by high concentrations of poverty and crime. They are isolated from basic adult and recreational supports, such as those offered by youth development programs; as young adults, they are isolated from employment opportunities. Furthermore, the decline in real incomes among low-income families coupled with discrimination in housing and reduction in construction of low-income housing has compounded the problems of minorities, particularly blacks. The effect has been to trap a growing number of poor families in dangerous, bleak, and socially disorganized neighborhoods.

Schools are a fundamental neighborhood institution that has historically provided the opportunity structure through which poor and disadvantaged people have gained access to the middle class. That has changed as a result of the post-World War II suburbanization of America and the abandonment of urban school systems by the middle class. Because school funding is tied to neighborhood wealth, the most adequately funded and highest quality schools are found not in the neighborhoods where the need is the greatest, but instead serve the children whose family and neighborhood environments already equip them with the knowledge and skills needed for success.

Reviving depressed urban areas will require a major commitment from federal and state governments and the private sector, including support for housing, transportation, economic development, and the social services required by poor and low-income residents. Strategies for urban revival, ranging from enterprise zones to community development banks, have been discussed, but few major initiatives have been started. If the nation chooses to increase the vitality of low-income neighborhoods, support will be needed to rebuild neighborhood infrastructures, including transportation networks and such basic community services as police, libraries, and parks and recreation opportunities. Affordable housing in inner cities and the fringe suburbs is urgently needed. The difficult problem of creating greater equity in school funding will also have to be addressed. Other types of programs to help families choose their neighborhood environments (e.g., vouchers) are also of great value. Finally, the issue of residential segregation will have to be addressed by all levels of government through the vigorous enforcement of fair housing laws and other civil rights laws and regulations as well as incentive programs.

In the absence of federal or state support, neighborhood residents and some local governments have developed programs that highlight different models of intervention. For example, community organizing and development efforts have resulted in neighborhood beautification, increased safety, community policing, improved housing stock, and the creation of new services for disadvantaged persons. Most of these efforts have been accomplished on a shoestring and have often involved young people in service organizations. These programs suggest ways in which limited federal and state funds can have a beneficial impact on communities and the young people who live in them. Clearly, however, improvements in housing, public service, schools, and public safety will require major public-sector commitments.

Health and Mental Health Services

There is no integrated health or mental health system in the United States. Moreover, individual programs are often built around and financially sustained by the treatment of specific pathology and physical disorders. Health insurance, when it exists, does not provide adequate coverage of preventive services, and about one-third of all parents cannot afford health insurance for themselves and their children. Overall, the health system remains an assortment of uncoordinated services, and access for young people is difficult. Hence, the availability and quality of service directed toward the major threats to adolescent health—illicit drug use, alcohol and tobacco use, violence, teenage pregnancy, and emotional distress—is entirely inadequate.

The panel is encouraged that health care reform and the need to provide insurance for those now without coverage has become a high priority in the national political agenda. As these reforms move forward, it should be remembered that for adolescents, insurance coverage is not sufficient; also needed are services directed toward disease prevention and health promotion. For adolescents, insurance mechanisms should support strengthening the primary care sector to encourage the provision of consistent, comprehensive, and coordinated services and, especially, prevention services: reducing smoking, alcohol, and drug consumption and preventing other behaviors that seriously compromise future health have an enormous payoff. Strategies such as restricting or banning tobacco and alcohol advertising directed toward young people should be considered, as well as higher excise taxes. The proliferation of firearms and their increasing use by adolescents—and even children—constitutes the single most serious threat to inner-city youth. Strategies to create a safe and healthy living environment for adolescents must address the problem of firearms. At a minimum, existing laws relating to the sale or transfer of firearms to minors should be rigorously enforced; measures to disarm this population should also be explored.

Education

Over the last decade, the nation's schools have been the object of many broad-based reform efforts—initiatives from the federal and state governments and the business community. In response, many school districts have undertaken reforms aimed at enhancing accountability throughout the education system. The call for more emphasis in basic skills has led to common curriculums and more requirements in the areas of math, reading, and science. In addition, schools are becoming the dominant setting for preventive health services, including screening, counseling substance abuse prevention, sex education, and violence prevention.

In the panel's judgment, these reform efforts are inadequate in two respects. First, only a few jurisdictions have taken on the politically charged question of inequitable funding. School-based management and parental involvement is not a substitute for inadequate resources. Breaking the link between family and neighborhood wealth and the resources available to individual schools is an urgent priority if the nation is going to improve the well-being of low-income adolescents. School "choice" proposals deserve attention as a means for allowing parents to enroll their children in better schools; however, serious questions have been raised about the impact of such reforms on the poorest schools in the worst neighborhoods. In addition, different schools would not ensure that low-achieving students receive effective instruction; as discussed in the report, many negative practices are the norm throughout the American school system, and low-achieving students may become further alienated and discouraged when transferred to schools where average achievement levels are higher than those in their previous schools.

Thus, our second point: there has been little attention to the widespread use of instructional practices that fail to improve the school performance of low-achieving students, and indeed, often diminish their motivation and achievement. Most schools continue to use counterproductive academic interventions—rigid ability grouping, grade retention, "pull-out" Chapter 1 programs, categorical dropout prevention programs—that have shown few benefits and many disadvantages for low-achieving students. Major changes in Chapter 1 programs appear to be on the horizon and may make that program more effective in assisting low-achieving students. However, serious research and classroom attention should be given to alternative practices that show promise for helping low-achieving students.

Some school districts are implementing alternatives to traditional practices that provide possible models for wider application. These include replacing rigid ability grouping and grade retention practices with programs to provide low achievers the vitality of instruction and high expectations usually directed to higher achievers. Because of the structural changes necessary to implement such alternatives, they are usually implemented with concurrent changes in school organization and staffing patterns. For example, rather than organizing a student's entire academic program around a designated ability track, alternatives include a mix of heterogeneous and "accelerated" classes or approaches that separate only the students at the extremes of ability. Alternatives to grade retention often determine "merit" through a range of performance-based assessments. Rather than being held back because of poor performance in one or two classes, students are allowed to advance in grade level while concurrently taking "bridging classes."

Transition from School to Work

The United States does not have a structured school-to-work transition system, leaving transitions largely to the market. Employment-oriented programs for young people are structurally isolated from the labor market and rarely give those participating in them the fundamental skills and knowledge to enter a field of employment and keep up with it as the specific demands of jobs in the field evolve. Instead, the emphasis is on improving their job search or general occupational skills. Few programs include initiatives to create new employment opportunities for young people, to encourage employers to accommodate to their needs. Furthermore, academic instruction, vocational education, and employment and training programs remain largely separate enterprises, despite the complementary nature of their missions.

Growing attention is being given at the national level to creating systems or mechanisms to help young people move into the labor market. Research on systems in other industrialized countries has found the greatest success in programs that not only prepare young people for employment, but also include an explicit goal of facilitating overall youth development. Often, the systems provide education and training through the integrated efforts of different entities, including a schooling sector (to facilitate basic skills), a manpower or employment training sector (for occupational training), and a private enterprise sector (for supervised work experience).

In a small number of U.S. communities, practitioners are implementing demonstration programs aimed at creating school-to-work transition systems that are consistent with the approaches used in many other industrialized countries. These models take a number of forms—cooperative education, vocational academies, apprenticeships, school-to-work transition programs, "second-chance" programs—but they all provide integrated and sequenced academic instruction, occupational training, and work experience.

Lacking a structure for school-to-work transition systems, most reforms in the United States have aimed at independently strengthening vocational education and employment and training. Evaluations suggest that the most successful efforts are those that provide a coherent and logical series of courses to young people, much like the approach used to facilitate academic learning. Evaluations of innovative employment and training programs have been disappointing, yet important lessons have been learned. Results indicate that single-component programs and those of short duration—whether for occupational training, academic remediation, work experience, or job search training—have few lasting effects on young people. Successful programs provide young people with a coordinated set of services, including academic remediation, counseling, peer group support, mentoring, and job placement services, over an extended period.

FACING RESPONSIBILITY

The nation's social institutions—including schools, foster care, health care, and the juvenile justice system—have been largely unable to respond to the needs of children and adolescents from high risk homes and neighborhoods. While the threats to positive adolescent development have increased over the past two decades, institutions have either deteriorated or failed to change. The underlying causes of the increased needs are complex, including demographic changes that have increased the proportion of adolescents living with a single parent and increases in numbers of low-income families and families living in impoverished neighborhoods. Federal and state responses to the situation have been limited in both scope and success.

In the absence of effective federal and state responses, families, communities, and adolescents have had no choice but to respond, and many have. For example, in the face of high-risk settings, many parents act creatively and effectively to mobilize personal and often limited resources to provide for their children. Despite hardship and stress, many are able to fully nurture their children. Some neighborhood residents, housing projects, and community coalitions organize to "take back the streets," provide mutual support, and develop opportunities for their children. Other communities have organized comprehensive youth development programs. Similarly, adolescents call on their own resiliency and that of their families to cope with high-risk settings, and most do succeed. But the attrition is both unacceptably and unnecessarily high.

Issues of Discrimination

On virtually all aggregate statistical measures for adults and adolescents—income, living standards, health, education, occupation, residential opportunities—blacks, Hispanics, and other minorities remain substantially behind whites. Much of this gap is due to income differentials, but a considerable amount is due to continuing discrimination. Employment and housing discrimination limits the choices available to parents in raising their children. A single act of discrimination—be it the denial of a job promotion or the denial of housing in a desirable neighborhood—

can dramatically change the life course of a family. Black adolescents, disproportionately placed in less rigorous and lower quality educational, vocational, and employment and training programs and who subsequently face discrimination in the labor market, are multiply disadvantaged in their efforts to move successfully into young adulthood.

Given the strong influence of family and neighborhood wealth on adolescent development, vigorous enforcement of nondiscrimination statutes in the areas of housing and employment is especially warranted. Such efforts would increase the economic security of black parents and provide improved access for their children to better neighborhoods and schools. Discrimination within the criminal and juvenile justice systems aggravate problems in an array of institutional settings. Because in some places community-level policing practices display discriminatory patterns, police and juvenile system interactions have become particularly difficult, and the juvenile and criminal justice systems are perceived with suspicion, hostility, distrust, and despair by minority citizens. Reduction in race-based inequalities throughout the justice system is critical to provide more equitable treatment for those who have contact with justice officials, as well as to improve relations between the police and minority communities.

Encouraging Change

Beginning a process of encouraging change will require significant commitments from governments at the federal, state, and local levels, and the panel recognizes that governments at all levels are already engaged in difficult reappraisals of current programs in the face of declining revenues. Yet this may be an appropriate time to reexamine the roles and expectations for each level of government and to think freshly about how to solve problems in a manner that is responsive to the needs of individuals and communities. The federal and state governments have a significant role in providing financial support, leadership, and incentives toward change. Yet effective change requires ground-level flexibility and discretion that cannot be directed from the top. Thus, many of the reforms that the panel believes are needed to make life better for adolescents and their families may well be more readily achieved through a realignment of authorities and responsibilities to encourage "bottom-up" decision making. Scholars of government finance and management have recently begun to write about rethinking federal, state, and local roles and funding as a way of bringing the resources needed to deal with problems closer to the people who are most likely to do it sensibly.

Increasing the resources available to states and localities is a necessary first step. But states and localities must also be willing to ease controls and show a greater degree of trust in providing legitimate program responsibility and accountability to community leaders, to program staff, and to young people themselves. Teachers and parents, for example, should play a greater role in school reform and have the resources to experiment with teaching methods and services that they believe will work in their neighborhoods. The legitimate need for accountability of public funds may involve more difficult auditing when programs are run at the community level rather than managed at the federal or state level. This should not blind policy makers to the costs associated with rigidly imposed standards and requirements that may be irrelevant to local needs or destructive of providers' ability to deliver effective services.

Under this approach, the federal role should be focused on improving the performance of the national economy and assuring the adequacy of "safety net" programs in income maintenance and health care for all residents. In addition, national leadership is needed to encourage and enable the design of integrated health and school-to-work transition systems, and new strategies for providing academic and vocational instruction in schools. At the same time, states and localities should have greater flexibility in the design and oversight of service delivery programs. Their priority should be to involve community-based institutions in the development and management of programs to meet the urgent need of adolescents for recreation, cultural enrichment, and legitimate opportunities to form attachments to adults and institutions and to contribute to the welfare of others and the community.

Chapter 10 reviewed some of the most promising strategies developed by locally based programs to respond to the diverse needs of adolescents. Most of these have not been rigorously or systematically evaluated. However, the panel consulted extensively with practitioners, and the major elements of programs that they believe to be critical are consistent with what theory-based research suggests. Accordingly, we suggest that communities be given more resources and more flexibility to experiment and to replicate successes. At the same time, the research community should give increased attention to developing better tools for evaluation and replication. Developing meaningful outcome measures should be a high priority.

AN AGENDA FOR RESEARCH

The findings and unresolved issues that have been identified in this report have important implications for the focus and orientation of future research on America's youths. Throughout its report, the panel has stressed that more and more young people in American society are exposed to critical settings—families, schools, neighborhoods, and systems of health care, welfare, and justice—that are under severe strain or in serious decline. Increasingly, these settings and institutions fail to provide adolescents with the support and resources needed for healthy development. Indeed, some of the settings actively jeopardize the young people who are living in them.

General Framework

The panel believes that a fundamental reorientation in society's approach to promoting adolescent development is needed. Consequently, there must also be reorientation in research and evaluation, accompanied by a different and more sustained pattern of funding. This new framework would have the following characteristics:

• It would give primary attention to achieving an understanding of the various settings in which adolescent development takes place in the course of everyday life—including families, neighborhoods, schools, and community organizations and programs.
• It would stress the interactive effects of multiple settings, in order to capture the full complexity of the social environment. Only by assessing adolescents in the context of their families and neighborhoods, and by assessing institutions and programs in the broader community context, can a valid understanding of adolescent development be achieved.
• It would require attention to both risk factors and protective factors—and to their interaction—at both the individual and social levels, in order to provide the fullest understanding of healthy adolescent development. Hence, it would encourage research protocols that capture individual differences simultaneously with assessments of social contexts and daily settings.
• It would dedicate support to long-term, longitudinal studies, which can illuminate processes of individual development and

change, as well as processes underlying change in communities and institutions.

Within this framework, research would shift its focus to those young people most at risk for not making a successful transition to young adulthood and would explicitly consider the effects of gender, race, and ethnicity on adolescents:

• It would give special attention to those youth who have hitherto been largely ignored in research on adolescent development—those from families with low incomes, those who are members of racial and ethnic minorities, and others with backgrounds of disadvantage and limited opportunity, such as immigrants, the homeless, and persons with physical and emotional disabilities.

• It would assess the effects of discrimination on neighborhoods and on the lives of families and adolescents, seeking to identify independent and interactive influences of class, race, gender, and ethnicity on adolescent development.

This new research orientation will require new methodologies and measures to assess the social context and the process of adolescent development. Research and evaluation studies should use multiple methods, recognizing the limitations of an exclusive reliance on single-discipline inquiries using traditional "objective" surveys and cross-sectional approaches. The research should be multidisciplinary and longitudinal; it must incorporate the unique advantages of qualitative and ethnographic methods for grasping the meaning of adolescent behavior in everyday situations. In order to simultaneously consider a process, program management, and outcome, multiple methods of research would be used:

• It would move beyond a sole emphasis on measuring youth problems (drug use, pregnancy, arrest) and accomplishments (graduation, employment) to include assessment of the individual and community attributes (alienation, responsibility, attachment, emotional health) that underlie the "status" outcomes.

• It would move beyond the isolated assessment of single settings or interventions by creating methodologies to examine the effects of a variety of influences on adolescents.

• It would get inside the "black box" of families, communities, schools, health care, and community-based programs to identify cross-cutting elements that support healthy adolescent development.

• It would encourage research on initiatives that explicitly seek to change the contexts of adolescent development, such as comprehensive programs and communitywide interventions; it would include studies of policies and interventions in other countries.

• It would study the process of change in schools, neighborhoods, organizations, and programs to identify the mechanisms that underlie the successful replication of good practice, with explicit attention to the technical, normative, and political barriers to change.

The Social Context of Adolescence

The panel's findings point to a clear and urgent need for research on the social contexts of young people in contemporary U.S. society. These are, at least, the family, the school, the neighborhood, and the systems of health care, welfare, and justice. Influencing all of these is the state and shape of the economy, with its specific effects on the labor market, employment, unemployment, and family income. Research has traditionally focused on adolescents as individuals and has given far less attention to the settings in which adolescents live. From the panel's perspective, however, the highest priority for future research should shift to studies of the contexts and settings of daily life, especially for adolescents from low-income and disadvantaged backgrounds.

Families

The role of the family as the primary socializing agency has been compromised by increasing family poverty, by long-term changes in family structure, and by the emergence of alternative agents of socialization that are more attractive to youth, such as the media and peer groups. Research is needed to trace out the mechanisms by which poverty (low income, unemployment, and underemployment) and changes in family structure (single-parent households, two-parent households with both parents working) influence family functioning. Understanding how families manage adversity or are overwhelmed by it, and how adolescent development can or cannot be insulated from it, should be the major objectives of inquiry in this setting. Furthermore, given the pervasive trend—across all income classes, but especially among the poor—toward single parenthood, research is urgently needed to understand the causes of these changes and the types of programs that might be effective in counteracting the most damaging effects on children and adolescents.

Family Support Systems

There is a great need for applied research on the effectiveness of family support programs, which are proliferating rapidly with little reference to the best allocation of resources. For labor-intensive case management programs, for example, research is needed to establish the optimum amount of time that a family requires from an advocate or case manager. It is also important to understand more clearly the extent to which family support programs actually have direct effects on adolescents. Research would also be useful to explore alternatives to families such as group homes or dormitories for adolescents who cannot live at home.

Schools

Probably nothing derails an adolescent's future more certainly than disconnecting from school, losing interest in learning, and, ultimately, dropping out of school. Adaptation to the school setting is necessary for the sequential acquisition of status and skills that provide access to future roles—whether further education, the military, or the labor market. Research on processes that sustain interest in and attachment to school—and on those that compromise that attachment—is therefore of critical importance. These processes may have to do with the availability of school resources, with such school practices as tracking, with the quality of the school climate, with school-family relations, with fear of violence in school buildings, with the adequacy of teacher training, or with other factors.

Research is also needed to explore what kinds of schools work best. Evaluation of alternatives to traditional school organization and instructional practice should focus on finding ways to improve the climate of schools for all students, with special attention to low achievers and minorities. Given the weight of evidence against traditional practices—such as grade retention, suspension, expulsion, and rigid forms of tracking—research is needed to guide educators toward alternatives that can be successfully implemented.

Neighborhoods

This report calls repeated attention to the deteriorating and dangerous conditions that characterize the urban neighborhoods in which increasing numbers of American youth live, especially those from low-income families and from disadvantaged racial and ethnic groups. We do not know how such circumstances influence adolescent growth and development. The physical condition of such settings (the anomie and dangers of high-rise housing, the decrepitude of the housing stock, the abandoned buildings and littered streets) and their social condition (the prevalence of gangs and organized drug markets, the lack of normative standards and informal social controls) have not been systematically examined for their impact on the young people in them. Research is therefore needed to determine the consequences of these conditions and to identify the elements of healthy, functioning neighborhoods that lead to healthy adolescent development. Such research needs to move beyond single settings to assess the mix of formal and informal support; descriptive research, mapping the supports available for adolescents in different communities, would be helpful in establishing a baseline. Community-level inquiries could examine the health and behavioral status of adolescents in comparable neighborhoods with and without programs or integrated service delivery systems.

Health Care

The lack of an integrated health care system in the United States has grave consequences for the health status of the adolescent population. The "system" is also reflected in studies of adolescent health: at present, most studies focus on isolated physical or behavioral characteristics. There is a need to broaden research to examine the effects of settings and services on individuals and communities, rather than on specific conditions. For example, do students in school with school-linked health centers enjoy better health than students who depend on other types of services? What are the most important components of primary care for adolescents and how do they differ from those for other age groups? The importance of comprehensive "one-stop" programs has been suggested. Research to document the relative efficacy of combined services versus category single-focus programs should be given high priority. The need for greater access to mental health services is often overlooked in the discussion of health delivery and finance. Research is needed to further document this need— and to determine the most effective prevention intervention and treatment.

Research should examine the qualities of health care settings (such as location, staff attributes, range of service provided) that are most likely to engage young people and sustain participation. Within this context, issues of confidentiality and consent need to be fully explored to identify and reduce barriers to appropriate service. As the country moves increasingly into managed care arrangements, research is needed to better document the effects of these systems on adolescents. Issues of access are particularly important. Greater use should be made of existing data to help identify research priorities and to answer research questions. Increased support for national health survey supplements that concern adolescents is of high priority, as is support of methods to improve such surveys. For example, the validity of information obtained from parents about adolescents is also a critical topic for study. However, the most important research question regarding adolescents and primary care is very simply how do we get them into the system?

School-to-Work Transition

The United States does not have a comprehensive school-to-work transition system, and the existing programs—vocational education and employment and training programs—provide marginal benefits to young people. On a policy level, there is a need for systematic evaluations of state, local, and foreign efforts to create school-to-work transition systems, with particular attention to the effects of such initiatives on adolescent outcomes. Specific interventions should be evaluated in the context of the overall education system, and evaluations should be consistent with this perspective. Similarly, employment and training programs need to be studied in the context of other community resources, including but not limited to the schools. Research should also examine how programs can be made more comprehensive by addressing a broader range of adolescent needs and competencies, and by providing services that offer continuity throughout the period of adolescence.

Juvenile and Criminal Justice

This report identifies a number of ways in which the juvenile and criminal justice systems fail to intervene before adolescent offenders become fully enmeshed in the adult criminal justice system. Like dropping out of school, contact with the juvenile justice system often acts to mortgage an adolescent's future by jeopardizing the school-to-work transition and by diminishing long-term employment prospects. Yet little research has monitored this process longitudinally, and there is little research on how this process varies across community settings or labor markets. Particular attention should be paid to ways in which the justice system seems to exacerbate racial, ethnic, and socioeconomic variations in life chances. Research is needed to develop alternatives to conviction and incarceration, including school and employment programs, that can alter developmental trajectories.

Child Welfare and Foster Care

The child welfare system, like the justice system, is overwhelmed by rising caseloads and is caught in a continuing controversy over the relative priority of family preservation versus the needs of children. Research is needed to identify strategies for strengthening families, especially those suffering from financial hardship and emotional stress; but research is also needed to evaluate the effects of these strategies. In particular, the paucity of research on adolescents in the foster care system severely limits policy and program initiatives. Research is needed to identify the unique risks faced by adolescents—in comparison with populations—and evaluations are necessary to assess different strategies for helping them make a successful transition into young adulthood.

Individual Differences in Adolescence

Although it is important to investigate the effects of dangerous and disadvantaged settings on all youths, it is also important to observe the variation in behavior and development among youths who grow up in similar settings. One source of such variation is individual differences in values, attitudes, beliefs, perceptions, social and self-definitions, expectations, and the like that play an important role in adolescent behavior and development.

The challenge is to map those individual differences that are logical reflections of socialization in critical settings—family, school, neighborhood—and that, at the same time, have implications for successful or unsuccessful adaptation in such contexts. Examples that seem promising on the basis of prior research include individual differences in the following characteristics: perceived self-efficacy or self-competence; values placed on achievement and health; perception of future opportunity or of life chances; attitudes about normative transgression; orientation to religion and involvement with church; self-definition, including ethnic or racial self-concept; and risk-taking propensity. Research should be done on how such characteristics develop, their organization into structures of personality, their linkage to variation in social context, and their interaction with context in influencing adolescent behavior and development.

Adolescent Risk Behavior

Increasing numbers of America's youth, those who live in affluence as well as poverty, engage in behaviors that compromise their development and jeopardize their futures, their health, and even their lives. The prevalence of risky behaviors among adolescents—drug use, unprotected sexual behavior, delinquency, violence, dropping out of school—warrants major research attention. The growing incidence of depression and the effects of exposure to violence must be considered. There has been considerable support for descriptive epidemiological monitoring of risky behaviors, but additional research is needed in several other key areas.

One such area is the organization of risky behaviors—their intraindividual covariation in the behavioral repertoires of youth. Prior research has found sufficient structures of covariation to warrant the label of "risky life-style," but this finding needs further examination, especially with the youth populations that are of concern in this report. Specifically, how do such structures or organizations of risky behaviors develop, what factors in the individual or the context promote or prevent harmful results from these behaviors, and how can one predict the link between risky behaviors and subsequent harm? Of equal research interest are the relationships among various risky behaviors and their relationship with behaviors that promote health. Such questions require longitudinal studies that can illuminate the process of behavioral development in all of its facets.

Comprehensive Intervention Programs

Current understanding of the needs of youth in high-risk settings suggests that no one single intervention has the power to change life-styles. Rather, it is postulated that a number of program components have to be put together to achieve a significant effect. A number of demonstration projects have been launched that measure the short-term effects of multicomponent, multiagency programs—such as community schools, school-based clinics, school-business collaboration, and communitywide youth development, substance abuse, and delinquency prevention programs. High priority should be given to research that evaluates the interactive effects of these complex programs over a long enough period to confirm or deny their validity. Previous experience with comprehensive programs that focused on middle school youth has shown short-term positive effects, but they tended to "wash out" by the time of high school graduation (or dropping out). Other items of research interest are the sequencing of components (the effects of early interventions versus later ones) and whether adolescents are better served in school-based or community-based programs, questions that can only be resolved through research and evaluation.

Much of the current policy research focuses on the categorical arrangement of programs—separate solutions for separate problems. The research agenda would be greatly enhanced if it included a review of how the federal government is organized to deal with the range of issues identified in this report, building on previous research, for example, that identified hundreds of federal agencies with responsibility for adolescent health services. Another major area of policy research involves the determination of how to move from demonstration projects to full-scale implementation. For example, if one comprehensive school-based family resource center appears to have a positive impact in a neighborhood, how can this model be replicated in other neighborhoods that want such an institution?

Other countries are believed to have created more caring social environments for youth, and this belief is supported by documented outcomes (levels of substance use, teenage pregnancy, etc.) that are more favorable than in the United States. Research should therefore be conducted that compares the policies and practices in various nations that are relevant to school, family, and neighborhoods. State governments also have a major role to play in the integration of human services and in assisting communities to develop coordinated systems for families and youth. Policy research should explore the various models of state government reform to identify successful approaches.

Monitoring the Status of the Adolescent Population

If it is true that young people are the nation's most precious resource, then the nation needs better means of measuring the overall effectiveness of the socialization process. Systematic efforts are needed to assess the adolescent population over time. Such efforts will require multifaceted measures that examine a range of adolescent attributes, including perceptions, behaviors, and accomplishments. Data collection must be organized to produce findings according to age, gender, race, ethnicity, and socioeconomic status.

The need to adequately monitor adolescents from low-income families is especially urgent. Relatively little is known about the exposure of the adolescent population to high-risk settings on a national and regional basis. In addition, studies do not adequately sample by race or ethnicity, and hence little is known about some of the most vulnerable populations. Finally, studies must allow for disaggregation into smaller age subgroups; for example, most national health surveys group young adolescents with children, and older adolescents with adults.

Reports about the problems facing children and adolescents generally conclude by reminding readers that the nation's youth constitute our future and urge steps to protect this vital resource: that is also the strongly held view of this panel. The problems are more serious than is often recognized, and if current trends continue, will become dramatically worse by the turn of the century.

In this report, we have attempted to document the pervasiveness and complexity of the problems and to suggest that it is time to focus more attention on the social environments in which adolescents live and grow. Environments are socially constructed and in a constant state of evolution, which means that the destructive effects we have described need not persist. Influencing change in a positive direction is often difficult, however, because understanding is always limited and everyone—policy makers, researchers, the public—is invested in current institutional practices—in health care, housing, education, criminal justice, child welfare, and employment. But as the century closes, the nation appears to be entering a period of reexamination and reform regarding many basic social institutions. This is therefore an appropriate time to urge that the needs of children and families be brought to the forefront and given priority attention.

Biographical Sketches of Panel Members and Staff

JOEL F. HANDLER is professor of law at the University of California, Los Angeles. Previously, he was the Vilas research professor and the George A. Wiley professor at the University of Wisconsin Law School and served on the senior research staff at the university's Institute for Research on Poverty. His primary research interests are in the areas of poverty law and administration, social welfare programs, race, social movements, and law reform activities. He has published a dozen books and numerous articles on these subjects. He has served on several committees of the National Research Council and chaired the Panel on Public Policies Contributing to the Deinstitutionalization of Children and Youth and the Panel on Political Participation and Administration of Justice of the Committee on the Status of Black Americans. He has been a Guggenheim Fellow and served as president of the Law and Society Association. He received an A.B. degree from Princeton University and a J.D. degree from Harvard Law School.

GORDON L. BERLIN is senior vice president at the Manpower Demonstration Research Corporation, an intermediary organization that tests new approaches to social welfare problems. He is also executive director of a Canadian nonprofit organization formed at the request of the Canadian government to undertake a two-province test of a wage subsidy program for single parents receiving public assistance. Previously, he was executive deputy ad-

257

ministrator for management, budget, and policy of the Human Resources Administration, New York City; program officer and deputy director at the Ford Foundation's urban poverty program; and a program analyst and project officer in the U.S. Department of Labor's Employment and Training Administration. Mr. Berlin is the author of numerous publications on youth, education, employment, and social welfare issues, including, *Toward a More Perfect Union* (with Andrew Sum), a report on basic skills, families, and the nation's economic future.

THOMAS D. COOK is professor of sociology, psychology, education, and public policy at Northwestern University, where he is also a faculty research associate at the Center for Urban Affairs and Policy Research. His research and teaching interests include urban policy, evaluation, and research methods. His books include *"Sesame Street" Revisited* (1975, with others); *Quasi-Experimentation: Design and Analysis Issues for Social Research in Field Settings* (1979, with D.T. Campbell); *Foundations of Program Evaluation: Twenty-Five Years of Theoretical Progress* (1991, with W. Shadish and L. Leviton); and *Meta-Analysis for Explanation* (1992, with Cooper, Cordray, Hartman, Hedges, Light, Louis, and Mosteller). He received a B.A. degree from Oxford University in German and French and a Ph.D. degree in communication research from Stanford University.

ALONZO A. CRIM is a professor at Georgia State University. His research, teaching, and administration interests include elementary school education, high school education, and adult education. Published works include "Preparing Students for Technology: The Atlanta Experiment" (with Boyd D. Odom) in *Curriculum Review* (March-April, 1987); "Desegregation in the Atlanta Public Schools: A Historical Overview" (with Nancy J. Emmons) in *School Desegregation Plans that Work* (1984); and "A Community of Believers" in *Educating Our Citizens: The Search for Excellence,* Center for National Policy, Alternatives for the 1980s—No. 9 (1983). He received a B.A. degree from Roosevelt College, an M.A. degree from the University of Chicago, and an Ed.D. degree from Harvard University.

SANFORD M. DORNBUSCH is Reed-Hodgson professor of human biology and professor of sociology and education at Stanford University. Formerly, he was director of the Stanford Center for the Study of Families, Children and Youth, and he is now chair of its advisory board; he also taught at Harvard and the University of Washington. He has received the Walter J. Gores Award for Excellence in Teaching at Stanford, and he has served as the elected head of both the academic senate and the advisory board. He is the first sociologist to have served as chair of three different sections of the American Sociological Association—methodology, social psychology, and sociology of education; he is currently the elected president of the Society for Research on Adolescence, the first nonpsychologist to receive that honor. Dornbusch is the author of numerous articles and the author or editor of six books, most recently *Feminism, Children, and the New Families* (1988). He received a B.A. degree from Syracuse University and M.A. and Ph.D. degrees from the University of Chicago, all in sociology.

JOY G. DRYFOOS is a researcher, writer, and lecturer. Previously, she was associated with the Alan Guttmacher Institute as director of research and planning and as a senior fellow. She has received support from the Carnegie Corporation since 1984 for a long-term youth-at-risk project with a focus on the integration of the knowledge base in four separate fields: substance abuse, delinquency, school failure, and teen pregnancy. Dryfoos's summary volume, *Adolescents-at-Risk: Prevalence and Prevention* (1990), presents strategies for developing more comprehensive programs at the community, state, and federal levels. Her current work focuses on school-based youth and family resource centers. Dryfoos serves on many advisory panels concerned with youth, including the Carnegie Task Force on Youth Development and Community Programs, Children's Initiative of the New York State Community Aid Association, and Girls Inc.; she was also recently appointed to the Alcohol, Drug, and Mental Health Block Grant Advisory Council of New York. She is a member of the Editorial Boards of the *American Journal of Public Health* and the *Journal of Adolescent Health Care*. She received a B.A. degree from Antioch College and an M.A. degree in urban sociology from Sarah Lawrence College.

ROBERTO M. FERNANDEZ is associate professor of sociology and faculty fellow at the Center for Urban Affairs and Policy Research at Northwestern University. Previously, he was an instructor and assistant professor in the Department of Sociology at the University of Arizona. Fernandez has published extensively in the areas of race and ethnic relations, formal organizations, and social networks. His current research examines the impact of the relocation of a firm from a central city in the suburbs on the employment chances of black, white, and Hispanic workers. He received a B.A. degree from Harvard College and a Ph.D. degree in sociology from the University of Chicago.

RICHARD B. FREEMAN is program director of the Program in Labor Studies of the National Bureau of Economic Research, professor of economics at Harvard University, and executive programme director of the Comparative Labour Market Institutions Programme at the Centre for Economic Performance of the London School of Economics. Previously, he taught at the University of Chicago and Yale University. Dr. Freeman has published over 100 articles dealing with topics in youth labor market problems, higher education, trade unionism, high-skilled labor markets, economic discrimination, social mobility, income distribution and equity in the marketplace. In addition, he has written 12 books, several of which have been translated into Japanese and Spanish. His recent books include *Labor Markets in Actions: Essays in Empirical Economics* (1989); *Immigration, Trade and the Labor Market* (1991); *Immigration and the Work Force: Economic Consequences for the United States and Source Areas* (1992); and *Capitalism and Generosity: Nonselfish Behavior in a Selfish Economy* (forthcoming). He received a Ph.D. degree in economics from Harvard University.

JOHN HAGAN is professor of sociology and law and Killam Research Fellow at the University of Toronto. His current research focuses on the causes and consequences of delinquency and crime in the life course and on the professional and personal lives of lawyers. In addition to more than 120 published papers on criminological and sociological topics, he has published seven books, one of which, *Structural Criminology* (1989), received awards from the Society for the Study of Social Problems and the American Sociological Association. He is a fellow of the Royal Society of Canada and the American Society of Criminology, a former president of the American Society of Criminology, a research fellow of Statistics Canada, and a fellow of the Canadian Institute of Advanced Research. He received a B.A. degree from the University of Illinois and M.A. and Ph.D. degrees from the University of Alberta.

CHARLES E. IRWIN, JR., is professor of pediatrics and director of the Division of Adolescent Medicine at the University of California, San Francisco School of Medicine. He also directs the Inter-disciplinary Adolescent Health Training Project at the University of California, San Francisco, and is a member of the Institute for Health Policy Studies. His research has focused on risk-taking behaviors during adolescence and how clinicians can more effectively identify adolescents who are at risk for engaging in health-compromising behaviors. He is the author of several publications on the development of risky behavior during adolescence and the editor of *Adolescent Social Behavior and Health* (1987). He is the recipient of the Society for Adolescent Medicine's Outstanding Achievement Award in 1985, the National Center for Youth Law/Youth Law Center's annual award recognizing his research in high-risk youth (in 1988) and the ambulatory Pediatric Association's Teaching Award for training physicians in behavioral sciences (in 1990). He received a B.S. degree in biology from Hobart College, a B.M.S. degree from Dartmouth Medical School, a M.D. degree from the University of California, San Francisco, and was a Robert Wood Johnson Foundation clinical scholar at the University of California, San Francisco-Stanford.

RICHARD JESSOR is a long-time member of the faculty in the Department of Psychology at the University of Colorado, Boulder. He currently also serves as director of the Institute of Behavioral Science and directs the MacArthur Foundation Research Network on Successful Adolescent Development Among Youth in High-Risk Settings. His areas of research include adolescent and young adult development, the social psychology of problem behavior, and psychosocial aspects of poverty. Jessor has been a consultant to numerous organizations, including the National Institute on Alcohol Abuse and Alcoholism; the National Institute on Drug Abuse, Health, and Welfare, Canada; and the World Health Organization. He has authored or edited approximately 100 publications, including 6 books. Jessor studied at the College of the City of New York and received a B.A. degree from Yale University, an M.A. degree from Columbia University in 1947, and a Ph.D. degree in clinical psychology from Ohio State University.

GLORIA JOHNSON-POWELL is professor of child psychiatry at Harvard Medical School and director of the Camille Cosby Center at the Judge Baker Children's Center in Boston. Her research and teaching interests include child psychiatry, mental retardation, pathology of child abuse, human behavior, mental health services to poor and minority group children, Head Start, and the Job Corps.

Publications include *Black Monday's Children: The Effects of School Desegregation,* (1973), *The Psycho-Social Development of Minority Group Children* (with J. Yamamoto, et al.) (1984), and *The Lasting Effects of Child Sexual Abuse* (with G.E. Wyatt, ed.) (1990). She received a B.A. degree from Mount Holyoke College and an M.D. degree from Meharry Medical College, Nashville; she completed a residency in psychiatry, a fellowship in child psychiatry, a research fellowship at the Center for Health Sciences, University of California, Los Angeles, and a fellowship in health policy at the RAND/UCLA Health Policy Institute.

AARON SHIRLEY is a pediatrician and director of the Jackson-Hinds Comprehensive Health Center in Jackson, Mississippi. His practice and interests include the correlation between health and education services, Head Start, human relations, rural medical practice, and health services for the poor. He received a B.S. degree from Tougaloo College and an M.D. degree from Meharry Medical College; he served a general rotating internship at Hubbard Hospital, Nashville, and a pediatric residency at the University of Mississippi Medical Center, Jackson, Mississippi.

BARBARA STARFIELD is professor and head of the Division of Health Policy at the Johns Hopkins University School of Public Health. Trained in pediatrics and epidemiology, she now devotes her energies to health services research and its translation into health policy at the national, state, and local levels. Her primary research interests are in primary care measurement, the relationship between the processes and outcomes of health care, quality of care, health status measurement (particularly for adolescents and children), and child health policy. She is a member of the Institute of Medicine and has served on several of its committees. She is currently chairing the Subcouncil on Medical Effectiveness and Outcomes of the National Advisory Council to the Agency for Health Care Policy and Research, and she recently chaired the Council on Research of the American Academy of Pediatrics. Starfield has published widely on the subject of child and youth health status and the impact of the health system on it. She received a B.A. from Swarthmore College, an M.D. from State University of New York, Downstate Medical Center, Brooklyn, and a M.P.H. from Johns Hopkins University.

LLOYD STREET is associate professor of human service studies at the College of Human Ecology, Cornell University. His research and teaching interests include race and crime, human service delivery, and program planning. Publications that reflect these interests include *The Transient Slum* (with Phil Brown), *Background for Planning* (with E. Fruedenberg), and *Race, Crime, and Community* (in press). He received B.A., M.A., and Ph.D. degrees in sociology and a post master's certificate in community organization research from the University of California, Berkeley.

R. SHEPARD ZELDIN, who served as study director for the panel, is now research director for the Center for Youth Development of the Academy for Education Development in Washington, D.C. His current research examines adolescent development as it occurs in schools and community-based youth programs. He also collaborates with community leaders and program managers nationwide to strengthen services on the basis of theory and research on youth development. Previously, he worked as an organizational consultant and education researcher and held senior positions in the legislative and executive branches of Virginia state government. He received a B.A. degree from Columbia University and a Ph.D. degree in human development and family studies from Cornell University.

Index

A

Ability grouping, *see* Tracking of students
Abortion, 92, 96
Abuse and neglect, 18, 19, 54-55, 185
and child welfare system, 4, 180-185 *passim*, 188-189
and health care system, 6, 88
Accidents, *see* Injuries
Adolescent Diversion Project (ADP), 215
Adoption, 186
Adoption Assistance and Child Welfare Act, 176-177
After High School, Then What?, 126
AIDS, *see* HIV
Aid to Families with Dependent Children (AFDC), 47, 91, 129, 176

Alcohol use, 84, 241
during pregnancy, 18
American Medical Association (AMA), 87
Anorexia nervosa, 90
Apprenticeship, 209
Arrest, 10, 42, 74, 152, 153, 157-158
Asian population, 65
Assault, 82, 152, *see also* Sexual assault and abuse
Assistance, *see* Welfare system
Attitude, *see* Demeanor
Authoritative parenting, 53, 54
Autism, 18
Autonomy, *see* Independence and autonomy issues

B

Basic skills, 32-33, 205, 210-211

265

Y